FANG-TASTIC FICTION

DEC   2010

ALA Editions purchases fund advocacy, awareness,
and accreditation programs for library professionals worldwide.

FANG-TASTIC FICTION

Twenty-First-Century Paranormal Reads

Patricia O'Brien Mathews

AMERICAN LIBRARY ASSOCIATION

Chicago   2011

After growing up as the high school principal's daughter in a small Ohio town (an adolescent's nightmare), **Patricia Mathews** inexplicably pursued a career in public education, working as a teacher, program coordinator, and curriculum and assessment designer. She currently has the best job of her life—working behind the reference desk at her local branch library. Before getting caught up in paranormal fiction, her favorite readings were narrative nonfiction and character-driven fiction. Now, however, she can't resist the heroes and heroines of urban fantasy. She lives in northeastern Ohio with her two cats, and although she watches them carefully, she has never caught them in the act of shape-shifting.

Printed in the United States of America

15   14   13   12   11   5   4   3   2   1

While extensive effort has gone into ensuring the reliability of the information in this book, the publisher makes no warranty, express or implied, with respect to the material contained herein.

ISBN: 978-0-8389-1073-3

Library of Congress Cataloging-in-Publication Data
Mathews, Patricia O'Brien.
    Fang-tastic fiction : twenty-first-century paranormal reads / Patricia O'Brien Mathews.
        p.   cm.
    Includes bibliographical references and index.
    ISBN 978-0-8389-1073-3 (alk. paper)
    1. Occult fiction, American—Bibliography. 2. Supernatural—Fiction—Bibliography. 3. American fiction—21st century—Bibliography. 4. Monographic series—Bibliography. 5. Sequels (Literature)—Bibliography. 6. Fiction in libraries—United States. 7. Readers' advisory services—United States. I. Title. II. Title: Fang-tastic fiction.
        Z1231.O28M38 2011
        [PS374.O28]
        016.813708037—dc22   2010032647

Cover design by Kirstin Krutsch

Text design in Berlin Sans and Janson Text by Karen Sheets de Gracia. Illustrations © GIGIBGM / Shutterstock, Inc.

♾ This paper meets the requirements of ANSI/NISO Z39.48-1992 (Permanence of Paper).

ALA Editions also publishes its books in a variety of electronic formats. For more information, visit the ALA Store at www.alastore.ala.org and select eEditions.

*To the memory of
Dad and Diana,
who would be stunned
by the subject matter
but extremely proud
of the achievement*

CONTENTS

ACKNOWLEDGMENTS

Thanks go to Karen Sigsworth, librarian extraordinaire, who has been totally supportive of this project every step of the way; to Susan Spivey, who helped with the reading and was always willing to have a vampire chat; to Donald J. Morrison, who produced an introductory piece for my *Fang-tastic Fiction* PowerPoint presentation that turned me into a vampire (what a rush!); to Mitch Brickell and Regina Paul, who taught me the finer points of writing and editing and trusted me with scary amounts of responsibility; and to a fantastic group of women friends who have always provided moral support during the bad times and shared the joy of the good times. Finally, I am grateful to all of the library patrons, mostly young women, who kept asking, "Which paranormal series should I read next?" I couldn't have done it without all of you.

introduction

At the heart of the vampire myth is a demon lover who is both elegant and deadly, a creature whose savagery is all the more shocking when taken with his seductive beauty and style.

from Anne Stuart's "Legends of Seductive Elegance," in *Dangerous Men and Adventurous Women: Romance Writers on the Appeal of Romance*

Defining Paranormal Fiction: What Is Included in This Bibliography?

The *American Heritage Dictionary of the English Language* defines *paranormal* as "beyond the range of normal experience or scientific explanation." If we used this broad definition to define paranormal fiction, the results would be a mix of fantasy, science fiction, and horror that could include futuristic, extra-terrestrial, time-travel, and all manner of supernatural adventures involving all manner of imaginary creatures.

This bibliography, however, uses a much more limited definition of *paranormal*. Included here are works of paranormal romance, fantasy, mystery, and suspense that are set, for the most part, in a relatively realistic modern world—a world inhabited by both humans and paranormal beings. Although a few series are set in the nineteenth century or earlier, most take place in real time in the late twentieth or early twenty-first century. Some may include a separate fantasy world, but characters generally move between that world and the real world. All include human characters.

This bibliography does not include works set totally in fantasy worlds in a dimension apart from human society, and it does not include extraterrestrial, futuristic, apocalyptic, dystopic, intergalactic, or technology-based science fiction. It also does not include horror fiction (i.e., fiction with the primary intent to scare or horrify the audience).

The works included have been published, for the most part, in the twenty-first century and are meant for adult readers. In some series, early books were written in the 1990s.

Titles in each series are listed in the order in which they were published, unless otherwise noted.

Modern versus Traditional Paranormal Fiction

One of the biggest changes in twenty-first-century paranormal fiction is the change in roles for the supernatural beings. Early literary vampires began as monstrous beasts, beyond even the fringes of human society (e.g., Bram Stoker's Dracula). Anne Rice and others portrayed more civilized vampires during the twentieth century, but they remained remote and unapproachable. Laurell K. Hamilton and Stephenie Meyer changed that image with, respectively, the ANITA BLAKE series and the TWILIGHT series. Instead of being bloodsucking monsters, vampires morphed into members of the human community and—most important of all—boyfriends! The same thing has happened with shape-shifters, demons, and other creatures of the night. Although some monstrous supernaturals are cast as villains in these novels, the supernatural leading man now has all of the traits of an all-American hero, with the added advantages of his super strength, magical talents, and utter gorgeousness.

Where Are They Shelved?

Whether you search online, at a bookstore, or in a library, you will find no consensus as to where paranormal fiction titles are shelved. Your best bet is to search the library catalog or bookstore database for individual titles or authors. Table 1 shows how selected series are categorized in libraries, on Amazon.com, and at Borders bookstores. Note the wide discrepancies in the classifications. Rachel Vincent's WERECATS and Jeaniene Frost's NIGHT

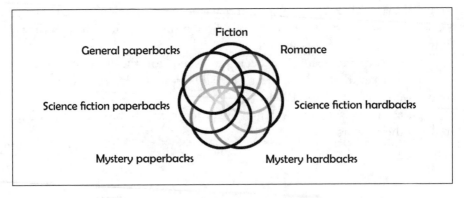

FIGURE 1 Where Are They Shelved?

TABLE 1   Examples of How Series Are Categorized

AUTHOR	SERIES	LIBRARIES	AMAZON.COM	BORDERS
Armstrong, Kelley	WOMEN OF THE OTHERWORLD	Science fiction, fiction, horror	Mystery/thriller	Science fiction/fantasy
Frost, Jeaniene	NIGHT HUNTRESS	Horror, fiction, romance	Fiction	Romance
Harris, Charlaine	SOUTHERN VAMPIRE (SOOKIE STACKHOUSE) MYSTERIES	Fiction, mystery	Contemporary fantasy	Science fiction/fantasy
Henry, Mark	AMANDA FERAL	Fiction, horror	Fiction/comic	Science fiction/fantasy
Vincent, Rachel	WERECATS	Fiction, science fiction, romance	Horror/occult	Romance
Wilson, F. Paul	REPAIRMAN JACK	Fiction, mystery, science fiction	Action and adventure	Horror

HUNTRESS, for example, are classified as both horror and romance—quite a stretch.

Most of these series are available in paperback form. Some series (e.g., Laurell K. Hamilton's ANITA BLAKE, Patricia Briggs's MERCY THOMPSON) exist in multiple forms: hardbacks, paperbacks, e-books, and graphic novels. Occasionally, one or two titles in a series go out of print but can still be found in libraries or in e-book format (a current trend), and this is noted in the series descriptions.

Not included in this bibliography are books published in the SILHOUETTE NOCTURNE series. This Harlequin imprint publishes sensual paranormal romances. NOCTURNE authors include Vivi Anna, Rhyannon Byrd, Doranna Durgin, Michele Hauf, and Patrice Michelle. These books go out of print quickly, usually within a few months of the publication date.

Series Annotations versus Title Annotations

One of the most important rules for reading the books in this bibliography is this: read them in series order—not in random order. Most readers' advisory sources list read-alikes by title rather than by series. That may lead the reader to a single book that falls anywhere in a series rather than to the first book in a series. In general, the reader gets more from the reading if he or she reads the books in the order in which they were written or in the order the author recommends. Many of these books will not be comprehensible if read in random order. They frequently have a story arc that begins in book 1 and develops throughout the series. Character development is generally heaviest in the early books of a series. Although authors attempt to provide background for the reader at the beginning of each book in a series, if a reader begins in the middle or at the end, he or she will miss a great deal of plot and character development that the early books provided. This is especially true for the urban fantasy (UF) and chick lit (CH) series. Reading a single title or starting from the middle or end of a series is like studying the developmental process of an oak tree by reading only about acorns or by beginning with the growth of leaves—you miss the critical steps of germination, growth, and maturation that help you understand the whole process. For these reasons, and with few exceptions, the annotations in this bibliography are for series—not for individual books—and the titles are presented in reading order, either chronological or according to an author's recommendation.

The Main Characters

Many of the vampire series include archetypal characters based on Bram Stoker's *Dracula*. Here is a character analysis from Charlie Huston's *Already Dead* (JOE PITT CASEBOOKS), in which Joe explains the role of humans:

> There are people that know about us. But they are few and most play a specific role. There are the Van Helsings, the righteous who stumble upon us and make it their mission to hunt us down. The Renfields . . . who glom on to us, half servile and half envious. The Lucys, both male and female, who have romanticized the whole vampire myth and dote over us like groupies. And the Minas, the ones who know the truth and don't care, the ones who fall in love. Van Helsings are killed, we use the Renfields and the Lucys to serve us and insulate us from the world. Minas are rare and precious beyond value. There is only one way to know if you have a true Mina: tell her or him what you are and what you do to stay alive. Not many make that final cut.
>
> Then there are the few men and women with true power and influence who know us. These are the ones to be feared. . . . But . . . We will never live in the open unless it is as freaks or prey. The

people who might guide us out of obscure myth will never risk their positions and reputations to say to the world, *"Hey, look, vampires are real!"* (Huston 2005, 64)

Although many of the main characters in these series are classified as "human," they usually have some nonhuman traits. Here are a few of the enhanced humans you will find in these series: psychics, necromancers, witches, sorcerers, warlocks, wizards, Knights Templar, ghost busters, demon hunters, voodoo priests, empaths, animal communicators, doppelgängers, and mirror walkers.

Another group of characters can be classified as the "walking dead": vampires, *dhampirs*, *chupacabras*, zombies, revenants, and reavers.

Shape-shifters are next in line. First, the "weres": wolves (the most common), cheetahs, lions, leopards, bears, sharks, swans, rats, and hyenas (usually the bad guys). Other shifters include skin walkers, dragons, and even gargoyles.

Aside from the obvious differences, most of the vampires and werewolves have stereotypical personalities in these stories. Vamps are sophisticated men of the world, whereas werewolves are blue-collar, all-American guys. Vamps generally live in cities—close to the crowds of humans who serve as their food source. Weres generally live in more rural areas—close to the fields and forests they need for moonlit runs and animal prey (for a comparison of vamps versus weres, see table 2).

Hmmm . . . Brad Pitt—vamp or were?

TABLE 2   Vamps vs. Weres

	VAMPIRES	WEREWOLVES
Clothing	Tuxedo	Blue jeans
Transportation	Bentley, Porsche	Pickup truck, Harley
Career	CEO, nightclub owner	Construction worker
Entertainment	Opera, theater	NASCAR races, line dancing
Exemplars	Carey Grant, George Clooney, Fred Astaire	Tommy Lee Jones, Toby Keith, Robert Duvall

Next, we have the representatives of heaven and hell:

Satan related: demons, incubi, succubi, fiends, hellhounds, and fallen angels

Heaven related: angels, archangels, guardian angels, seraphim, cherubim, and nephilim

Mythology related: gods and goddesses, valkyries, furies, and lamia

Finally, we have the "fae"—the fairy creatures: imps, fairies, elves, garden sprites, pixies, fauns, druids, mermaids, sibyls, ghosts, shadow dwellers, banshees, trolls, ghouls, and boggles.

Variant spellings abound in these stories, with archaic spellings almost always beating out contemporary spellings: *vampires/vampyres*; *dhampir/dhampire/dhamphir/dhampyr*; *daemon/daimon/demon*; and—always—*magick* (supposedly to differentiate it from ordinary magicians' magic). This book uses the "creature" spellings that individual authors use.

Paranormal Plots

Although some authors have created inventive plots, these favorites appear repeatedly:

- Corrupt supernatural council members attack the hero or heroine.
- Human religious fanatics attack the supernaturals.
- Demonic creatures attempt to come through a portal and attack humans.
- Mad scientists or crazy doctors kidnap and experiment on the supernaturals.
- A secret government agency kidnaps supernaturals to build an unbeatable army.
- An ancient evil is reborn and must be stopped.

Plots can be very simple (e.g., villain threatens heroine; hero defeats villain), but many plots veer toward the complex. Vicki Pettersson's SIGNS OF THE ZODIAC is one of the most complicated.

In a recent *New Yorker* interview, Nora Roberts gave her tongue-in-cheek thoughts on the complexity of paranormal plots: "I hope to write the first romantic suspense time-travel paranormal thriller set in Mongolia dealing with Siamese twins who tragically fall in love with the same woman who may or may not be Annie Oakley" (Collins 2009, 62).

Plot Types

Modern paranormal fiction series fall (loosely) into five very different plot types:

> Soul-mate romances
>
> Urban fantasy
>
> Chick lit
>
> Cozy mysteries
>
> Historical series

Some of the works, particularly the soul-mate romances, are also historical romances, so that designation is included as well.

Soul-Mate Romance (SMR) Series

In his *Symposium*, Plato presents Aristophanes' satiric theory of the origin of love. Humankind, Plato's Aristophanes says, was first created with two heads and two sets of appendages—arms, legs, and so on. There were three genders: children of the earth (female-female), children of the sun (male-male), and children of the moon (male-female). They were very powerful, and when they began to plot against the gods, Zeus decided to limit their power and double their number by splitting them in half. To punish them further, each half would then spend its lifetime searching for its matching half. This is a very simplistic synopsis of Aristophanes' philosophy on love, but as you can see, this is really the very beginning of the mythology of the soul mate—forever seeking his or her other half.

Soul-mate romances are closely related to traditional romance fiction. In any romance story, the focus is on the heroine and her hero as they fall in love (lust) at first sight. In the paranormal SMR series, the hero is generally a paranormal being (e.g., vampire, werewolf, demon). By the end of the book, the couple marries, or at least heads off into a happy future together. There may be bumps along the way (ah, those stressful second thoughts and annoying plot intrusions!), but these books concentrate on the romantic relationship and end with the feeling that the couple will live happily ever after. Although similar to regular romantic relationships, soul-mate bonds are much stronger in soul-mate romances than in traditional romances. In fact, the soul-mate bond is for life: if one dies, the other will also die, almost immediately.

In most SMR series, there is a definite process for becoming soul mates. Here is a summary of the steps that Katie MacAlister's hero must take in her DARK ONES series, as spelled out in *A Girl's Guide to Vampires*. Most of the SMR series use some form of this process:

1. Marks the heroine as his own
2. Protects her from afar
3. Conducts first exchange of body fluids (kiss)
4. Entrusts heroine with his life
5. Conducts second exchange (much more intimate than the first exchange)
6. Seeks the heroine's help in overcoming his darker self
7. Conducts the ultimate exchange—their lifeblood

These heroes spend a great deal of time analyzing their attraction to their potential soul mates. From series to series, the heroines' characteristics are very similar. She is usually attractive—in her own way, of course—and she is smart, sassy, independent, and stubborn. She is frequently adopted, or has lost her parents at an early age, or one parent deserted her during infancy. The adoption characteristic is a common one throughout all the types of modern paranormal fiction. Many of the heroines have some type of supernatural ability—generally attributed to the absent parent(s) .

The heroine also spends a great deal of time admiring the hero's physical beauty. His hair is not just brown or blond. It is glossy chocolate or golden sand or molten copper or silky jet. My favorite is leafy green—the hair color of one of Meredith Gentry's lovers in Laurell K. Hamilton's series of the same name. And his hair is not just leafy green; it is ankle-length leafy green.

Just as hair is not just brown, eyes are not just brown or blue, either. They are stormy gray, translucent jade, liquid emerald, blue flame, or quicksilver.

Both the male and the female protagonists in these books are obsessed with their soul mate's scent. It's a big part of their attraction to each other. Cinnamon and cloves are the front-runners here for the men, and vanilla and raspberries are most common for the heroines.

All of the heroes dress in a type of uniform: tight black leather pants or jeans and black silk shirt or T-shirt. Both the men and the women wear so much leather that it's a wonder there is a cow left alive.

"Dark Yearning: Searching for a Soul Mate" is a typical—if concise— soul-mate story made up of quotations from seven SMR works included in this book.

. . . .

Dark Yearning: Searching for a Soul Mate

A Story Created from Real Soul-Mate Romances

by Patricia O'Brien Mathews

LOVE AT FIRST SIGHT

HER: My blood warmed just looking at him. He was striking. If you liked the GQ type. He wore a dark, tailored suit cut to fit his broad shoulders. His angled features gave away nothing as he watched us. I felt his eyes, hidden in shadows, sweep over every inch of my body. . . . Something inside me felt like I knew him. . . . Everything about him was polished, except for the way his thick, ebony hair curled around his collar. . . . His eyes flashed orange, then yellow. Holy Moses . . . I stood there . . . staring up at this magical enigma. (Angela Fox's *Accidental Demon Slayer*)

HIM: He knew the instant he set eyes on her, though he never would have guessed she'd be the one, had that intoxicating scent not wrapped around him like a vise. But it was her. The innocent-looking little waif with the long auburn braid, . . . tortoise-shell glasses perched smartly on the bridge of her small nose. She was wearing a tight white polo shirt with faded blue jeans. . . . A simple outfit . . . but on her it looked downright sinful. . . . A fierce, possessive wave of heat poured through his veins while his mouth watered, and it was only with a conscious effort that Mason controlled the urge to pant like a randy dog. (Rhyannon Byrd's *Last Wolf Watching*)

SECOND THOUGHTS

HER: "I want you to go. Now. And never come back." She blinked back her tears, her hand closing over the crucifix at her throat. . . . Savanah shook her head in disbelief. A hundred years was longer than most people lived. But it didn't change anything. He was still a Vampire. He had still lied to her. For all she knew, he could be the one who had killed her father. (Amanda Ashley's *Night's Pleasure*)

HIM: "Nikolai sighed. He had no idea what he was doing, with her or with himself. She made him feel. . . . Feel? Was that It? He hadn't really felt much of anything more than indifference for such a long time. His life was composed of endurance, duty, hatred, and occasional envy . . . and his kind didn't associate with her kind. She was food. More than that, she was mortal and still had her immortal soul. She wasn't just sustenance. She was an enemy. The worst kind . . . and he wanted her. (Dina James's "Play Dead," in *The Mammoth Book of Vampire Romance*)

. . . .

. . . .

PLOT INTERVENTION: A human religious fanatic tries to kill the supernatural hero, OR wicked witches cast an evil spell on the couple, OR bad humans make a pact with bad supernaturals, OR a dangerous sorcerer weaves black magic to entrap the hero, OR a secret government agency captures the hero for experimentation, OR a vicious demon comes to town, OR a nasty rogue tries to move in on the hero's territory, OR a fallen angel wants the heroine as his mate, OR bad guys from the hero's mysterious past catch up with him, OR a powerful rival tries to kidnap the heroine, OR, OR, OR . . . And then, back to the soul-mate search.

TOO LATE NOW

HER: Beneath my hands, his shoulders shuddered as he fought the red wave of hunger that swept through him. I knew, in a distant part of my mind, that I should be horrified, sickened by what I was offering, by what I craved him to do, but the truth was, I ached to have him feed off me. . . . I gasped and arched back, my eyes open but blind with the overwhelmingly erotic sensation of his mouth moving on my neck, his mind bound so tightly with mine that I could taste my own blood as it slipped down his throat. Within him the endless night that howled so cruelly faded a little, the torment easing as I gave myself up to the moment, trusting that he wouldn't harm me, locked in an embrace more arousing than anything I'd ever known. (Katie MacAlister's *Sex, Lies, and Vampires*)

HIM: He had to stop now, while he could, before his lust for blood overcame his desire for her sweet flesh. . . . He knew he should let her go before it was too late, before his hunger overcame his good sense, before he succumbed to the need burning through him. He could scarcely remember the last time he had embraced a woman he had not regarded as prey. But this woman was more than mere sustenance. Her body fit his perfectly, her voice sang to his soul, her gaze warmed the cold dark places in his heart, shone like the sun in the depths of his hell-bound spirit. (Amanda Ashley's *Desire after Dark*)

HAPPILY EVER AFTER

THEM: "You have made me so completely happy. I'm afraid to hold on to this feeling. . . . I'm scared to death that it's only a dream."

"Not a dream," he said gently, caressing the stray tear from her cheek. "And you can hold on to me if you feel afraid. I'm going to be here beside you as long as you'll have me."

"Forever," she said, beaming up at him.

Nikolai nodded. "Yes, love. Forever." (Lara Adrian's *Veil of Midnight*)

. . . .

Urban Fantasy (UF) Series

According to Tim Holman, head of the science fiction and fantasy publisher Orbit, the rise of urban fantasy has been "the biggest category shift within the science fiction/fantasy market in the last ten years in the U.S." Holman points out that, in July 2009, twenty-eight of the top fifty fantasy best sellers in the United States were UF titles. Holman stresses the importance of urban fantasy: "Remove urban fantasy from the current [science fiction and fantasy] bestseller charts, and they collapse. Most of the bestselling authors disappear; many of the most successful new authors launched over recent years disappear; many of the authors with most rapidly growing sales disappear" (Holman 2009, n.p.). Figure 2, an adaptation of Holman's graph, shows the rise in popularity of urban fantasy between 2004 and 2008.

So . . . there is no doubt that urban fantasy is selling well, but what exactly is it?

In the *Encyclopedia of Fantasy*, the editor John Clute distinguishes urban fantasy from other sorts of contemporary fantasy by the role of the urban setting in the story: "UFs are normally texts where fantasy and the mundane world intersect and interweave throughout a tale which is significantly *about* a real city" (Clute and Grant 1997, 975).

Clute goes on to trace urban fantasy back as far as Charles Dickens, who "tended to imagine internal kingdoms within the city . . . which operated as microcosms and parodies of the larger reality" (Clute and Grant 1997, 975), as in *A Christmas Carol* and *A Tale of Two Cities*. Clute sees modern urban fantasy as having "intensified the model developed by Dickens" (Clute and Grant 1997, 976).

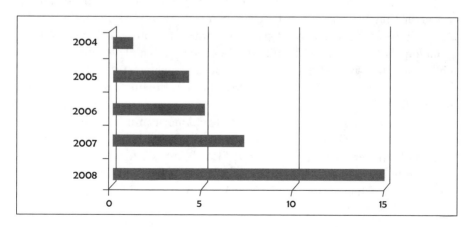

FIGURE 2   **UF Growth among Top 20 Fantasy Bestsellers**

. . . .

Here is an example of Dickens's sense of place as he describes dark and dreary Victorian London:

> It was a foggy day in London, and the fog was heavy and dark. Animate London, with smarting eyes and irritated lungs, was blinking, wheezing, and choking; inanimate London was a sooty spectre, divided in purpose between being visible and invisible, and so being wholly neither. Gaslights flared in the shops with a haggard and unblest air, as knowing themselves to be night-creatures that had no business abroad under the sun; while the sun itself when it was for a few moments dimly indicated through circling eddies of fog, showed as if it had gone out and were collapsing flat and cold. Even in the surrounding country it was a foggy day, but there the fog was grey, whereas in London it was, at about the boundary line, dark yellow, and a little within it brown, and then browner, and then browner, until at the heart of the City—which call Saint Mary Axe—it was rusty-black. From any point of the high ridge of land northward, it might have been discerned that the loftiest buildings made an occasional struggle to get their heads above the foggy sea, and especially that the great dome of Saint Paul's seemed to die hard; but this was not perceivable in the streets at their feet, where the whole metropolis was a heap of vapour charged with muffled sound of wheels, and enfolding a gigantic catarrh.

> Charles Dickens, *Our Mutual Friend*

> Source: www.gutenberg.org/files/883/883.txt

. . . .

But what are twenty-first-century paranormal readers really searching for when they ask for urban fantasy? Nanette Wargo Donohue is on the mark when she says that what patrons want is fiction with "tough female protagonists . . . , stronger distinctions between good and evil, grittier urban landscapes, first-person narration, and sexual tension, often between the female protagonist and a male character who toes the line between good and evil" (2008, 64).

Some urban fantasy is closely related to American noir fiction (i.e., the hard-boiled detective story), with its jaded hero living as an outsider in a bleak and sinister city. See chapter 1, "Read-Alikes," for a list of series in which the protagonist is an investigator or a detective. Prime examples are Jim Butcher's DRESDEN FILES, P. N. Elrod's VAMPIRE FILES, and Mark Del Franco's CONNOR GREY.

In general, the UF protagonist is an insecure loner with some type of supernatural power. He or she lives in an urban environment in the contemporary world and has a cynical outlook on life, embracing sarcasm and an antagonistic attitude as protective devices to maintain distance from unwanted relationships. The protagonist is often adopted, with birth parent(s) who deserted or died during his or her infancy; the otherworldliness of the parent(s) is generally the source of the supernatural gift(s). Female protagonists frequently have red hair.

The reader should definitely start at the beginning of a UF series and read through it chronologically, as the story arc generally extends over several books and the reader must reach back to previous books for background information.

Some urban fantasy is not very urban. For example, Charlaine Harris's SOUTHERN VAMPIRE (SOOKIE STACKHOUSE) MYSTERIES series takes place primarily in small-town Bontemps, Louisiana, although some books in the series are set in large cities like Chicago and Dallas. The series does, however, meet other UF criteria.

At least one series fits all UF criteria except time period. Barb Hendee and J. C. Hendee's NOBLE DEAD SAGA is as dark and urban as the typical UF series, but it takes place in medieval Europe. The series would probably appeal more to a UF reader than to a historical series reader.

Many of the UF protagonists are young, and the events of the series carry them through coming-of-age experiences. The characters go through huge changes throughout the series and emerge as very different persons. A prime example of this is Laurell K. Hamilton's ANITA BLAKE. The character of Anita in book 1 is very different from the Anita in book 19. Other examples include Rob Thurman's CAL LEANDROS, Trisha Baker's CRIMSON, Jenna Black's MORGAN KINGSLEY, EXORCIST, Patricia Briggs's MERCY THOMPSON, Kim Harrison's THE HOLLOWS, and Karen Chance's CASSANDRA PALMER.

Chick Lit (CH) Series

Writing in *Library Journal*, Rebecca Vnuk says that "chick lit . . . is distinguished by its humor—wisecracking characters or ridiculous situations, usually involving work or dating." She goes on to list other attributes: "Look also for a big helping of pop culture—great shoes, trendy drinks, celebrities, jobs in publishing. The characters' ages should also tip you off. Chick lit almost always posits young women setting out to make their mark in the world. Add to this mix an urban setting and a heroine who interacts with the world (whereas in a typical romance, the action is highly internal, mainly between the heroine and the hero), and, presto! you've got yourself a chick lit book" (Vnuk 2005, 42).

Paranormal chick lit has all of those features. In addition, these attractive, young, female protagonists are all supernaturals, from psychic to succubus to vampire to witch, and they all have one or more magical talents, from mind reading to super strength to ghost busting to raising the dead. Paranormal chick lit has much more humor than other types of paranormal fiction. Sensuality levels are frequently high.

Cozy Mystery (COZ) Series

Paranormal COZ series are relatively rare. In these novels, protagonists are intuitive men or women with supernatural abilities who see themselves as amateur detectives. The story generally involves one or more murders that take place in a small town or village where the protagonist is a popular member of the community, members of which may or may not know about the protagonist's magical talents or supernatural status. The local police department views the protagonist as a nuisance—at first. Cozy mysteries generally have no profanity and no sexual details. The reader usually gets no graphic description of the actual violence of the murder(s) to be solved: the dead body just turns up. Plots tend to have several false trails, with lots of misleading clues. The protagonist generally uses his or her supernatural abilities to solve the crime(s).

Historical (HIS) Series

Historical series stories take place in the past, usually in the nineteenth century, but sometimes earlier. Historical stories that are also SMR or CH stories are labeled as such in this book: (HIS, SMR) or (CH, HIS).

Rating Violence, Sensuality, and Humor

A reader generally searches for a book or series that has certain characteristics that have proved likable in past reading experiences. Because three prominent characteristics, or variables, in modern paranormal fiction are violence, sensuality, and humor, this bibliography rates each series with an index for each of those:

V = Violence Index

    1 (yelling and shouting) to **5** (bloodthirsty brutality)

S = Sensuality Index

    1 (chaste) to **5** (multiple explicit sexual scenes)

H = Humor Index

    1 (serious) to **5** (hilarious)

    To further explain the Sensuality Index, if the series rates a 1 or 2, there is friendly or passionate kissing. If the rating is a 3, there is sexual activity with few, if any, details. A 4 or 5 rating means multiple sex scenes with details, from few to many. A 5+ rating means that the graphic sex includes some over-the-top scenes (e.g., multiple partners, sadomasochism, extreme bloodlust).

    Chapter 2, "Series Characteristics," includes lists of series categorized according to these ratings.

Why Are the Ratings Important?

Consider these five series, all SMR series: Stephenie Meyer's TWILIGHT (V3, S2, H3); Nina Bangs's CASTLE OF DARK DREAMS (V2, S5, H5); Kresley Cole's IMMORTALS AFTER DARK (V4, S5, H3); Jenna Black's GUARDIANS OF THE NIGHT (V4, S5, H3); and Amanda Ashley's DARK SERIES (V3, S3, H2)— figure 3 shows their profiles.

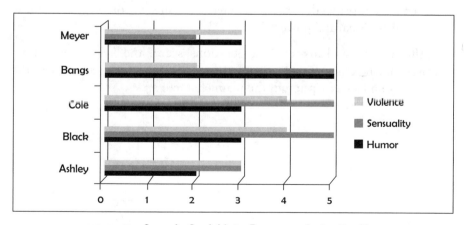

FIGURE 3　Sample Soul-Mate Romance Series Profiles

Obviously, there are major differences. Among the five series, the closest matches would be Cole and Black, with identical profiles. If the reader wants a Meyer read-alike, on this list, Ashley is the closest match, with a bit more sensuality and slightly less humor than Meyer. If the reader wants lots of laughs, Bangs is the obvious choice. If the reader is looking for sensuality, Bangs, Cole, and Black fill the bill. The point to remember is that paranormal novels are not equal when it comes to violence, sensuality, and humor.

How Can This Book Be Used to Find Read-Alikes?

Chapter 1, "Read-Alikes: Categorizing the Series," provides a breakdown of the series by plot type, gender of protagonist, supernatural trait of protagonist, level of violence, level of sensuality, and level of humor.

In using this book to search for a read-alike series, the first step would be to determine which characteristic is most important to the reader. Here are some questions to ask:

- Are you looking for a romance? An urban fantasy? Chick lit?
- Do you want a female protagonist or a male protagonist?
- Do you like lots of laughs, or is humor not important?
- Do you like over-the-top sexual scenes, or not much sexual action?
- Is violence your thing, or are you looking for a more peaceful story?
- Do you like to read about vampires? Shape-shifters? Demons? Hunters? Paranormal detectives? The fae? Witches or sorcerers? Humans with supernatural powers?

After you ask and answer these questions, search the lists on the following pages for matches. Finally, turn to the annotations for a summary of the series plots and a description of the main characters.

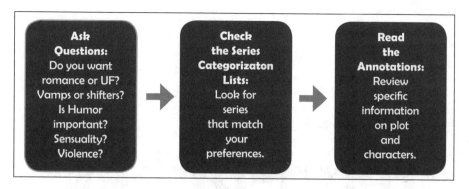

FIGURE 4   How to Find Read-Alikes

CHAPTER 1

read-alikes

categorizing the series

PLOT: Soul-Mate Romance (SMR)

Adair, Cherry: T-FLAC NIGHT TRILOGY—V4, S4, H3

Adams, C. T., and Cathy Clamp: TALES OF THE SAZI—V4, S3–4, H1

Adrian, Lara: THE MIDNIGHT BREED—V3, S4, H2

Allen, Harper: CROSSE TRIPLETS—V5, S3, H3 (CH, SMR)

Andersen, Jessica: THE FINAL PROPHECY—V5, S4, H1

Arthur, Keri: MYTH AND MAGIC SERIES—V5, S5, H2

Ashley, Amanda: DARK SERIES—V3, S3, H2

Ashley, Amanda: NIGHT SERIES—V3, S3, H2

Ashley, Jennifer: SHIFTERS UNBOUND—V3, S4, H3

Ashley, Jennifer, Joy Nash, and Robin Popp: THE IMMORTALS—V3, S5, H3

Bangs, Nina: CASTLE OF DARK DREAMS—V2, S5, H5

Bangs, Nina: GODS OF THE NIGHT—V3, S3, H3

Bangs, Nina: MACKENZIE VAMPIRES—V2, S3, H5

Barbieri, Elaine: WOLF SERIES—V2, S1, H1 (HIS, SMR)

Bardsley, Michele: BROKEN HEART VAMPIRES—V3, S4, H4

Bast, Anya: ELEMENTAL WITCHES—V4, S5, H2

Bast, Anya: THE EMBRACED—V4, S5+, H1

Black, Jenna: GUARDIANS OF THE NIGHT—V4, S5, H3

Black, Shayla: THE DOOMSDAY BRETHREN—V4, S4, H1

Blair, Annette: ACCIDENTAL WITCH TRILOGY—V0, S4, H4

Blair, Annette: TRIPLET WITCH TRILOGY—V1, S5, H4

Blair, Annette: WORKS LIKE MAGICK—V3, S4, H4

Blue, Lucy: BOUND IN DARKNESS—V4, S3, H1 (HIS, SMR)

Briggs, Patricia: ALPHA AND OMEGA—V3, S3, H3 (SMR, UF)

Brook, Meljean: THE GUARDIANS—V4, S4, H3

Burton, Jaci: DEMON HUNTER—V4, S4, H2

Byrd, Rhyannon: PRIMAL INSTINCT—V5, S4, H1

Cassidy, Dakota: ACCIDENTAL FRIENDS—V3, S5, H5 (CH, SMR)

Castle, Kendra Leigh: MACINNES WEREWOLVES TRILOGY—V3, S5, H5

Cole, Kresley: IMMORTALS AFTER DARK—V4, S5, H3

Cooke, Deborah: DRAGONFIRE—V4, S4, H2

Day, Alyssa: WARRIORS OF POSEIDON—V3, S4, H3

Dean, Cameron: CANDACE STEELE, VAMPIRE KILLER—V3, S5, H2
    (SMR, UF)

Dodd, Christina: THE CHOSEN ONES—V3, S4, H3

Dodd, Christina: DARKNESS CHOSEN—V4, S4, H2

Eden, Cynthia: MIDNIGHT TRILOGY—V4, S4, H2

Elias, Amelia: GUARDIANS' LEAGUE—V3, S4, H3

Fallon, Linda: SHADES SERIES—V3, S4, H2 (HIS, SMR)

Feehan, Christine: THE CARPATHIANS (DARK) SERIES—V5, S5, H1

Feehan, Christine: DRAKE SISTERS—V3, S5, H3

Feehan, Christine: GHOSTWALKERS—V4, S4, H2

Feehan, Christine: LEOPARD—V4, S4, H1

Frank, Jacquelyn: THE GATHERERS—V4, S4, H1

Frank, Jacquelyn: NIGHTWALKERS—V4, S5, H3

Frank, Jacquelyn: SHADOWDWELLERS—V4, S5, H1

Greiman, Lois: WITCHES OF MAYFAIR—V4, S4, H2 (HIS, SMR)

Handeland, Lori: NIGHTCREATURE—V4, S4, H3

Hansen, Jamie Leigh: *Betrayal; Cursed* (no series title)—V3, S3, H1

Havens, Candace: CARUTHERS SISTERS—V5, S3, H4 (CH, SMR)

Herron, Rita: THE DEMONBORN—V4, S5, H1

Hill, Joey W.: VAMPIRE QUEEN—V5, S5+, H1

Holling, Jen: MACDONELL BRIDES—V3, S4, H3 (HIS, SMR)

Holly, Emma: FITZ CLARE CHRONICLES/UPYR—V4, S4, H2 (HIS, SMR)

Hooper, Kay: BISHOP/SPECIAL CRIMES UNIT—V5, S3, H2

Howard, Linda, and Linda Jones: SPIRIT WARRIORS—V5, S4, H1

Ione, Larissa: DEMONICA—V5, S4, H3

Ivy, Alexandra: GUARDIANS OF ETERNITY—V4, S4, H3

James, Allyson: DRAGON SERIES—V2, S5, H3

Kantra, Virginia: CHILDREN OF THE SEA—V4, S4, H2

Klasky, Mindy: AS YOU WISH—V1, S3, H4 (CH, SMR)

Kenner, Julie: SUPERHERO CENTRAL—V2, S3–4, H4 (CH, SMR)

Kenyon, Sherrilyn: DARK-HUNTERS—V3, S4, H3

Kenyon, Sherrilyn: DREAM-HUNTERS—V3, S4, H3

Knight, Angela: MAGEVERSE—V5, S5, H3

Knight, Deidre: GODS OF MIDNIGHT—V4, S4, H2

Kohler, Sharie: MOON CHASERS—V4, S5, H2

Krinard, Susan: FANE—V4, S4, H2 (HIS, SMR)

Lane, Amy: LITTLE GODDESS—V5, S5, H3

Laurenston, Shelly: PRIDE—V4, S5, H5

Laurey, Rosemary: VAMPIRE SERIES—V3, S4, H2

Leigh, Lora: BREEDS—V4, S5, H1

Leto, Julie: PHANTOM—V3, S4, H2

Liu, Marjorie M.: DIRK AND STEELE—V3, S3, H1

Love, Kathy: THE YOUNG BROTHERS—V4, S4, H4

MacAlister, Katie: AISLING GREY, GUARDIAN—V3, S4, H5

MacAlister, Katie: DARK ONES—V2, S5, H5

MacAlister, Katie: SILVER DRAGON—V3, S4, H5

Maverick, Liz, Marjorie M. Liu, Patti O'Shea, Carolyn Jewel, and Jade Lee: CRIMSON CITY—V4, S4, H1

Mayhue, Melissa: DAUGHTERS OF THE GLEN—V3, S4, H3

McCarthy, Erin: CUTTERSVILLE GHOSTS—V1, S5, H4

McCarthy, Erin: SEVEN DEADLY SINS—V1, S5, H3

McCarthy, Erin: VEGAS VAMPIRES—V3, S5, H5

McCleave, Annette: SOUL GATHERERS—V3, S4, H1

McCray, Cheyenne: MAGIC—V5, S5, H2

Meyer, Stephenie: THE TWILIGHT SAGA—V3, S2 (books 1–3), S4 (book 4), H3

Moning, Karen: HIGHLANDER SERIES—V3, S4, H2 (HIS, SMR)

Morgan, Alexis: PALADINS OF DARKNESS—V4, S5, H2

Morgan, Alexis: TALIONS—V4, S4, H2

O'Shea, Patti: LIGHT WARRIORS—V4, S4 (book 1 = 5+), H1

Palmer, Pamela: FERAL WARRIORS—V5, S4, H1

Parks, Lydia: EROTIC VAMPIRE SERIES—V5, S5+, H1

Popp, Robin T.: NIGHT SLAYER—V3, S4, H1

Reinke, Sara: THE BRETHREN—V5, S4, H1

Roberts, Nora: SIGN OF SEVEN TRILOGY—V4, S4, H4

Rowe, Stephanie: IMMORTALLY SEXY—V2, S3, H5

Rush, Jaime: OFFSPRING—V4, S4, H1

Russe, Savannah: SISTERHOOD OF THE SIGHT—V3, S4, H2

St. Giles, Jennifer: SHADOWMEN—V3, S4, H1

Sands, Lynsay: ARGENEAU VAMPIRES—V4, S4, H3

Shayne, Maggie: *Bloodline* (novel)—V3, S4, H1

Shayne, Maggie: IMMORTAL WITCHES—V3, S4, H2 (HIS, SMR)

Shayne, Maggie: WINGS IN THE NIGHT—V4, S4, H3

Showalter, Gena: ALIEN HUNTRESS—V4, S4, H2

Showalter, Gena: ATLANTIS—V4, S4, H3

Showalter, Gena: LORDS OF THE UNDERWORLD—V4, S4, H3

Silver, Eve: COMPACT OF SORCERERS—V5, S5, H2

Singh, Nalini: PSY-CHANGELINGS—V3, S4, H3

Sizemore, Susan: LAWS OF THE BLOOD—V4, S3, H2

Sizemore, Susan: PRIMES—V4, S4, H2

Smith, Kathryn: BROTHERHOOD OF BLOOD—V3, S5, H2 (HIS, SMR)

Sparks, Kerrelyn: LOVE AT STAKE—V4, S5, H4 (CH, SMR)

Spear, Terry: WOLF SERIES—V4, S4, H2

Spencer, Jorrie: STRENGTH—V4, S4, H2

Squires, Susan: THE COMPANION—V5, S5, H1 (HIS, SMR)

Stone, Juliana: JAGUAR WARRIOR—V4, S4, H1

Thompson, Ronda: WILD WULFS OF LONDON—V4, S4, H2 (HIS, SMR)

Thompson, Vicki Lewis: HEX SERIES—V1, S4, H5

Viehl, Lynn: THE DARKYN SERIES—V5, S5, H3

Walker, Shiloh: THE HUNTERS—V3, S4, H1

Ward, J. R.: BLACK DAGGER BROTHERHOOD—V5, S5, H3

Ward, J. R.: FALLEN ANGELS—V4, S4, H2

Warren, Christine: THE OTHERS—V4, S4, H4

Whiteside, Diane: TEXAS VAMPIRES—V4, S5, H2

Wilks, Eileen: WORLD OF THE LUPI—V4, S4, H3

Windsor, Anna: DARK CRESCENT SISTERHOOD—V4, S5, H3

York, Rebecca: MOON SERIES—V4, S4–5+, H1

PLOT: URBAN FANTASY (UF)

Acevedo, Mario: FELIX GOMEZ—V5, S3, H3

Adams, C. T., and Cathy Clamp: THRALL—V5, S4, H1

Aguirre, Ann: CORINE SOLOMON—V4, S2, H1

Andrews, Ilona: KATE DANIELS—V5, S2, H3

Andrews, Toni: MERCY HOLLINGS—V3, S4, H3

Armintrout, Jennifer: BLOOD TIES—V5, S4–5, H1

Armstrong, Kelley: WOMEN OF THE OTHERWORLD—V4, S4, H4

Arthur, Keri: RILEY JENSEN, GUARDIAN—V5, S5, H2

Bacon-Smith, Camille: DAEMONS, INC.—V4, S3, H1

Baker, Trisha: CRIMSON—V5, S5, H0

Banks, L. A.: CRIMSON MOON—V4, S4, H2

Banks, L. A.: VAMPIRE HUNTRESS LEGEND—V4, S4, H2

Benedict, Lyn: SHADOWS INQUIRIES—V4, S3, H3

Bickle, Laura: ANYA KALINCZYK—V3, S4, H2

Black, Jenna: MORGAN KINGSLEY, EXORCIST—V4, S51, H3

Boyd, Donna: DEVONCROIX DYNASTY—V4, S4, H1

Brennan, Allison: SEVEN DEADLY SINS—V4, S2 (book 1), S4 (book 2), H1

Briggs, Patricia: ALPHA AND OMEGA—V3, S3, H3 (SMR, UF)

Briggs, Patricia: MERCY THOMPSON—V3, S4, H3

Butcher, Jim: DRESDEN FILES—V4, S3, H4

Butler, Octavia: *Fledgling* (novel)—V4, S4, H1

Caine, Rachel: OUTCAST SEASON—V4, S2, H1

Caine, Rachel: WEATHER WARDEN—V5, S3, H1

Carey, Mike: FELIX CASTOR—V5, S3, H3

Chance, Karen: CASSANDRA PALMER—V3, S4, H2

Chance, Karen: DORINA BASARAB, DHAMPIR—V3, S4, H3

Child, Maureen: QUEEN OF THE OTHERWORLD—V3, S4, H4

Crane, Carolyn: JUSTINE JONES: DISILLUSIONIST—V3, S4, H2

Cunningham, Elaine: CHANGELING DETECTIVE AGENCY—V4, S3, H2

Day, S. J.: MARKED—V5, S5, H2

Dean, Cameron: CANDACE STEELE, VAMPIRE KILLER—V3, S5, H2 (SMR, UF)

Del Franco, Mark: CONNOR GREY—V3, S1, H3

Del Franco, Mark: LAURA BLACKSTONE—V4, S2–3, H3

Devlin, Delilah: DARK REALM—V1, S5+, H1

Douglas, Carole Nelson: DELILAH STREET, PARANORMAL INVESTIGATOR—V4, S4, H4

Drake, Jocelynn: DARK DAYS—V4, S4, H1

Durgin, Doranna: THE RECKONERS—V4, S2, H2

Elrod, P. N.: VAMPIRE FILES—V4, S3, H3

Farren, Mick: RENQUIST QUARTET—V5, S3, H1

Foster, L. L.: SERVANT—V5, S4, H2

Fox, Andrew: FAT WHITE VAMPIRE—V5, S3, H5

Frost, Jeaniene: NIGHT HUNTRESS—V5, S4, H3

Frost, Jeaniene: NIGHT HUNTRESS WORLD—V5, S4, H3

Frost, P. R.: TESS NONCOIRÉ—V4, S3, H2

Galenorn, Yasmine: SISTERS OF THE MOON—V4, S4, H2

Garey, Terri: NICKI STYX—V2, S3, H4

Gideon, Nancy: MOONLIGHT—V4, S4, H1

Gilman, Laura Anne: PARANORMAL SCENE INVESTIGATIONS—V3, S2, H2

Gilman, Laura Anne: RETRIEVERS—V5, S3, H3

Green, Chris Marie: VAMPIRE BABYLON—V4, S4, H1

Green, Simon R.: NIGHTSIDE—V5, S1, H3

Green, Simon R.: SECRET HISTORIES—V4, S2, H4

Gustainis, Justin: QUINCEY MORRIS, SUPERNATURAL INVESTIGATOR—V3, S3, H3

Haddock, Nancy: OLDEST CITY VAMPIRE—V3, S5, H4

Hamilton, Laurell K.: ANITA BLAKE, VAMPIRE HUNTER—V5, S2 (books 1–5), S5 (books 6–19), H3

Hamilton, Laurell K.: MEREDITH GENTRY—V4, S5, H2

Handeland, Lori: PHOENIX CHRONICLES—V4, S4, H2

Harris, Charlaine: HARPER CONNELLY—V3, S2 (books 1–2), S3 (books 3–4), H3

Harris, Charlaine: SOUTHERN VAMPIRE (SOOKIE STACKHOUSE) MYSTERIES—V3, S4, H3

Harrison, Kim: THE HOLLOWS—V4, S5, H3

Hart, Raven, and Virginia Ellis: SAVANNAH VAMPIRES—V5, S5, H3

Hecht, Daniel: CREE BLACK—V3, S2, H2

Hendee, Barb: VAMPIRE MEMORIES—V4, S1, H1

Hilburn, Lynda: KISMET KNIGHT, VAMPIRE PSYCHOLOGIST—V5, S5, H3

Holzner, Nancy: DEADTOWN—V3, S2, H2

Huff, Tanya: SMOKE TRILOGY—V4, S3, H4

Huff, Tanya: VICTORIA NELSON/BLOOD SERIES—V4, S3, H3

Hunter, Faith: JANE YELLOWROCK—V5, S2, H2

Huston, Charlie: JOE PITT CASEBOOKS—V5, S2, H2

James, Allyson: STORMWALKER—V4, S4, H2

Kane, Stacia: DOWNSIDE GHOSTS—V5, S4, H1

Kane, Stacia: MEGAN CHASE—V4, S4, H3

Kenner, Julie: BLOOD LILY CHRONICLES—V4, S2, H1

Kenner, Julie: DEMON-HUNTING SOCCER MOM—V5, S3, H5

Kessler, Jackie: HELL ON EARTH—V4, S5, H5

Kittredge, Caitlin: BLACK LONDON—V4, S3, H2

Kittredge, Caitlin: NOCTURNE CITY—V5, S4, H3

Levitt, John: DOG DAYS—V4, S3, H3

Lewis, J. F.: VOID CITY—V5, S3, H3

Liu, Marjorie M.: HUNTER KISS—V3, S2, H1

MacInerney, Karen: TALES OF AN URBAN WEREWOLF—V2, S3, H4

McGuire, Seanan: OCTOBER DAYE—V4, S1, H2

Mead, Richelle: DARK SWAN—V4, S5, H3

Mead, Richelle: GEORGINA KINCAID—V2, S4, H4

Moning, Karen: FEVER SERIES—V4, S3, H1

Monk, Devon: ALLIE BECKSTROM—V4, S4, H1

Murphy, C. E.: NEGOTIATOR TRILOGY—V3, S3, H2

Murphy, C. E.: WALKER PAPERS—V3, S1, H3

Neill, Chloe: CHICAGOLAND VAMPIRES—V4, S2, H3

Pettersson, Vicki: SIGNS OF THE ZODIAC—V4, S3, H1

Phoenix, Adrian: THE MAKER'S SONG—V5, S5, H1

Pratt, T. A.: MARLA MASON—V3, S3, H4

Rardin, Jennifer: JAZ PARKS—V5, S2, H3

Resnick, Laura: ESTHER DIAMOND—V4, S3, H3

Richardson, Kat: GREYWALKER—V3, S3, H1

Robertson, Linda: CIRCLE/PERSEPHONE ALCMEDI—V3, S3, H2

Rowen, Michelle: LIVING IN EDEN—V3, S3, H3

Rowland, Diana: KARA GILLIAN—V3, S4, H3

Saintcrow, Lilith: DANTE VALENTINE—V4, S3, H1

Saintcrow, Lilith: JILL KISMET—V5, S3, H2

Showalter, Gena: TALES OF AN EXTRAORDINARY GIRL—V4, S4, H3

Simmons, Wm. Mark: CHRIS CSÉJTHE: HALF/LIFE CHRONICLES—V5, S3, H4

Singh, Nalini: GUILD HUNTER—V4, S3, H3

Smith, Kathryn: NIGHTMARE CHRONICLES—V3, S4, H2

Smith-Ready, Jeri: WVMP RADIO—V5, S4, H3

Sniegoski, Thomas E.: REMY CHANDLER—V4, S2, H2

Stein, Jeanne C.: ANNA STRONG CHRONICLES—V4, S3, H2

Strout, Anton: SIMON CANDEROUS—V4, S3, H4

Sunny: DEMON PRINCESS CHRONICLES—V5, S5, H2

Sunny: MONÉRE: CHILDREN OF THE MOON—V5, S5, H2

Thurman, Rob: CAL LEANDROS—V5, S3, H4

Thurman, Rob: TRICKSTER—V4, S2, H4

Troop, Alan F.: DRAGON DELASANGRE—V5, S3, H1

Vaughn, Carrie: KITTY NORVILLE—V3, S3, H3

Vincent, Rachel: WERECATS—V5, S4, H3

Warren, J. D.: WORLD OF THE STORM RAVENS—V2, S2, H4

Weldon, Phaedra: ZOË MARTINIQUE—V4, S2, H2

Wellington, David: LAURA CAXTON—V5, S3, H0

Wells, Jaye: SABINA KANE—V4, S3, H3

Wilson, F. Paul: REPAIRMAN JACK—V5, S3, H4

Wisdom, Linda: HEX SERIES—V5, S4, H5

PLOT: CHICK LIT (CH)

Acosta, Marta: CASA DRACULA—V3, S4, H4

Allen, Harper: CROSSE TRIPLETS—V5, S3, H3 (CH, SMR)

Alt, Madelyn: BEWITCHING MYSTERIES—V3, S2, H3

Austen, Jane, and Seth Grahame-Smith: *Pride and Prejudice and Zombies* (novel)—V5, S1, H4 (CH, HIS spoof)

Bartlett, Gerry: GLORY ST. CLAIRE—V4, S5, H4

Benson, Amber: CALLIOPE REAPER-JONES—V3, S2, H5

Blackwell, Juliet: WITCHCRAFT MYSTERIES—V3, S3, H3

Blair, Annette: VINTAGE MAGIC—V2, S2, H4 (CH, COZ)

Carriger, Gail: THE PARASOL PROTECTORATE—V4, S3, H4 (CH, HIS)

Cassidy, Dakota: ACCIDENTAL FRIENDS—V3, S5, H5 (CH, SMR)

Cassidy, Dakota: DEMONIC ROMANCE—V2, S4, H5 (CH, SMR)

Child, Maureen: FIEND—V4, S4, H5

Daniels, Casey: PEPPER MARTIN MYSTERIES—V3, S3, H4

Davidson, MaryJanice: FRED THE MERMAID—V2, S4, H4

Davidson, MaryJanice: QUEEN BETSY—V4, S4, H4

Fox, Angela: DEMON SLAYERS—V3, S5, H5

Hallaway, Tate: GARNET LACEY—V3, S3, H4

Harper, Molly: NICE GIRLS—V3, S3, H4

Harper, Nina: Succubus Series—V4, S5, H4

Havens, Candace: Bronwyn the Witch—V3, S3, H4

Havens, Candace: Caruthers Sisters—V5, S3, H4 (CH, SMR)

Henry, Mark: Amanda Feral—V5, S4, H5

Kenner, Julie: Superhero Central—V2, S3–4, H4 (CH, SMR)

Klasky, Mindy: As You Wish—V1, S3, H4 (CH, SMR)

Laurie, Victoria: Ghost Hunter Mysteries—V2, S2, H3

Laurie, Victoria: Psychic Eye Mysteries—V3, S3, H3

Lockwood, Cara: Demon Series—V3, S2, H5

McCray, Cheyenne: Night Tracker—V5, S4, H2

Raye, Kimberly: Dead End Dating—V3–4, S2–4, H4

Rowen, Michelle: Immortality Bites—V3, S4, H3

Russe, Savannah: Darkwing Chronicles—V5, S5, H2

Swendson, Shanna: Enchanted, Inc. Series—V2, S2, H3

PLOT: Cozy Mystery (COZ)

Blair, Annette: Vintage Magic—V2, S2, H4 (CH, COZ)

Damsgaard, Shirley: Ophelia and Abby Mysteries—V3, S2, H3

James, Dean: Simon Kirby-Jones Mysteries—V2, S2, H5

PLOT: Historical (HIS)

Austen, Jane, and Seth Grahame-Smith: *Pride and Prejudice and Zombies* (novel)—V5, S1, H4 (CH, HIS spoof)

Barbieri, Elaine: Wolf Series—V2, S1, H1 (HIS, SMR)

Blue, Lucy: Bound in Darkness—V4, S3, H1 (HIS, SMR)

Carriger, Gail: The Parasol Protectorate—V4, S3, H4 (CH, HIS)

Elrod, P. N.: *Quincey Morris, Vampire* (novel)—V3, S3, H2

Fallon, Linda: Shades Series—V3, S4, H2 (HIS, SMR)

Finlay, C. C.: Traitor to the Crown—V4, S2, H2

Gleason, Colleen: Gardella Vampire Chronicles—V4, S4, H2

Greiman, Lois: WITCHES OF MAYFAIR—V4, S4, H2 (HIS, SMR)

Hendee, Barb, and J. C. Hendee: NOBLE DEAD SAGA—V4, S3, H2

Holling, Jen: MACDONELL BRIDES—V3, S4, H3 (HIS, SMR)

Holly, Emma: FITZ CLARE CHRONICLES/UPYR—V4, S4, H2 (HIS, SMR)

Krinard, Susan: FANE—V4, S4, H2 (HIS, SMR)

Krinard, Susan: HISTORICAL WEREWOLF SERIES—V3, S4, H1 (HIS, SMR)

Maclaine, Jenna: CIN CRAVEN—V3, S4, H3

Moning, Karen: HIGHLANDER SERIES—V3, S4, H2 (HIS, SMR)

Shayne, Maggie: IMMORTAL WITCHES—V3, S4, H2 (HIS, SMR)

Smith, Kathryn: BROTHERHOOD OF BLOOD—V3, S5, H2 (HIS, SMR)

Squires, Susan: THE COMPANION—V5, S5, H1 (HIS, SMR)

Thompson, Ronda: WILD WULFS OF LONDON—V4, S4, H2 (HIS, SMR)

Yarbro, Chelsea Quinn: SAINT-GERMAIN—V4, S4, H3

PROTAGONIST: FEMALE

Acosta, Marta: CASA DRACULA—V3, S4, H4 (CH)

Adams, C. T., and Cathy Clamp: TALES OF THE SAZI—V4, S3–4, H1 (SMR)

Adams, C. T., and Cathy Clamp: THRALL—V5, S4, H1 (UF)

Aguirre, Ann: CORINE SOLOMON—V4, S2, H1 (UF)

Allen, Harper: CROSSE TRIPLETS—V5, S3, H3 (CH, SMR)

Alt, Madelyn: BEWITCHING MYSTERIES—V3, S2, H3 (CH)

Andrews, Ilona: KATE DANIELS—V5, S2, H3 (UF)

Andrews, Toni: MERCY HOLLINGS—V3, S4, H3 (UF)

Armintrout, Jennifer: BLOOD TIES—V5, S4–5, H1 (UF)

Armstrong, Kelley: WOMEN OF THE OTHERWORLD—V4, S4, H4 (UF)

Arthur, Keri: MYTH AND MAGIC SERIES—V5, S5, H2 (SMR)

Arthur, Keri: RILEY JENSEN, GUARDIAN—V5, S5, H2 (UF)

Austen, Jane, and Seth Grahame-Smith: *Pride and Prejudice and Zombies* (novel)—V5, S1, H4 (CH, HIS spoof)

Baker, Trisha: CRIMSON—V5, S5, H0 (UF)

Banks, L. A.: CRIMSON MOON—V4, S4, H2 (UF)

Banks, L. A.: VAMPIRE HUNTRESS LEGEND—V4, S4, H2 (UF)

Barbieri, Elaine: WOLF SERIES—V2, S1, H1 (HIS, SMR)

Bardsley, Michele: BROKEN HEART VAMPIRES—V3, S4, H4 (SMR)

Bartlett, Gerry: GLORY ST. CLAIRE—V4, S5, H4 (CH)

Benedict, Lyn: SHADOWS INQUIRIES—V4, S3, H3 (UF)

Benson, Amber: CALLIOPE REAPER-JONES—V3, S2, H5 (CH)

Bickle, Laura: ANYA KALINCZYK—V3, S4, H2 (UF)

Black, Jenna: MORGAN KINGSLEY, EXORCIST—V4, S5+, H3 (UF)

Blackwell, Juliet: WITCHCRAFT MYSTERIES—V3, S3, H3 (CH)

Blair, Annette: ACCIDENTAL WITCH TRILOGY—V0, S4, H4 (SMR)

Blair, Annette: TRIPLET WITCH TRILOGY—V1, S5, H4 (SMR)

Blair, Annette: VINTAGE MAGIC—V2, S2, H4 (CH, COZ)

Blair, Annette: WORKS LIKE MAGICK—V3, S4, H4 (SMR)

Brennan, Allison: SEVEN DEADLY SINS—V4, S2 (book 1), S4 (book 2), H1 (UF)

Briggs, Patricia: ALPHA AND OMEGA—V3, S3, H3 (SMR, UF)

Briggs, Patricia: MERCY THOMPSON—V3, S4, H3 (UF)

Butler, Octavia: *Fledgling* (novel)—V4, S4, H1 (UF)

Caine, Rachel: OUTCAST SEASON—V4, S2, H1 (UF)

Caine, Rachel: WEATHER WARDEN—V5, S3, H1 (UF)

Carriger, Gail: THE PARASOL PROTECTORATE—V4, S3, H4 (CH, HIS)

Cassidy, Dakota: ACCIDENTAL FRIENDS—V3, S5, H5 (CH, SMR)

Cassidy, Dakota: DEMONIC ROMANCE—V2, S4, H5 (CH, SMR)

Chance, Karen: CASSANDRA PALMER—V3, S4, H2 (UF)

Chance, Karen: DORINA BASARAB, DHAMPIR—V3, S4, H3 (UF)

Child, Maureen: FIEND—V4, S4, H5 (CH)

Child, Maureen: QUEEN OF THE OTHERWORLD—V3, S4, H4 (UF)

Cole, Kresley: IMMORTALS AFTER DARK—V4, S5, H3 (SMR)

Crane, Carolyn: JUSTINE JONES: DISILLUSIONIST—V3, S4, H2 (UF)

Cunningham, Elaine: CHANGELING DETECTIVE AGENCY—V4, S3, H2 (UF)

Damsgaard, Shirley: OPHELIA AND ABBY MYSTERIES—V3, S2, H3 (COZ)

Daniels, Casey: PEPPER MARTIN MYSTERIES—V3, S3, H4 (CH)

Davidson, MaryJanice: FRED THE MERMAID—V2, S4, H4 (CH)

Davidson, MaryJanice: QUEEN BETSY—V4, S4, H4 (CH)

Dean, Cameron: CANDACE STEELE, VAMPIRE KILLER—V3, S5, H2 (SMR, UF)

Del Franco, Mark: LAURA BLACKSTONE—V4, S2–3, H3 (UF)

Douglas, Carole Nelson: DELILAH STREET, PARANORMAL INVESTIGATOR— V4, S4, H4 (UF)

Drake, Jocelynn: DARK DAYS—V4, S4, H1 (UF)

Durgin, Doranna: THE RECKONERS—V4, S2, H2 (UF)

Fallon, Linda: SHADES SERIES—V3, S4, H2 (HIS, SMR)

Feehan, Christine: DRAKE SISTERS—V3, S5, H3 (SMR)

Foster, L. L.: SERVANT—V5, S4, H2 (UF)

Fox, Angela: DEMON SLAYERS—V3, S5, H5 (CH)

Frost, Jeaniene: NIGHT HUNTRESS—V5, S4, H3 (UF)

Frost, P. R.: TESS NONCOIRÉ—V4, S3, H2 (UF)

Galenorn, Yasmine: SISTERS OF THE MOON—V4, S4, H2 (UF)

Garey, Terri: NICKI STYX—V2, S3, H4 (UF)

Gideon, Nancy: MOONLIGHT—V4, S4, H1 (UF)

Gilman, Laura Anne: PARANORMAL SCENE INVESTIGATIONS—V3, S2, H2 (UF)

Gilman, Laura Anne: RETRIEVERS—V5, S3, H3 (UF)

Gleason, Colleen: GARDELLA VAMPIRE CHRONICLES—V4, S4, H2 (HIS)

Green, Chris Marie: VAMPIRE BABYLON—V4, S4, H1 (UF)

Greiman, Lois: WITCHES OF MAYFAIR—V4, S4, H2 (HIS, SMR)

Haddock, Nancy: OLDEST CITY VAMPIRE—V3, S5, H4 (UF)

Hallaway, Tate: GARNET LACEY—V3, S3, H4 (CH)

Hamilton, Laurell K.: ANITA BLAKE, VAMPIRE HUNTER—V5, S2 (books 1–5), S5 (books 6–19), H3 (UF)

Hamilton, Laurell K.: MEREDITH GENTRY—V4, S5, H2 (UF)

Handeland, Lori: PHOENIX CHRONICLES—V4, S4, H2 (UF)

Harper, Molly: NICE GIRLS—V3, S3, H4 (CH)

Harper, Nina: SUCCUBUS SERIES—V4, S5, H4 (CH)

Harris, Charlaine: HARPER CONNELLY—V3, S2 (books 1–2), S3 (books 3–4), H3 (UF)

Harris, Charlaine: SOUTHERN VAMPIRE (SOOKIE STACKHOUSE) MYSTERIES—
V3, S4, H3 (UF)

Harrison, Kim: THE HOLLOWS—V4, S5, H3 (UF)

Havens, Candace: BRONWYN THE WITCH—V3, S3, H4 (CH)

Havens, Candace: CARUTHERS SISTERS—V5, S3, H4 (CH, SMR)

Hecht, Daniel: CREE BLACK—V3, S2, H2 (UF)

Hendee, Barb: VAMPIRE MEMORIES—V4, S1, H1 (UF)

Hendee, Barb, and J. C. Hendee: NOBLE DEAD SAGA—V4, S3, H2 (HIS)

Henry, Mark: AMANDA FERAL—V5, S4, H5 (CH)

Hilburn, Lynda: KISMET KNIGHT, VAMPIRE PSYCHOLOGIST—V5, S5, H3 (UF)

Hill, Joey W.: VAMPIRE QUEEN—V5, S5+, H1 (SMR)

Holling, Jen: MACDONELL BRIDES—V3, S4, H3 (HIS, SMR)

Holzner, Nancy: DEADTOWN—V3, S2, H2 (UF)

Huff, Tanya: VICTORIA NELSON/BLOOD SERIES—V4, S3, H3 (UF)

Hunter, Faith: JANE YELLOWROCK—V5, S2, H2 (UF)

James, Allyson: STORMWALKER—V4, S4, H2 (UF)

Kane, Stacia: DOWNSIDE GHOSTS—V5, S4, H1 (UF)

Kane, Stacia: MEGAN CHASE—V4, S4, H3 (UF)

Kenner, Julie: BLOOD LILY CHRONICLES—V4, S2, H1 (UF)

Kenner, Julie: DEMON-HUNTING SOCCER MOM—V5, S3, H5 (UF)

Kessler, Jackie: HELL ON EARTH—V4, S5, H5 (UF)

Kittredge, Caitlin: BLACK LONDON—V4, S3, H2 (UF)

Kittredge, Caitlin: NOCTURNE CITY—V5, S4, H3 (UF)

Klasky, Mindy: AS YOU WISH—V1, S3, H4 (CH, SMR)

Kohler, Sharie: MOON CHASERS—V4, S5, H2 (SMR)

Lane, Amy: LITTLE GODDESS—V5, S5, H3 (SMR)

Laurie, Victoria: GHOST HUNTER MYSTERIES—V2, S2, H3 (CH)

Laurie, Victoria: PSYCHIC EYE MYSTERIES—V3, S3, H3 (CH)

Liu, Marjorie M.: HUNTER KISS—V3, S2, H1 (UF)

Lockwood, Cara: DEMON SERIES—V3, S2, H5 (CH)

MacAlister, Katie: AISLING GREY, GUARDIAN—V3, S4, H5 (SMR)

MacAlister, Katie: SILVER DRAGON—V3, S4, H5 (SMR)

MacInerney, Karen: TALES OF AN URBAN WEREWOLF—V2, S3, H4 (UF)

Maclaine, Jenna: CIN CRAVEN—V3, S4, H3 (HIS)

Mayhue, Melissa: DAUGHTERS OF THE GLEN—V3, S4, H3 (SMR)

McCray, Cheyenne: MAGIC—V5, S5, H2 (SMR)

McCray, Cheyenne: NIGHT TRACKER—V5, S4, H2 (CH)

McGuire, Seanan: OCTOBER DAYE—V4, S1, H2 (UF)

Mead, Richelle: DARK SWAN—V4, S5, H3 (UF)

Mead, Richelle: GEORGINA KINCAID—V2, S4, H4 (UF)

Meyer, Stephenie: THE TWILIGHT SAGA—V3, S2 (books 1–3), S4 (book 4), H3 (SMR)

Moning, Karen: FEVER SERIES—V4, S3, H1 (UF)

Monk, Devon: ALLIE BECKSTROM—V4, S4, H1 (UF)

Murphy, C. E.: NEGOTIATOR TRILOGY—V3, S3, H2 (UF)

Murphy, C. E.: WALKER PAPERS—V3, S1, H3 (UF)

Neill, Chloe: CHICAGOLAND VAMPIRES—V4, S2, H3 (UF)

Pettersson, Vicki: SIGNS OF THE ZODIAC—V4, S3, H1 (UF)

Pratt, T. A.: MARLA MASON—V3, S3, H4 (UF)

Rardin, Jennifer: JAZ PARKS—V5, S2, H3 (UF)

Raye, Kimberly: DEAD END DATING—V3–4, S2–4, H4 (CH)

Resnick, Laura: ESTHER DIAMOND—V4, S3, H3 (UF)

Richardson, Kat: GREYWALKER—V3, S3, H1 (UF)

Robertson, Linda: CIRCLE/PERSEPHONE ALCMEDI—V3, S3, H2 (UF)

Rowe, Stephanie: IMMORTALLY SEXY—V2, S3, H5 (SMR)

Rowen, Michelle: IMMORTALITY BITES—V3, S4, H3 (CH)

Rowen, Michelle: LIVING IN EDEN—V3, S3, H3 (UF)

Rowland, Diana: KARA GILLIAN—V3, S4, H3 (UF)

Russe, Savannah: DARKWING CHRONICLES—V5, S5, H2 (CH)

Russe, Savannah: SISTERHOOD OF THE SIGHT—V3, S4, H2 (SMR)

Saintcrow, Lilith: DANTE VALENTINE—V4, S3, H1 (UF)

Saintcrow, Lilith: JILL KISMET—V5, S3, H2 (UF)

Shayne, Maggie: IMMORTAL WITCHES—V3, S4, H2 (HIS, SMR)

Showalter, Gena: ALIEN HUNTRESS—V4, S4, H2 (SMR)

Showalter, Gena: TALES OF AN EXTRAORDINARY GIRL—V4, S4, H3 (UF)

Singh, Nalini: GUILD HUNTER—V4, S3, H3 (UF)

Smith, Kathryn: NIGHTMARE CHRONICLES—V3, S4, H2 (UF)

Stein, Jeanne C.: ANNA STRONG CHRONICLES—V4, S3, H2 (UF)

Sunny: DEMON PRINCESS CHRONICLES—V5, S5, H2 (UF)

Sunny: MONÉRE: CHILDREN OF THE MOON—V5, S5, H2 (UF)

Swendson, Shanna: ENCHANTED, INC. SERIES—V2, S2, H3 (CH)

Thurman, Rob: TRICKSTER—V4, S2, H4 (UF)

Vaughn, Carrie: KITTY NORVILLE—V3, S3, H3 (UF)

Vincent, Rachel: WERECATS—V5, S4, H3 (UF)

Weldon, Phaedra: ZOË MARTINIQUE—V4, S2, H2 (UF)

Wellington, David: LAURA CAXTON—V5, S3, H0 (UF)

Wells, Jaye: SABINA KANE—V4, S3, H3 (UF)

Wilks, Eileen: WORLD OF THE LUPI—V4, S4, H3 (SMR)

Windsor, Anna: DARK CRESCENT SISTERHOOD—V4, S5, H3 (SMR)

Wisdom, Linda: HEX SERIES—V5, S4, H5 (UF)

PROTAGONIST: MALE

Acevedo, Mario: FELIX GOMEZ—V5, S3, H3 (UF)

Adair, Cherry: T-FLAC NIGHT TRILOGY—V4, S4, H3 (SMR)

Ashley, Jennifer, Joy Nash, and Robin Popp: THE IMMORTALS—V3, S5, H3 (SMR)

Bacon-Smith, Camille: DAEMONS, INC.—V4, S3, H1 (UF)

Bangs, Nina: CASTLE OF DARK DREAMS—V2, S5, H5 (SMR)

Bangs, Nina: GODS OF THE NIGHT—V3, S3, H3 (SMR)

Bangs, Nina: MACKENZIE VAMPIRES—V2, S3, H5 (SMR)

Bast, Anya: THE EMBRACED—V4, S5+, H1 (SMR)

Black, Jenna: GUARDIANS OF THE NIGHT—V4, S5, H3 (SMR)

Black, Shayla: THE DOOMSDAY BRETHREN—V4, S4, H1 (SMR)

Blue, Lucy: BOUND IN DARKNESS—V4, S3, H1 (HIS, SMR)

Boyd, Donna: DEVONCROIX DYNASTY—V4, S4, H1 (UF)

Burton, Jaci: Demon Hunter—V4, S4, H2 (SMR)

Butcher, Jim: Dresden Files—V4, S3, H4 (UF)

Carey, Mike: Felix Castor—V5, S3, H3 (UF)

Castle, Kendra Leigh: MacInnes Werewolves Trilogy—V3, S5, H5 (SMR)

Cole, Kresley: Immortals after Dark—V4, S5, H3 (SMR)

Cooke, Deborah: Dragonfire—V4, S4, H2 (SMR)

Day, Alyssa: Warriors of Poseidon—V3, S4, H3 (SMR)

Del Franco, Mark: Connor Grey—V3, S1, H3 (UF)

Dodd, Christina: Darkness Chosen—V4, S4, H2 (SMR)

Elias, Amelia: Guardians' League—V3, S4, H3 (SMR)

Elrod, P. N.: *Quincey Morris, Vampire* (novel)—V3, S3, H2 (HIS)

Elrod, P. N.: Vampire Files—V4, S3, H3 (UF)

Fallon, Linda: Shades Series—V3, S4, H2 (HIS, SMR)

Farren, Mick: Renquist Quartet—V5, S3, H1 (UF)

Feehan, Christine: The Carpathians (Dark) Series—V5, S5, H1 (SMR)

Feehan, Christine: GhostWalkers—V4, S4, H2 (SMR)

Feehan, Christine: Leopard—V4, S4, H1 (SMR)

Finlay, C. C.: Traitor to the Crown—V4, S2, H2 (HIS)

Fox, Andrew: Fat White Vampire—V5, S3, H5 (UF)

Green, Simon R.: Nightside—V5, S1, H3 (UF)

Green, Simon R.: Secret Histories—V4, S2, H4 (UF)

Gustainis, Justin: Quincey Morris, Supernatural Investigator—V3, S3, H3 (UF)

Hart, Raven, and Virginia Ellis: Savannah Vampires—V5, S5, H3 (UF)

Herron, Rita: The Demonborn—V4, S5, H1 (SMR)

Holly, Emma: Fitz Clare Chronicles/Upyr—V4, S4, H2 (HIS, SMR)

Huff, Tanya: Smoke Trilogy—V4, S3, H4 (UF)

Huston, Charlie: Joe Pitt Casebooks—V5, S2, H2 (UF)

Ione, Larissa: Demonica—V5, S4, H3 (SMR)

Ivy, Alexandra: Guardians of Eternity—V4, S4, H3 (SMR)

James, Dean: Simon Kirby-Jones Mysteries—V2, S2, H5 (COZ)

Kantra, Virginia: CHILDREN OF THE SEA—V4, S4, H2 (SMR)

Kenyon, Sherrilyn: DARK-HUNTERS—V3, S4, H3 (SMR)

Knight, Angela: MAGEVERSE—V5, S5, H3 (SMR)

Knight, Deidre: GODS OF MIDNIGHT—V4, S4, H2 (SMR)

Kohler, Sharie: MOON CHASERS—V4, S5, H2 (SMR)

Laurey, Rosemary: VAMPIRE SERIES—V3, S4, H2 (SMR)

Leigh, Lora: BREEDS—V4, S5, H1 (SMR)

Leto, Julie: PHANTOM—V3, S4, H2 (SMR)

Levitt, John: DOG DAYS—V4, S3, H3 (UF)

Lewis, J. F.: VOID CITY—V5, S3, H3 (UF)

Liu, Marjorie M.: DIRK AND STEELE—V3, S3, H1 (SMR)

Love, Kathy: THE YOUNG BROTHERS—V4, S4, H4 (SMR)

MacAlister, Katie: DARK ONES—V2, S5, H5 (SMR)

McCarthy, Erin: SEVEN DEADLY SINS—V1, S5, H3 (SMR)

McCray, Cheyenne: MAGIC—V5, S5, H2 (SMR)

Morgan, Alexis: PALADINS OF DARKNESS—V4, S5, H2 (SMR)

Morgan, Alexis: TALIONS—V4, S4, H2 (SMR)

Parks, Lydia: EROTIC VAMPIRE SERIES—V5, S5+, H1 (SMR)

Phoenix, Adrian: THE MAKER'S SONG—V5, S5, H1 (UF)

Reinke, Sara: THE BRETHREN—V5, S4, H1 (SMR)

Roberts, Nora: SIGN OF SEVEN TRILOGY—V4, S4, H4 (SMR)

St. Giles, Jennifer: SHADOWMEN—V3, S4, H1 (SMR)

Sands, Lynsay: ARGENEAU VAMPIRES—V4, S4, H3 (SMR)

Showalter, Gena: ATLANTIS—V4, S4, H3 (SMR)

Silver, Eve: COMPACT OF SORCERERS—V5, S5, H2 (SMR)

Simmons, Wm. Mark: CHRIS CSÉJTHE: HALF/LIFE CHRONICLES—V5, S3, H4 (UF)

Smith, Kathryn: BROTHERHOOD OF BLOOD—V3, S5, H2 (HIS, SMR)

Sparks, Kerrelyn: LOVE AT STAKE—V4, S5, H4 (CH, SMR)

Strout, Anton: SIMON CANDEROUS—V4, S3, H4 (UF)

Thurman, Rob: CAL LEANDROS—V5, S3, H4 (UF)

Troop, Alan F.: DRAGON DELASANGRE—V5, S3, H1 (UF)

Viehl, Lynn: THE DARKYN SERIES—V5, S5, H3 (SMR)

Ward, J. R.: BLACK DAGGER BROTHERHOOD—V5, S5, H3 (SMR)

Ward, J. R.: FALLEN ANGELS—V4, S4, H2 (SMR)

Whiteside, Diane: TEXAS VAMPIRES—V4, S5, H2 (SMR)

Wilson, F. Paul: REPAIRMAN JACK—V5, S3, H4 (UF)

Yarbro, Chelsea Quinn: SAINT-GERMAIN—V4, S4, H3 (HIS)

York, Rebecca: MOON SERIES—V4, S4–5+, H1 (SMR)

PROTAGONIST: VAMPIRE

Acevedo, Mario: FELIX GOMEZ—V5, S3, H3 (UF)

Acosta, Marta: CASA DRACULA—V3, S4, H4 (CH)

Adams, C. T., and Cathy Clamp: THRALL—V5, S4, H1 (UF)

Adrian, Lara: THE MIDNIGHT BREED—V3, S4, H2 (SMR)

Armintrout, Jennifer: BLOOD TIES—V5, S4–5, H1 (UF)

Ashley, Amanda: DARK SERIES—V3, S3, H2 (SMR)

Ashley, Amanda: NIGHT SERIES—V3, S3, H2 (SMR)

Baker, Trisha: CRIMSON—V5, S5, H0 (UF)

Bangs, Nina: CASTLE OF DARK DREAMS—V2, S5, H5 (SMR)

Bangs, Nina: MACKENZIE VAMPIRES—V2, S3, H5 (SMR)

Bardsley, Michele: BROKEN HEART VAMPIRES—V3, S4, H4 (SMR)

Bartlett, Gerry: GLORY ST. CLAIRE—V4, S5, H4 (CH)

Bast, Anya: THE EMBRACED—V4, S5+, H1 (SMR)

Black, Jenna: GUARDIANS OF THE NIGHT—V4, S5, H3 (SMR)

Blue, Lucy: BOUND IN DARKNESS—V4, S3, H1 (HIS, SMR)

Butler, Octavia: *Fledgling* (novel)—V4, S4, H1 (UF)

Cassidy, Dakota: ACCIDENTAL FRIENDS—V3, S5, H5 (CH, SMR)

Chance, Karen: DORINA BASARAB, DHAMPIR—V3, S4, H3 (UF)

Davidson, MaryJanice: QUEEN BETSY—V4, S4, H4 (CH)

Dean, Cameron: CANDACE STEELE, VAMPIRE KILLER—V3, S5, H2 (SMR, UF)

Devlin, Delilah: DARK REALM—V1, S5+, H1 (UF)

Drake, Jocelynn: DARK DAYS—V4, S4, H1 (UF)

Eden, Cynthia: MIDNIGHT TRILOGY—V4, S4, H2 (SMR)

Elias, Amelia: GUARDIANS' LEAGUE—V3, S4, H3 (SMR)

Elrod, P. N.: *Quincey Morris, Vampire* (novel)—V3, S3, H2 (HIS)

Elrod, P. N.: VAMPIRE FILES—V4, S3, H3 (UF)

Farren, Mick: RENQUIST QUARTET—V5, S3, H1 (UF)

Feehan, Christine: THE CARPATHIANS (DARK) SERIES—V5, S5, H1 (SMR)

Fox, Andrew: FAT WHITE VAMPIRE—V5, S3, H5 (UF)

Frank, Jacquelyn: NIGHTWALKERS—V4, S5, H3 (SMR)

Frost, Jeaniene: NIGHT HUNTRESS—V5, S4, H3 (UF)

Frost, Jeaniene: NIGHT HUNTRESS WORLD—V5, S4, H3 (UF)

Galenorn, Yasmine: SISTERS OF THE MOON—V4, S4, H2 (UF)

Gleason, Colleen: GARDELLA VAMPIRE CHRONICLES—V4, S4, H2 (HIS)

Haddock, Nancy: OLDEST CITY VAMPIRE—V3, S5, H4 (UF)

Harper, Molly: NICE GIRLS—V3, S3, H4 (CH)

Hart, Raven, and Virginia Ellis: SAVANNAH VAMPIRES—V5, S5, H3 (UF)

Hendee, Barb: VAMPIRE MEMORIES—V4, S1, H1 (UF)

Hill, Joey W.: VAMPIRE QUEEN—V5, S5+, H1 (SMR)

Holly, Emma: FITZ CLARE CHRONICLES/UPYR—V4, S4, H2 (HIS, SMR)

Huff, Tanya: SMOKE TRILOGY—V4, S3, H4 (UF)

Huff, Tanya: VICTORIA NELSON/BLOOD SERIES—V4, S3, H3 (UF)

Huston, Charlie: JOE PITT CASEBOOKS—V5, S2, H2 (UF)

Ivy, Alexandra: GUARDIANS OF ETERNITY—V4, S4, H3 (SMR)

James, Dean: SIMON KIRBY-JONES MYSTERIES—V2, S2, H5 (COZ)

Kenyon, Sherrilyn: DARK-HUNTERS—V3, S4, H3 (SMR)

Knight, Angela: MAGEVERSE—V5, S5, H3 (SMR)

Laurey, Rosemary: VAMPIRE SERIES—V3, S4, H2 (SMR)

Lewis, J. F.: VOID CITY—V5, S3, H3 (UF)

Love, Kathy: THE YOUNG BROTHERS—V4, S4, H4 (SMR)

MacAlister, Katie: DARK ONES—V2, S5, H5 (SMR)

Maclaine, Jenna: CIN CRAVEN—V3, S4, H3 (HIS)

Maverick, Liz, Marjorie M. Liu, Patti O'Shea, Carolyn Jewel, and Jade Lee: CRIMSON CITY—V4, S4, H1 (SMR)

McCarthy, Erin: VEGAS VAMPIRES—V3, S5, H5 (SMR)

Meyer, Stephenie: THE TWILIGHT SAGA—V3, S2 (books 1–3), S4 (book 4), H3 (SMR)

Neill, Chloe: CHICAGOLAND VAMPIRES—V4, S2, H3 (UF)

Parks, Lydia: EROTIC VAMPIRE SERIES—V5, S5+, H1 (SMR)

Phoenix, Adrian: THE MAKER'S SONG—V5, S5, H1 (UF)

Popp, Robin T.: NIGHT SLAYER—V3, S4, H1 (SMR)

Raye, Kimberly: DEAD END DATING—V3–4, S2–4, H4 (CH)

Reinke, Sara: THE BRETHREN—V5, S4, H1 (SMR)

Rowen, Michelle: IMMORTALITY BITES—V3, S4, H3 (CH)

Russe, Savannah: DARKWING CHRONICLES—V5, S5, H2 (CH)

Sands, Lynsay: ARGENEAU VAMPIRES—V4, S4, H3 (SMR)

Shayne, Maggie: WINGS IN THE NIGHT—V4, S4, H3 (SMR)

Showalter, Gena: LORDS OF THE UNDERWORLD—V4, S4, H3 (SMR)

Simmons, Wm. Mark: CHRIS CSÉJTHE: HALF/LIFE CHRONICLES—V5, S3, H4 (UF)

Sizemore, Susan: LAWS OF THE BLOOD—V4, S3, H2 (SMR)

Sizemore, Susan: PRIMES—V4, S4, H2 (SMR)

Smith, Kathryn: BROTHERHOOD OF BLOOD—V3, S5, H2 (HIS, SMR)

Smith-Ready, Jeri: WVMP RADIO—V5, S4, H3 (UF)

Sparks, Kerrelyn: LOVE AT STAKE—V4, S5, H4 (CH, SMR)

Squires, Susan: THE COMPANION—V5, S5, H1 (HIS, SMR)

Stein, Jeanne C.: ANNA STRONG CHRONICLES—V4, S3, H2 (UF)

Viehl, Lynn: THE DARKYN SERIES—V5, S5, H3 (SMR)

Walker, Shiloh: THE HUNTERS—V3, S4, H1 (SMR)

Ward, J. R.: BLACK DAGGER BROTHERHOOD—V5, S5, H3 (SMR)

Warren, Christine: THE OTHERS—V4, S4, H4 (SMR)

Wells, Jaye: SABINA KANE—V4, S3, H3 (UF)

Whiteside, Diane: TEXAS VAMPIRES—V4, S5, H2 (SMR)

Yarbro, Chelsea Quinn: SAINT-GERMAIN—V4, S4, H3 (HIS)

PROTAGONIST: Werewolf or Other Shape-Shifter

Adams, C. T., and Cathy Clamp: Tales of the Sazi—V4, S3–4, H1 (SMR) (wolves)

Armstrong, Kelley: Women of the Otherworld—V4, S4, H4 (UF) (wolves)

Arthur, Keri: Myth and Magic Series—V5, S5, H2 (SMR) (sea dragon)

Arthur, Keri: Riley Jensen, Guardian—V5, S5, H2 (UF) (*dhampir*)

Ashley, Jennifer: Shifters Unbound—V3, S4, H3 (SMR) (various)

Bangs, Nina: Gods of the Night—V3, S3, H3 (SMR) (prehistoric creatures)

Banks, L. A.: Crimson Moon—V4, S4, H2 (UF) (wolves)

Blair, Annette: Works like Magick—V3, S4, H4 (SMR) (dragon)

Boyd, Donna: Devoncroix Dynasty—V4, S4, H1 (UF) (wolves)

Briggs, Patricia: Alpha and Omega—V3, S3, H3 (SMR, UF) (wolves)

Briggs, Patricia: Mercy Thompson—V3, S4, H3 (UF) (coyote, wolves)

Byrd, Rhyannon: Primal Instinct—V5, S4, H1 (SMR) (various)

Cassidy, Dakota: Accidental Friends—V3, S5, H5 (CH, SMR) (wolves)

Castle, Kendra Leigh: MacInnes Werewolves Trilogy—V3, S5, H5 (SMR) (wolves)

Cole, Kresley: Immortals after Dark—V4, S5, H3 (SMR) (wolves)

Cooke, Deborah: Dragonfire—V4, S4, H2 (SMR) (dragons)

Davidson, MaryJanice: Fred the Mermaid—V2, S4, H4 (CH) (mermaid)

Dodd, Christina: Darkness Chosen—V4, S4, H2 (SMR) (various)

Eden, Cynthia: Midnight Trilogy—V4, S4, H2 (SMR) (various)

Feehan, Christine: Leopard—V4, S4, H1 (SMR) (various big cats)

Gideon, Nancy: Moonlight—V4, S4, H1 (UF) (werewolf)

Handeland, Lori: Nightcreature—V4, S4, H3 (SMR) (wolves)

Holzner, Nancy: Deadtown—V3, S2, H2 (UF) (Cerddorion—shifts into any sentient being)

Hunter, Faith: Jane Yellowrock—V5, S2, H2 (UF) (skin walker)

James, Allyson: Dragon Series—V2, S5, H3 (SMR) (dragons)

Kantra, Virginia: Children of the Sea—V4, S4, H2 (SMR) (selkies)

Kittredge, Caitlin: Nocturne City—V5, S4, H3 (UF) (wolves)

Knight, Angela: MAGEVERSE—V5, S5, H3 (SMR) (various)

Kohler, Sharie: MOON CHASERS—V4, S5, H2 (SMR) (wolves)

Krinard, Susan: FANE—V4, S4, H2 (HIS, SMR) (from fae to human form)

Krinard, Susan: HISTORICAL WEREWOLF SERIES—V3, S4, H1 (HIS, SMR)
(dragons)

Laurenston, Shelly: PRIDE—V4, S5, H5 (SMR) (various)

Leigh, Lora: BREEDS—V4, S5, H1 (SMR) (wolves, big cats, coyotes)

MacAlister, Katie: AISLING GREY, GUARDIAN—V3, S4, H5 (SMR) (dragons)

MacAlister, Katie: SILVER DRAGON—V3, S4, H5 (SMR) (dragons)

MacInerney, Karen: TALES OF AN URBAN WEREWOLF—V2, S3, H4 (UF)
(wolves)

Maverick, Liz, Marjorie M. Liu, Patti O'Shea, Carolyn Jewel, and Jade Lee:
CRIMSON CITY—V4, S4, H1 (SMR) (wolves)

Palmer, Pamela: FERAL WARRIORS—V5, S4, H1 (SMR) (various)

St. Giles, Jennifer: SHADOWMEN—V3, S4, H1 (SMR) (from shadowmen to
human form)

Singh, Nalini: PSY-CHANGELINGS—V3, S4, H3 (SMR) (wolves, leopards)

Spear, Terry: WOLF SERIES—V4, S4, H2 (SMR) (wolves)

Spencer, Jorrie: STRENGTH—V4, S4, H2 (SMR) (wolves)

Thompson, Ronda: WILD WULFS OF LONDON—V4, S4, H2 (HIS, SMR)
(werewolves)

Troop, Alan F.: DRAGON DELASANGRE—V5, S3, H1 (UF) (dragon)

Vaughn, Carrie: KITTY NORVILLE—V3, S3, H3 (UF) (wolf)

Vincent, Rachel: WERECATS—V5, S4, H3 (UF) (cats)

Walker, Shiloh: THE HUNTERS—V3, S4, H1 (SMR) (various)

Warren, Christine: THE OTHERS—V4, S4, H4 (SMR) (various)

Warren, J. D.. WORLD OF THE STORM RAVENS—V2, S2, H4 (UF) (ravens)

Wilks, Eileen: WORLD OF THE LUPI—V4, S4, H3 (SMR) (wolf)

York, Rebecca: MOON SERIES—V4, S4–5+, H1 (SMR) (wolf)

PROTAGONIST: DEMON

Bacon-Smith, Camille: DAEMONS, INC.—V4, S3, H1 (UF)

Bangs, Nina: CASTLE OF DARK DREAMS—V2, S5, H5 (SMR)

Frank, Jacquelyn: NIGHTWALKERS—V4, S5, H3 (SMR)

Harper, Nina: SUCCUBUS SERIES—V4, S5, H4 (CH)

Herron, Rita: THE DEMONBORN—V4, S5, H1 (SMR)

Ione, Larissa: DEMONICA—V5, S4, H3 (SMR)

Kane, Stacia: MEGAN CHASE—V4, S4, H3 (UF)

Kenner, Julie: BLOOD LILY CHRONICLES—V4, S2, H1 (UF)

Kessler, Jackie: HELL ON EARTH—V4, S5, H5 (UF)

MacAlister, Katie: AISLING GREY, GUARDIAN—V3, S4, H5 (SMR)

MacAlister, Katie: SILVER DRAGON—V3, S4, H5 (SMR)

McCarthy, Erin: SEVEN DEADLY SINS—V1, S5, H3 (SMR)

Mead, Richelle: GEORGINA KINCAID—V2, S4, H4 (UF)

PROTAGONIST: HUNTER OF DEMONS, VAMPIRES, OR WEREWOLVES

Andersen, Jessica: THE FINAL PROPHECY—V5, S4, H1 (SMR)

Ashley, Jennifer, Joy Nash, and Robin Popp: THE IMMORTALS—V3, S5, H3 (SMR)

Austen, Jane, and Seth Grahame-Smith: *Pride and Prejudice and Zombies* (novel)—V5, S1, H4 (CH, HIS spoof)

Banks, L. A.: VAMPIRE HUNTRESS LEGEND—V4, S4, H2 (UF)

Black, Jenna: MORGAN KINGSLEY, EXORCIST—V4, S5+, H3 (UF)

Brennan, Allison: SEVEN DEADLY SINS—V4, S2, H1 (UF)

Brook, Meljean: THE GUARDIANS—V4, S4, H3 (SMR)

Burton, Jaci: DEMON HUNTER—V4, S4, H2 (SMR)

Child, Maureen: FIEND—V4, S4, H5 (CH)

Child, Maureen: QUEEN OF THE OTHERWORLD—V3, S4, H4 (UF)

Dean, Cameron: CANDACE STEELE, VAMPIRE KILLER—V3, S5, H2 (SMR, UF)

Drake, Jocelynn: DARK DAYS—V4, S4, H1 (UF)

Foster, L. L.: SERVANT—V5, S4, H2 (UF)

Fox, Angela: DEMON SLAYERS—V3, S5, H5 (CH)

Frost, Jeaniene: NIGHT HUNTRESS—V5, S4, H3 (UF)

Frost, P. R.: TESS NONCOIRÉ—V4, S3, H2 (UF)

Gustainis, Justin: QUINCEY MORRIS, SUPERNATURAL INVESTIGATOR—V3, S3, H3 (UF)

Hamilton, Laurell K.: ANITA BLAKE, VAMPIRE HUNTER—V5, S2 (books 1–5), S5 (books 6–19), H3 (UF)

Handeland, Lori: NIGHTCREATURE—V4, S4, H3 (SMR)

Handeland, Lori: PHOENIX CHRONICLES—V4, S4, H2 (UF)

Havens, Candace: CARUTHERS SISTERS—V5, S3, H4 (CH, SMR)

Hendee, Barb, and J. C. Hendee: NOBLE DEAD SAGA—V4, S3, H2 (HIS)

Herron, Rita: THE DEMONBORN—V4, S5, H1 (SMR)

Hunter, Faith: JANE YELLOWROCK—V5, S2, H2 (UF)

Ione, Larissa: DEMONICA—V5, S4, H3 (SMR)

Kenner, Julie: BLOOD LILY CHRONICLES—V4, S2, H1 (UF)

Kenner, Julie: DEMON-HUNTING SOCCER MOM—V5, S3, H5 (UF)

Kohler, Sharie: MOON CHASERS—V4, S5, H2 (SMR)

Liu, Marjorie M.: HUNTER KISS—V3, S2, H1 (UF)

Mead, Richelle: DARK SWAN—V4, S5, H3 (UF)

Morgan, Alexis: PALADINS OF DARKNESS—V4, S5, H2 (SMR)

Morgan, Alexis: TALIONS—V4, S4, H2 (SMR)

Pratt, T. A.: MARLA MASON—V3, S3, H4 (UF)

Roberts, Nora: SIGN OF SEVEN TRILOGY—V4, S4, H4 (SMR)

Saintcrow, Lilith: JILL KISMET—V5, S3, H2 (UF)

Showalter, Gena: ALIEN HUNTRESS—V4, S4, H2 (SMR)

Silver, Eve: COMPACT OF SORCERERS—V5, S5, H2 (SMR)

Singh, Nalini: GUILD HUNTER—V4, S3, H3 (UF)

Thurman, Rob: CAL LEANDROS—V5, S3, H4 (UF)

Thurman, Rob: TRICKSTER—V4, S2, H4 (UF)

Walker, Shiloh: THE HUNTERS—V3, S4, H1 (SMR)

Wellington, David: LAURA CAXTON—V5, S3, H0 (UF)

Wells, Jaye: SABINA KANE—V4, S3, H3 (UF)

Wilson, F. Paul: REPAIRMAN JACK—V5, S3, H4 (UF)

PROTAGONIST: INVESTIGATOR OR DETECTIVE

Acevedo, Mario: FELIX GOMEZ—V5, S3, H3 (UF)

Benedict, Lyn: SHADOWS INQUIRIES—V4, S3, H3 (UF)

Butcher, Jim: DRESDEN FILES—V4, S3, H4 (UF)

Cunningham, Elaine: CHANGELING DETECTIVE AGENCY—V4, S3, H2 (UF)

Daniels, Casey: PEPPER MARTIN MYSTERIES—V3, S3, H4 (CH)

Del Franco, Mark: CONNOR GREY—V3, S1, H3 (UF)

Douglas, Carole Nelson: DELILAH STREET, PARANORMAL INVESTIGATOR—
V4, S4, H4 (UF)

Elrod, P. N.: VAMPIRE FILES—V4, S3, H3 (UF)

Gideon, Nancy: MOONLIGHT—V4, S4, H1 (UF)

Green, Chris Marie: VAMPIRE BABYLON—V4, S4, H1 (UF)

Green, Simon R.: NIGHTSIDE—V5, S1, H3 (UF)

Gustainis, Justin: QUINCEY MORRIS, SUPERNATURAL INVESTIGATOR—V3, S3,
H3 (UF)

Harris, Charlaine: HARPER CONNELLY—V3, S2 (books 1–2), S3 (books 3–4),
H3 (UF)

Hecht, Daniel: CREE BLACK—V3, S2, H2 (UF)

Hooper, Kay: BISHOP/SPECIAL CRIMES UNIT—V5, S3, H2 (SMR)

Huff, Tanya: VICTORIA NELSON/BLOOD SERIES—V4, S3, H3 (UF)

Kittredge, Caitlin: BLACK LONDON—V4, S3, H2 (UF)

Kittredge, Caitlin: NOCTURNE CITY—V5, S4, H3 (UF)

Laurie, Victoria: PSYCHIC EYE MYSTERIES—V3, S3, H3 (CH)

Liu, Marjorie M.: DIRK AND STEELE—V3, S3, H1 (SMR)

McCray, Cheyenne: NIGHT TRACKER—V5, S4, H2 (CH)

Rowland, Diana: KARA GILLIAN—V3, S4, H3 (UF)

PROTAGONIST: FAE OR OTHER SUPERNATURAL CREATURE

Andersen, Jessica: THE FINAL PROPHECY—V5, S4, H1 (SMR) (magical
warriors)

Bangs, Nina: CASTLE OF DARK DREAMS—V2, S5, H5 (SMR) (immortal
warrior)

Brook, Meljean: The Guardians—V4, S4, H3 (SMR) (guardian angels)

Caine, Rachel: Outcast Season—V4, S2, H1 (UF) (djin, or genie)

Chance, Karen: Cassandra Palmer—V3, S4, H2 (UF) (clairvoyant, descendant of Apollo's priestess)

Child, Maureen: Queen of the Otherworld—V3, S4, H4 (UF) (fae)

Cole, Kresley: Immortals after Dark—V4, S5, H3 (SMR) (valkyries)

Cunningham, Elaine: Changeling Detective Agency—V4, S3, H2 (UF) (elf)

Davidson, MaryJanice: Fred the Mermaid—V2, S4, H4 (CH) (mermaid)

Day, Alyssa: Warriors of Poseidon—V3, S4, H3 (SMR) (immortal warriors)

Del Franco, Mark: Connor Grey—V3, S1, H3 (UF) (Druid)

Del Franco, Mark: Laura Blackstone—V4, S2–3, H3 (UF) (Druid)

Foster, L. L.: Servant—V5, S4, H2 (UF) (paladin)

Frank, Jacquelyn: The Gatherers—V4, S4, H1 (SMR) (gatherers who collect the energy that keeps them alive)

Frank, Jacquelyn: Shadowdwellers—V4, S5, H1 (SMR) (shadow dwellers)

Galenorn, Yasmine: Sisters of the Moon—V4, S4, H2 (UF) (half fairy)

Green, Simon R.: Secret Histories—V4, S2, H4 (UF) (Druid)

Hamilton, Laurell K.: Meredith Gentry—V4, S5, H2 (UF) (fairy princess)

Hansen, Jamie Leigh: *Betrayal; Cursed* (no series title)—V3, S3, H1 (SMR) (various)

Harris, Charlaine: Southern Vampire (Sookie Stackhouse) Mysteries—V3, S4, H3 (UF) (Sookie has some fairy blood)

Henry, Mark: Amanda Feral—V5, S4, H5 (CH) (ghoul)

Howard, Linda, and Linda Jones: Spirit Warriors—V5, S4, H1 (SMR) (warrior spirits and their human conduits)

Kenyon, Sherrilyn: Dark-Hunters—V3, S4, H3 (SMR) (immortal warriors)

Kenyon, Sherrilyn: Dream-Hunters—V3, S4, H3 (SMR) (gods and goddesses)

Klasky, Mindy: As You Wish—V1, S3, H4 (CH, SMR) (wish-granting genie)

Knight, Angela: MAGEVERSE—V5, S5, H3 (SMR) (immortal Arthurian characters)

Knight, Deidre: GODS OF MIDNIGHT—V4, S4, H2 (SMR) (immortal warriors)

Krinard, Susan: FANE—V4, S4, H2 (HIS, SMR) (sidhe)

Leto, Julie: PHANTOM—V3, S4, H2 (SMR) (cursed brothers)

MacAlister, Katie: SILVER DRAGON—V3, S4, H5 (SMR) (doppelgänger, dragons)

Mayhue, Melissa: DAUGHTERS OF THE GLEN—V3, S4, H3 (SMR) (fae)

McCarthy, Erin: SEVEN DEADLY SINS—V1, S5, H3 (SMR) (fallen angel)

McCleave, Annette: SOUL GATHERERS—V3, S4, H1 (SMR) (soul gatherers)

McCray, Cheyenne: MAGIC—V5, S5, H2 (SMR) (D'Danann—fae warriors)

McCray, Cheyenne: NIGHT TRACKER—V5, S4, H2 (CH) (Drow—dark elf)

Moning, Karen: HIGHLANDER SERIES—V3, S4, H2 (HIS, SMR) (Knights Templar and Berserker warriors)

Morgan, Alexis: PALADINS OF DARKNESS—V4, S5, H2 (SMR) (immortal warriors)

Morgan, Alexis: TALIONS—V4, S4, H2 (SMR) (Kyth—uses human energy)

Murphy, C. E.: NEGOTIATOR TRILOGY—V3, S3, H2 (UF) (gargoyle)

O'Shea, Patti: LIGHT WARRIORS—V4, S4 (book 1 = 5+), H1 (SMR) (Gineal—magical warriors)

Palmer, Pamela: FERAL WARRIORS—V5, S4, H1 (SMR) (shape-shifting immortal warriors)

Pettersson, Vicki: SIGNS OF THE ZODIAC—V4, S3, H1 (UF) (warriors with enhanced strength and senses)

St. Giles, Jennifer: SHADOWMEN—V3, S4, H1 (SMR) (shadowmen warriors)

Showalter, Gena: ATLANTIS—V4, S4, H3 (SMR) (nymphs, dragons)

Showalter, Gena: LORDS OF THE UNDERWORLD—V4, S4, H3 (SMR) (immortals who are demon controlled)

Singh, Nalini: GUILD HUNTER—V4, S3, H3 (UF) (angels)

Smith, Kathryn: NIGHTMARE CHRONICLES—V3, S4, H2 (UF) (a nightmare, daughter of Morpheus)

Sniegoski, Thomas E.: REMY CHANDLER—V4, S2, H2 (UF) (former angel)

Stone, Juliana: JAGUAR WARRIOR—V4, S4, H1 (SMR) (immortal warriors)

Sunny: Demon Princess Chronicles—V5, S5, H2 (UF) (daughter of lord of hell)

Sunny: Monére: Children of the Moon—V5, S5, H2 (UF) (queen of moon children)

Thurman, Rob: Cal Leandros—V5, S3, H4 (UF) (Auphe, or elf)

Thurman, Rob: Trickster—V4, S2, H4 (UF) (trickster)

Walker, Shiloh: The Hunters—V3, S4, H1 (SMR) (fallen angel)

Ward, J. R.: Fallen Angels—V4, S4, H2 (SMR) (fallen angel)

Weldon, Phaedra: Zoë Martinique—V4, S2, H2 (UF) (wraith—travels out of body)

Windsor, Anna: Dark Crescent Sisterhood—V4, S5, H3 (SMR) (sybils)

PROTAGONIST: Witch, Warlock, Wizard, Shaman, Sorcerer, Exorcist, Necromancer, Mage

Adair, Cherry: T-FLAC Night Trilogy—V4, S4, H3 (SMR) (wizards)

Andrews, Ilona: Kate Daniels—V5, S2, H3 (UF) (mage)

Bast, Anya: Elemental Witches—V4, S5, H2 (SMR) (witch)

Black, Jenna: Morgan Kingsley, Exorcist—V4, S5+, H3 (UF) (exorcist)

Black, Shayla: The Doomsday Brethren—V4, S4, H1 (SMR) (wizards)

Blackwell, Juliet: Witchcraft Mysteries—V3, S3, H3 (CH) (witch)

Blair, Annette: Accidental Witch Trilogy—V0, S4, H4 (SMR) (witch)

Blair, Annette: Triplet Witch Trilogy—V1, S5, H4 (SMR) (witch)

Butcher, Jim: Dresden Files—V4, S3, H4 (UF) (wizard)

Carey, Mike: Felix Castor—V5, S3, H3 (UF) (exorcist-spiritualist)

Damsgaard, Shirley: Ophelia and Abby Mysteries—V3, S2, H3 (COZ) (witches)

Del Franco, Mark: Connor Grey—V3, S1, H3 (UF) (wizard)

Feehan, Christine: Drake Sisters—V3, S5, H3 (SMR) (witches)

Finlay, C. C.: Traitor to the Crown—V4, S2, H2 (HIS) (witches)

Gilman, Laura Anne: Paranormal Scene Investigations—V3, S2, H2 (UF) (witch)

Gilman, Laura Anne: Retrievers—V5, S3, H3 (UF) (witch, psychometrist)

Greiman, Lois: WITCHES OF MAYFAIR—V4, S4, H2 (HIS, SMR) (witches)

Hallaway, Tate: GARNET LACEY—V3, S3, H4 (CH) (witch)

Hamilton, Laurell K.: ANITA BLAKE, VAMPIRE HUNTER—V5, S2 (books 1–5), S5 (books 6–19), H3 (UF) (necromancer)

Harrison, Kim: THE HOLLOWS—V4, S5, H3 (UF) (witch)

Havens, Candace: BRONWYN THE WITCH—V3, S3, H4 (CH) (witch)

Holling, Jen: MACDONELL BRIDES—V3, S4, H3 (HIS, SMR) (witches)

Huff, Tanya: SMOKE TRILOGY—V4, S3, H4 (UF) (wizard)

James, Allyson: STORMWALKER—V4, S4, H2 (UF) (stormwalker—mage who channels energy from storms)

Levitt, John: DOG DAYS—V4, S3, H3 (UF) (wizardlike abilities)

McCray, Cheyenne: MAGIC—V5, S5, H2 (SMR) (witches)

Mead, Richelle: DARK SWAN—V4, S5, H3 (UF) (shaman)

Monk, Devon: ALLIE BECKSTROM—V4, S4, H1 (UF) (hound—a type of wizard)

Murphy, C. E.: WALKER PAPERS—V3, S1, H3 (UF) (shaman)

Pratt, T. A.: MARLA MASON—V3, S3, H4 (UF) (sorcerer)

Robertson, Linda: CIRCLE/PERSEPHONE ALCMEDI—V3, S3, H2 (UF) (witch)

Saintcrow, Lilith: DANTE VALENTINE—V4, S3, H1 (UF) (necromancer)

Shayne, Maggie: IMMORTAL WITCHES—V3, S4, H2 (HIS, SMR) (witches)

Silver, Eve: COMPACT OF SORCERERS—V5, S5, H2 (SMR) (sorcerer)

Thompson, Vicki Lewis: HEX SERIES—V1, S4, H5 (SMR) (a witch and a wizard)

Wells, Jaye: SABINA KANE—V4, S3, H3 (UF) (mage)

Wisdom, Linda: HEX SERIES—V5, S4, H5 (UF) (witch)

PROTAGONIST: HUMAN WITH SUPERNATURAL CONNECTION OR TALENT

Aguirre, Ann: CORINE SOLOMON—V4, S2, H1 (UF) (psychometrist)

Alt, Madelyn: BEWITCHING MYSTERIES—V3, S2, H3 (CH) (empath)

Andrews, Ilona: KATE DANIELS—V5, S2, H3 (UF) (magical powers)

Andrews, Toni: MERCY HOLLINGS—V3, S4, H3 (UF) (hypnotherapist)

Barbieri, Elaine: WOLF SERIES—V2, S1, H1 (HIS, SMR) (sees ghosts)

Benson, Amber: CALLIOPE REAPER-JONES—V3, S2, H5 (CH) (Death's daughter)

Bickle, Laura: ANYA KALINCZYK—V3, S4, H2 (UF) (absorbs ghosts)

Blair, Annette: VINTAGE MAGIC—V2, S2, H4 (CH, COZ) (psychometrist)

Caine, Rachel: WEATHER WARDEN—V5, S3, H1 (UF) (controls weather)

Carriger, Gail: THE PARASOL PROTECTORATE—V4, S3, H4 (CH, HIS) (no soul)

Cassidy, Dakota: DEMONIC ROMANCE—V2, S4, H5 (CH, SMR) (sees dead people)

Chance, Karen: CASSANDRA PALMER—V3, S4, H2 (UF) (clairvoyant)

Crane, Carolyn: JUSTINE JONES: DISILLUSIONIST—V3, S4, H2 (UF) (channels emotions into others)

Daniels, Casey: PEPPER MARTIN MYSTERIES—V3, S3, H4 (CH) (sees dead people)

Day, S. J.: MARKED—V5, S5, H2 (UF) (has angelic mark)

Dodd, Christina: THE CHOSEN ONES—V3, S4, H3 (SMR) (various mental and physical talents)

Douglas, Carole Nelson: DELILAH STREET, PARANORMAL INVESTIGATOR—V4, S4, H4 (UF) (mirror walker)

Durgin, Doranna: THE RECKONERS—V4, S2, H2 (UF) (communicates with ghosts)

Fallon, Linda: SHADES SERIES—V3, S4, H2 (HIS, SMR) (sees ghosts)

Feehan, Christine: GHOSTWALKERS—V4, S4, H2 (SMR) (medically enhanced DNA)

Garey, Terri: NICKI STYX—V2, S3, H4 (UF) (sees dead people)

Gilman, Laura Anne: RETRIEVERS—V5, S3, H3 (UF) (retriever)

Green, Chris Marie: VAMPIRE BABYLON—V4, S4, H1 (UF) (mental pushes)

Green, Simon R.: NIGHTSIDE—V5, S1, H3 (UF) (various magical talents)

Harris, Charlaine: HARPER CONNELLY—V3, S2 (books 1–2), S3 (books 3–4), H3 (UF) (communicates with dead people)

Hecht, Daniel: CREE BLACK—V3, S2, H2 (UF) (sees ghosts)

Hilburn, Lynda: KISMET KNIGHT, VAMPIRE PSYCHOLOGIST—V5, S5, H3 (UF) (psychologist for vamps)

Hooper, Kay: BISHOP/SPECIAL CRIMES UNIT—V5, S3, H2 (SMR) (each team member has a different psychic skill)

Kane, Stacia: DOWNSIDE GHOSTS—V5, S4, H1 (UF) (ghostbuster)

Kane, Stacia: MEGAN CHASE—V4, S4, H3 (UF) (psychic, part demon)

Kenner, Julie: SUPERHERO CENTRAL—V2, S3–4, H4 (CH, SMR) (super strength, flying skills)

Lane, Amy: LITTLE GODDESS—V5, S5, H3 (SMR) (various sex-derived powers)

Laurie, Victoria: GHOST HUNTER MYSTERIES—V2, S2, H3 (CH) (medium)

Laurie, Victoria: PSYCHIC EYE MYSTERIES—V3, S3, H3 (CH) (psychic)

Liu, Marjorie M.: DIRK AND STEELE—V3, S3, H1 (SMR) (each team member has a different paranormal skill)

Lockwood, Cara: DEMON SERIES—V3, S2, H5 (CH) (prophet)

McCarthy, Erin: CUTTERSVILLE GHOSTS—V1, S5, H4 (SMR) (townspeople see ghosts)

Rardin, Jennifer: JAZ PARKS—V5, S2, H3 (UF) (some magical skills, has a spirit guide)

Richardson, Kat: GREYWALKER—V3, S3, H1 (UF) (sees ghosts and auras)

Rowe, Stephanie: IMMORTALLY SEXY—V2, S3, H5 (SMR) (immortal guardian)

Rowen, Michelle: LIVING IN EDEN—V3, S3, H3 (UF) (psychics)

Rowland, Diana: KARA GILLIAN—V3, S4, H3 (UF) (summons demons)

Rush, Jaime: OFFSPRING—V4, S4, H1 (SMR) (various psychic abilities)

Russe, Savannah: SISTERHOOD OF THE SIGHT—V3, S4, H2 (SMR) (various magical skills)

Saintcrow, Lilith: JILL KISMET—V5, S3, H2 (UF) (psychic abilities)

Showalter, Gena: TALES OF AN EXTRAORDINARY GIRL—V4, S4, H3 (UF) (controls elements)

Singh, Nalini: PSY-CHANGELINGS—V3, S4, H3 (SMR) (various psychic abilities)

Strout, Anton: SIMON CANDEROUS—V4, S3, H4 (UF) (psychometrist)

Swendson, Shanna: ENCHANTED, INC. SERIES—V2, S2, H3 (CH) (immune to magic)

Wilson, F. Paul: REPAIRMAN JACK—V5, S3, H4 (UF) (outfights Rakoshi)

York, Rebecca: MOON SERIES—V4, S4–5+, H1 (SMR) (various)

LEVEL OF VIOLENCE: 0–2 (LITTLE OR NO VIOLENCE)

Bangs, Nina: CASTLE OF DARK DREAMS—**V2,** S5, H5 (SMR)

Bangs, Nina: MACKENZIE VAMPIRES—**V2,** S3, H5 (SMR)

Barbieri, Elaine: WOLF SERIES—**V2,** S1, H1 (HIS, SMR)

Blair, Annette: ACCIDENTAL WITCH TRILOGY—**V0,** S4, H4 (SMR)

Blair, Annette: TRIPLET WITCH TRILOGY—**V1,** S5, H4 (SMR)

Blair, Annette: VINTAGE MAGIC—**V2,** S2, H4 (CH, COZ)

Davidson, MaryJanice: FRED THE MERMAID—**V2,** S4, H4 (CH)

Devlin, Delilah: DARK REALM—**V1,** S5+, H1 (UF)

Garey, Terri: NICKI STYX—**V2,** S3, H4 (UF)

James, Allyson: DRAGON SERIES—**V2,** S5, H3 (SMR)

James, Dean: SIMON KIRBY-JONES MYSTERIES—**V2,** S2, H5 (COZ)

Kenner, Julie: SUPERHERO CENTRAL—**V2,** S3–4, H4 (CH, SMR)

Laurie, Victoria: GHOST HUNTER MYSTERIES—**V2,** S2, H3 (CH)

MacAlister, Katie: DARK ONES—**V2,** S5, H5 (SMR)

MacInerney, Karen: TALES OF AN URBAN WEREWOLF—**V2,** S3, H4 (UF)

McCarthy, Erin: CUTTERSVILLE GHOSTS—**V1,** S5, H4 (SMR)

McCarthy, Erin: SEVEN DEADLY SINS—**V1,** S5, H3 (SMR)

Mead, Richelle: GEORGINA KINCAID—**V2,** S4, H4 (UF)

Rowe, Stephanie: IMMORTALLY SEXY—**V2,** S3, H5 (SMR)

Swendson, Shanna: ENCHANTED, INC. SERIES—**V2,** S2, H3 (CH)

Warren, J. D.: WORLD OF THE STORM RAVENS—**V2,** S2, H4 (UF)

LEVEL OF VIOLENCE: 4–5 (VERY VIOLENT)

Acevedo, Mario: FELIX GOMEZ—**V5,** S3, H3 (UF)

Adair, Cherry: T-FLAC NIGHT TRILOGY—**V4,** S4, H3 (SMR)

Adams, C. T., and Cathy Clamp: TALES OF THE SAZI—**V4,** S3–4, H1 (SMR)

Adams, C. T., and Cathy Clamp: THRALL—**V5,** S4, H1 (UF)

Aguirre, Ann: CORINE SOLOMON—**V4,** S2, H1 (UF)

Allen, Harper: CROSSE TRIPLETS—**V5,** S3, H3 (CH, SMR)

Andersen, Jessica: THE FINAL PROPHECY—**V5,** S4, H1 (SMR)

Andrews, Ilona: KATE DANIELS—**V5,** S2, H3 (UF)

Armintrout, Jennifer: BLOOD TIES—**V5,** S4–5, H1 (UF)

Armstrong, Kelley: WOMEN OF THE OTHERWORLD—**V4,** S4, H4 (UF)

Arthur, Keri: MYTH AND MAGIC SERIES—**V5,** S5, H2 (SMR)

Arthur, Keri: RILEY JENSEN, GUARDIAN—**V5,** S5, H2 (UF)

Austen, Jane, and Seth Grahame-Smith: *Pride and Prejudice and Zombies* (novel)—**V5,** S1, H4 (CH, HIS spoof)

Bacon-Smith, Camille: DAEMONS, INC.—**V4,** S3, H1 (UF)

Baker, Trisha: CRIMSON—**V5,** S5, H0 (UF)

Banks, L. A.: CRIMSON MOON—**V4,** S4, H2 (UF)

Banks, L. A.: VAMPIRE HUNTRESS LEGEND—**V4,** S4, H2 (UF)

Bartlett, Gerry: GLORY ST. CLAIRE—**V4,** S5, H4 (CH)

Bast, Anya: ELEMENTAL WITCHES—**V4,** S5, H2 (SMR)

Bast, Anya: THE EMBRACED—**V4,** S5+, H1 (SMR)

Benedict, Lyn: SHADOWS INQUIRIES—**V4,** S3, H3 (UF)

Black, Jenna: GUARDIANS OF THE NIGHT—**V4,** S5, H3 (SMR)

Black, Jenna: MORGAN KINGSLEY, EXORCIST—**V4,** S5+, H3 (UF)

Black, Shayla: THE DOOMSDAY BRETHREN—**V4,** S4, H1 (SMR)

Blue, Lucy: BOUND IN DARKNESS—**V4,** S3, H1 (HIS, SMR)

Boyd, Donna: DEVONCROIX DYNASTY—**V4,** S4, H1 (UF)

Brennan, Allison: SEVEN DEADLY SINS—**V4,** S2, H1 (UF)

Brook, Meljean: THE GUARDIANS—**V4,** S4, H3 (SMR)

Burton, Jaci: DEMON HUNTER—**V4,** S4, H2 (SMR)

Butcher, Jim: DRESDEN FILES—**V4,** S3, H4 (UF)

Butler, Octavia: *Fledgling* (novel)—**V4,** S4, H1 (UF)

Byrd, Rhyannon: PRIMAL INSTINCT—**V5,** S4, H1 (SMR)

Caine, Rachel: OUTCAST SEASON—**V4,** S2, H1 (UF)

Caine, Rachel: WEATHER WARDEN—**V5,** S3, H1 (UF)

Carey, Mike: FELIX CASTOR—**V5,** S3, H3 (UF)

Carriger, Gail: THE PARASOL PROTECTORATE—**V4,** S3, H4 (CH, HIS)

Child, Maureen: FIEND—**V4,** S4, H5 (CH)

Cole, Kresley: IMMORTALS AFTER DARK—**V4,** S5, H3 (SMR)

Cooke, Deborah: DRAGONFIRE—**V4,** S4, H2 (SMR)

Cunningham, Elaine: CHANGELING DETECTIVE AGENCY—**V4,** S3, H2 (UF)

Davidson, MaryJanice: QUEEN BETSY—**V4,** S4, H4 (CH)

Day, S. J.: MARKED—**V5,** S5, H2 (UF)

Del Franco, Mark: LAURA BLACKSTONE—**V4,** S2, H2 (UF)

Dodd, Christina: DARKNESS CHOSEN—**V4,** S4, H2 (SMR)

Douglas, Carole Nelson: DELILAH STREET, PARANORMAL INVESTIGATOR—**V4,** S4, H4 (UF)

Drake, Jocelynn: DARK DAYS—**V4,** S4, H1 (UF)

Durgin, Doranna: THE RECKONERS—**V4,** S2, H2 (UF)

Eden, Cynthia: MIDNIGHT TRILOGY—**V4,** S4, H2 (SMR)

Elrod, P. N.: VAMPIRE FILES—**V4,** S3, H3 (UF)

Farren, Mick: RENQUIST QUARTET—**V5,** S3, H1 (UF)

Feehan, Christine: THE CARPATHIANS (DARK) SERIES—**V5,** S5, H1 (SMR)

Feehan, Christine: GHOSTWALKERS—**V4,** S4, H2 (SMR)

Feehan, Christine: LEOPARD—**V4,** S4, H1 (SMR)

Finlay, C. C.: TRAITOR TO THE CROWN—**V4,** S2, H2 (HIS)

Foster, L. L.: SERVANT—**V5,** S4, H2 (UF)

Fox, Andrew: FAT WHITE VAMPIRE—**V5,** S3, H5 (UF)

Frank, Jacquelyn: THE GATHERERS—**V4,** S4, H1 (SMR)

Frank, Jacquelyn: NIGHTWALKERS—**V4,** S5, H3 (SMR)

Frank, Jacquelyn: SHADOWDWELLERS—**V4,** S5, H1 (SMR)

Frost, Jeaniene: NIGHT HUNTRESS—**V5,** S4, H3 (UF)

Frost, Jeaniene: NIGHT HUNTRESS WORLD—**V5,** S4, H3 (UF)

Frost, P. R.: TESS NONCOIRÉ—**V4,** S3, H2 (UF)

Galenorn, Yasmine: SISTERS OF THE MOON—**V4,** S4, H2 (UF)

Gideon, Nancy: MOONLIGHT—**V4,** S4, H1 (UF)

Gilman, Laura Anne: RETRIEVERS—**V5,** S3, H3 (UF)

Gleason, Colleen: GARDELLA VAMPIRE CHRONICLES—**V4,** S4, H2 (HIS)

Green, Chris Marie: VAMPIRE BABYLON—**V4,** S4, H1 (UF)

Green, Simon R.: NIGHTSIDE—**V5,** S1, H3 (UF)

Green, Simon R.: SECRET HISTORIES—**V4,** S2, H4 (UF)

Greiman, Lois: WITCHES OF MAYFAIR—**V4,** S4, H2 (HIS, SMR)

Hamilton, Laurell K.: ANITA BLAKE, VAMPIRE HUNTER—**V5,** S2 (books 1–5), S5 (books 6–19), H3 (UF)

Hamilton, Laurell K.: MEREDITH GENTRY—**V4,** S5, H2 (UF)

Handeland, Lori: NIGHTCREATURE—**V4,** S4, H3 (SMR)

Handeland, Lori: PHOENIX CHRONICLES—**V4,** S4, H2 (UF)

Harper, Nina: SUCCUBUS SERIES—**V4,** S5, H4 (CH)

Harrison, Kim: THE HOLLOWS—**V4,** S5, H3 (UF)

Hart, Raven, and Virginia Ellis: SAVANNAH VAMPIRES—**V5,** S5, H3 (UF)

Havens, Candace: CARUTHERS SISTERS—**V5,** S3, H4 (CH, SMR)

Hendee, Barb: VAMPIRE MEMORIES—**V4,** S1, H1 (UF)

Hendee, Barb, and J. C. Hendee: NOBLE DEAD SAGA—**V4,** S3, H2 (HIS)

Henry, Mark: AMANDA FERAL—**V5,** S4, H5 (CH)

Herron, Rita: THE DEMONBORN—**V4,** S5, H1 (SMR)

Hilburn, Lynda: KISMET KNIGHT, VAMPIRE PSYCHOLOGIST—**V5,** S5, H3 (UF)

Hill, Joey W.: VAMPIRE QUEEN—**V5,** S5+, H1 (SMR)

Holly, Emma: FITZ CLARE CHRONICLES/UPYR—**V4,** S4, H2 (HIS, SMR)

Hooper, Kay: BISHOP/SPECIAL CRIMES UNIT—**V5,** S3, H2 (SMR)

Howard, Linda, and Linda Jones: SPIRIT WARRIORS—**V5,** S4, H1 (SMR)

Huff, Tanya: SMOKE TRILOGY—**V4,** S3, H4 (UF)

Huff, Tanya: VICTORIA NELSON/BLOOD SERIES—**V4,** S3, H3 (UF)

Hunter, Faith: JANE YELLOWROCK—**V5,** S2, H2 (UF)

Huston, Charlie: JOE PITT CASEBOOKS—**V5,** S2, H2 (UF)

Ione, Larissa: DEMONICA—**V5,** S4, H3 (SMR)

Ivy, Alexandra: GUARDIANS OF ETERNITY—**V4,** S4, H3 (SMR)

James, Allyson: STORMWALKER—**V4,** S4, H2 (UF)

Kane, Stacia: DOWNSIDE GHOSTS—**V5,** S4, H1 (UF)

Kane, Stacia: MEGAN CHASE—**V4,** S4, H3 (UF)

Kantra, Virginia: CHILDREN OF THE SEA—**V4,** S4, H2 (SMR)

Kenner, Julie: BLOOD LILY CHRONICLES—**V4,** S2, H1 (UF)

Kenner, Julie: DEMON-HUNTING SOCCER MOM—**V5,** S3, H5 (UF)

Kessler, Jackie: HELL ON EARTH—**V4,** S5, H5 (UF)

Kittredge, Caitlin: Black London—**V4**, S3, H2 (UF)

Kittredge, Caitlin: Nocturne City—**V5**, S4, H3 (UF)

Knight, Angela: Mageverse—**V5**, S5, H3 (SMR)

Knight, Deidre: Gods of Midnight—**V4**, S4, H2 (SMR)

Kohler, Sharie: Moon Chasers—**V4**, S5, H2 (SMR)

Krinard, Susan: Fane—**V4**, S4, H2 (HIS, SMR)

Lane, Amy: Little Goddess—**V5**, S5, H3 (SMR)

Laurenston, Shelly: Pride—**V4**, S5, H5 (SMR)

Leigh, Lora: Breeds—**V4**, S5, H1 (SMR)

Levitt, John: Dog Days—**V4**, S3, H3 (UF)

Lewis, J. F.: Void City—**V5**, S3, H3 (UF)

Love, Kathy: The Young Brothers—**V4**, S4, H4 (SMR)

Maverick, Liz, Marjorie M. Liu, Patti O'Shea, Carolyn Jewel, and Jade Lee: Crimson City—**V4**, S4, H1 (SMR)

McCray, Cheyenne: Magic—**V5**, S5, H2 (SMR)

McGuire, Seanan: October Daye—**V4**, S1, H2 (UF)

Mead, Richelle: Dark Swan—**V4**, S5, H3 (UF)

Moning, Karen: Fever Series—**V4**, S3, H1 (UF)

Monk, Devon: Allie Beckstrom—**V4**, S4, H1 (UF)

Morgan, Alexis: Paladins of Darkness—**V4**, S5, H2 (SMR)

Morgan, Alexis: Talions—**V4**, S4, H2 (SMR)

Neill, Chloe: Chicagoland Vampires—**V4**, S2, H3 (UF)

O'Shea, Patti: Light Warriors—**V4**, S4 (book 1 = 5+), H1 (SMR)

Palmer, Pamela: Feral Warriors—**V5**, S4, H1 (SMR)

Parks, Lydia: Erotic Vampire Series—**V5**, S5+, H1 (SMR)

Pettersson, Vicki: Signs of the Zodiac—**V4**, S3, H1 (UF)

Phoenix, Adrian: The Maker's Song—**V5**, S5, H1 (UF)

Rardin, Jennifer: Jaz Parks—**V5**, S2, H3 (UF)

Raye, Kimberly: Dead End Dating—**V3–4**, S2–4, H4 (CH)

Reinke, Sara: The Brethren—**V5**, S4, H1 (SMR)

Resnick, Laura: Esther Diamond—**V4**, S3, H3 (UF)

Roberts, Nora: Sign of Seven Trilogy—**V4**, S4, H4 (SMR)

Rush, Jaime: OFFSPRING—**V4**, S4, H1 (SMR)

Russe, Savannah: DARKWING CHRONICLES—**V5**, S5, H2 (CH)

Saintcrow, Lilith: DANTE VALENTINE—**V4**, S3, H1 (UF)

Saintcrow, Lilith: JILL KISMET—**V5**, S3, H2 (UF)

Sands, Lynsay: ARGENEAU VAMPIRES—**V4**, S4, H3 (SMR)

Shayne, Maggie: WINGS IN THE NIGHT—**V4**, S4, H3 (SMR)

Showalter, Gena: ALIEN HUNTRESS—**V4**, S4, H2 (SMR)

Showalter, Gena: ATLANTIS—**V4**, S4, H3 (SMR)

Showalter, Gena: LORDS OF THE UNDERWORLD—**V4**, S4, H3 (SMR)

Showalter, Gena: TALES OF AN EXTRAORDINARY GIRL—**V4**, S4, H3 (UF)

Silver, Eve: COMPACT OF SORCERERS—**V5**, S5, H2 (SMR)

Simmons, Wm. Mark: CHRIS CSÉJTHE: HALF/LIFE CHRONICLES—**V5**, S3, H4 (UF)

Singh, Nalini: GUILD HUNTER—**V4**, S3, H3 (UF)

Sizemore, Susan: LAWS OF THE BLOOD—**V4**, S3, H2 (SMR)

Sizemore, Susan: PRIMES—**V4**, S4, H2 (SMR)

Smith-Ready, Jeri: WVMP RADIO—**V5**, S4, H3 (UF)

Sniegoski, Thomas E.: REMY CHANDLER—**V4**, S2, H2 (UF)

Sparks, Kerrelyn: LOVE AT STAKE—**V4**, S5, H4 (CH, SMR)

Spear, Terry: WOLF SERIES—**V4**, S4, H2 (SMR)

Spencer, Jorrie: STRENGTH—**V4**, S4, H2 (SMR)

Squires, Susan: THE COMPANION—**V5**, S5, H1 (HIS, SMR)

Stein, Jeanne C.: ANNA STRONG CHRONICLES—**V4**, S3, H2 (UF)

Stone, Juliana: JAGUAR WARRIOR—**V4**, S4, H1 (SMR)

Strout, Anton: SIMON CANDEROUS—**V4**, S3, H4 (UF)

Sunny: DEMON PRINCESS CHRONICLES—**V5**, S5, H2 (UF)

Sunny: MONÉRE: CHILDREN OF THE MOON—**V5**, S5, H2 (UF)

Thompson, Ronda: WILD WULFS OF LONDON—**V4**, S4, H2 (HIS, SMR)

Thurman, Rob: CAL LEANDROS—**V5**, S3, H4 (UF)

Thurman, Rob: TRICKSTER—**V4**, S2, H4 (UF)

Troop, Alan F.: DRAGON DELASANGRE—**V5**, S3, H1 (UF)

Viehl, Lynn: THE DARKYN SERIES—**V5**, S5, H3 (SMR)

Vincent, Rachel: WERECATS—**V5,** S4, H3 (UF)

Ward, J. R.: BLACK DAGGER BROTHERHOOD—**V5,** S5, H3 (SMR)

Ward, J. R.: FALLEN ANGELS—**V4,** S4, H2 (SMR)

Warren, Christine: THE OTHERS—**V4,** S4, H4 (SMR)

Weldon, Phaedra: ZOË MARTINIQUE—**V4,** S2, H2 (UF)

Wellington, David: LAURA CAXTON—**V5,** S3, H0 (UF)

Wells, Jaye: SABINA KANE—**V4,** S3, H3 (UF)

Whiteside, Diane: TEXAS VAMPIRES—**V4,** S5, H2 (SMR)

Wilks, Eileen: WORLD OF THE LUPI—**V4,** S4, H3 (SMR)

Wilson, F. Paul: REPAIRMAN JACK—**V5,** S3, H4 (UF)

Windsor, Anna: DARK CRESCENT SISTERHOOD—**V4,** S5, H3 (SMR)

Wisdom, Linda: HEX SERIES—**V5,** S4, H5 (UF)

Yarbro, Chelsea Quinn: SAINT-GERMAIN—**V4,** S4, H3 (HIS)

York, Rebecca: MOON SERIES—**V4,** S4–5+, H1 (SMR)

LEVEL OF SENSUALITY: 0–2 (LITTLE OR NO SEX)

Aguirre, Ann: CORINE SOLOMON—V4, **S2,** H1 (UF)

Alt, Madelyn: BEWITCHING MYSTERIES—V3, **S2,** H3 (CH)

Andrews, Ilona: KATE DANIELS—V5, **S2,** H3 (UF)

Austen, Jane, and Seth Grahame-Smith: *Pride and Prejudice and Zombies* (novel)—V5, **S1,** H4 (CH, HIS spoof)

Barbieri, Elaine: WOLF SERIES—V2, **S1,** H1 (HIS, SMR)

Benson, Amber: CALLIOPE REAPER-JONES—V3, **S2,** H5 (CH)

Blair, Annette: VINTAGE MAGIC—V2, **S2,** H4 (CH, COZ)

Brennan, Allison: SEVEN DEADLY SINS—V4, **S2** (book 1), **S4** (book 2), H1 (UF)

Caine, Rachel: OUTCAST SEASON—V4, **S2,** H1 (UF)

Damsgaard, Shirley: OPHELIA AND ABBY MYSTERIES—V3, **S2,** H3 (COZ)

Del Franco, Mark: CONNOR GREY—V3, **S1,** H3 (UF)

Del Franco, Mark: LAURA BLACKSTONE—V4, **S2–3,** H3 (UF)

Durgin, Doranna: THE RECKONERS—V4, **S2,** H2 (UF)

Finlay, C. C.: TRAITOR TO THE CROWN—V4, **S2,** H2 (HIS)

Gilman, Laura Anne: Paranormal Scene Investigations—V3, **S2**, H2 (UF)

Green, Simon R.: Nightside—V5, **S1**, H3 (UF)

Green, Simon R.: Secret Histories—V4, **S2**, H4 (UF)

Hamilton, Laurell K.: Anita Blake, Vampire Hunter—V5, **S2** (books 1–5), **S5** (books 6–19), H3 (UF)

Hecht, Daniel: Cree Black—V3, **S2**, H2 (UF)

Hendee, Barb: Vampire Memories—V4, **S1**, H1 (UF)

Holzner, Nancy: Deadtown—V3, **S2**, H2 (UF)

Hunter, Faith: Jane Yellowrock—V5, **S2**, H2 (UF)

James, Dean: Simon Kirby-Jones Mysteries—V2, **S2**, H5 (COZ)

Kenner, Julie: Blood Lily Chronicles—V4, **S2**, H1 (UF)

Laurie, Victoria: Ghost Hunter Mysteries—V2, **S2**, H3 (CH)

Liu, Marjorie M.: Hunter Kiss—V3, **S2**, H1 (UF)

Lockwood, Cara: Demon Series—V3, **S2**, H5 (CH)

McGuire, Seanan: October Daye—V4, **S1**, H2 (UF)

Meyer, Stephenie: The Twilight Saga—V3, **S2** (books 1–3), **S4** (book 4), H3 (SMR)

Murphy, C. E.: Walker Papers—V3, **S1**, H3 (UF)

Neill, Chloe: Chicagoland Vampires—V4, **S2**, H3 (UF)

Rardin, Jennifer: Jaz Parks—V5, **S2**, H3 (UF)

Raye, Kimberly: Dead End Dating—V3–4, **S2–4**, H4 (CH)

Sniegoski, Thomas E.: Remy Chandler—V4, **S2**, H2 (UF)

Swendson, Shanna: Enchanted, Inc. Series—V2, **S2**, H3 (CH)

Warren, J. D.: World of the Storm Ravens—V2, **S2**, H4 (UF)

Weldon, Phaedra: Zoë Martinique—V4, **S2**, H2 (UF)

LEVEL OF SENSUALITY: 4–5 (Lots of Graphic Sex)

Acosta, Marta: Casa Dracula—V3, **S4**, H4 (CH)

Adair, Cherry: T-FLAC Night Trilogy—V4, **S4**, H3 (SMR)

Adams, C. T., and Cathy Clamp: Thrall—V5, **S4**, H1 (UF)

Adrian, Lara: The Midnight Breed—V3, **S4**, H2 (SMR)

Andersen, Jessica: The Final Prophecy—V5, **S4**, H1 (SMR)

Andrews, Toni: MERCY HOLLINGS—V3, **S4,** H3 (UF)

Armintrout, Jennifer: BLOOD TIES—V5, **S4–5,** H1 (UF)

Armstrong, Kelley: WOMEN OF THE OTHERWORLD—V4, **S4,** H4 (UF)

Arthur, Keri: MYTH AND MAGIC SERIES—V5, **S5,** H2 (SMR)

Arthur, Keri: RILEY JENSEN, GUARDIAN—V5, **S5,** H2 (UF)

Ashley, Jennifer: SHIFTERS UNBOUND—V3, **S4,** H3 (SMR)

Ashley, Jennifer, Joy Nash, and Robin Popp: THE IMMORTALS—V3, **S5,** H3 (SMR)

Baker, Trisha: CRIMSON—V5, **S5,** H0 (UF)

Bangs, Nina: CASTLE OF DARK DREAMS—V2, **S5,** H5 (SMR)

Banks, L. A.: CRIMSON MOON—V4, **S4,** H2 (UF)

Banks, L. A.: VAMPIRE HUNTRESS LEGEND—V4, **S4,** H2 (UF)

Bardsley, Michele: BROKEN HEART VAMPIRES—V3, **S4,** H4 (SMR)

Bartlett, Gerry: GLORY ST. CLAIRE—V4, **S5,** H4 (CH)

Bast, Anya: ELEMENTAL WITCHES—V4, **S5,** H2 (SMR)

Bast, Anya: THE EMBRACED—V4, **S5+,** H1 (SMR)

Bickle, Laura: ANYA KALINCZYK—V3, **S4,** H2 (UF)

Black, Jenna: GUARDIANS OF THE NIGHT—V4, **S5,** H3 (SMR)

Black, Jenna: MORGAN KINGSLEY, EXORCIST—V4, **S5+,** H3 (UF)

Black, Shayla: THE DOOMSDAY BRETHREN—V4, **S4,** H1 (SMR)

Blair, Annette: ACCIDENTAL WITCH TRILOGY—V0, **S4,** H4 (SMR)

Blair, Annette: TRIPLET WITCH TRILOGY—V1, **S5,** H4 (SMR)

Blair, Annette: WORKS LIKE MAGICK—V3, **S4,** H4 (SMR)

Boyd, Donna: DEVONCROIX DYNASTY—V4, **S4,** H1 (UF)

Briggs, Patricia: MERCY THOMPSON—V3, **S4,** H3 (UF)

Brook, Meljean: THE GUARDIANS—V4, **S4,** H3 (SMR)

Burton, Jaci: DEMON HUNTER—V4, **S4,** H2 (SMR)

Butler, Octavia: *Fledgling* (novel)—V4, **S4,** H1 (UF)

Byrd, Rhyannon: PRIMAL INSTINCT—V5, **S4,** H1 (SMR)

Cassidy, Dakota: ACCIDENTAL FRIENDS—V3, **S5,** H5 (CH, SMR)

Cassidy, Dakota: DEMONIC ROMANCE—V2, **S4,** H5 (CH, SMR)

Castle, Kendra Leigh: MACINNES WEREWOLVES TRILOGY—V3, **S5,** H5 (SMR)

Chance, Karen: CASSANDRA PALMER—V3, **S4,** H2 (UF)

Chance, Karen: DORINA BASARAB, DHAMPIR—V3, **S4,** H3 (UF)

Child, Maureen: FIEND—V4, **S4,** H5 (CH)

Child, Maureen: QUEEN OF THE OTHERWORLD—V3, **S4,** H4 (UF)

Cole, Kresley: IMMORTALS AFTER DARK—V4, **S5,** H3 (SMR)

Cooke, Deborah: DRAGONFIRE—V4, **S4,** H2 (SMR)

Crane, Carolyn: JUSTINE JONES: DISILLUSIONIST—V3, **S4,** H2 (UF)

Davidson, MaryJanice: FRED THE MERMAID—V2, **S4,** H4 (CH)

Davidson, MaryJanice: QUEEN BETSY—V4, **S4,** H4 (CH)

Day, Alyssa: WARRIORS OF POSEIDON—V3, **S4,** H3 (SMR)

Day, S. J.: MARKED—V5, **S5,** H2 (UF)

Dean, Cameron: CANDACE STEELE, VAMPIRE KILLER—V3, **S5,** H2 (SMR, UF)

Devlin, Delilah: DARK REALM—V1, **S5+,** H1 (UF)

Dodd, Christina: THE CHOSEN ONES—V3, **S4,** H3 (SMR)

Dodd, Christina: DARKNESS CHOSEN—V4, **S4,** H2 (SMR)

Douglas, Carole Nelson: DELILAH STREET, PARANORMAL INVESTIGATOR— V4, **S4,** H4 (UF)

Drake, Jocelynn: DARK DAYS—V4, **S4,** H1 (UF)

Eden, Cynthia: MIDNIGHT TRILOGY—V4, **S4,** H2 (SMR)

Elias, Amelia: GUARDIANS' LEAGUE—V3, **S4,** H3 (SMR)

Fallon, Linda: SHADES SERIES—V3, **S4,** H2 (HIS, SMR)

Feehan, Christine: THE CARPATHIANS (DARK) SERIES—V5, **S5,** H1 (SMR)

Feehan, Christine: DRAKE SISTERS—V3, **S5,** H3 (SMR)

Feehan, Christine: GHOSTWALKERS—V4, **S4,** H2 (SMR)

Feehan, Christine: LEOPARD—V4, **S4,** H1 (SMR)

Foster, L. L.: SERVANT—V5, **S4,** H2 (UF)

Fox, Angela: DEMON SLAYERS—V3, **S5,** H5 (CH)

Frank, Jacquelyn: THE GATHERERS—V4, **S4,** H1 (SMR)

Frank, Jacquelyn: NIGHTWALKERS—V4, **S5,** H3 (SMR)

Frank, Jacquelyn: SHADOWDWELLERS—V4, **S5,** H1 (SMR)

Frost, Jeaniene: Night Huntress—V5, **S4,** H3 (UF)

Frost, Jeaniene: Night Huntress World—V5, **S4,** H3 (UF)

Galenorn, Yasmine: Sisters of the Moon—V4, **S4,** H2 (UF)

Gideon, Nancy: Moonlight—V4, **S4,** H1 (UF)

Gleason, Colleen: Gardella Vampire Chronicles—V4, **S4,** H2 (HIS)

Green, Chris Marie: Vampire Babylon—V4, **S4,** H1 (UF)

Greiman, Lois: Witches of Mayfair—V4, **S4,** H2 (HIS, SMR)

Haddock, Nancy: Oldest City Vampire—V3, **S5,** H4 (UF)

Hamilton, Laurell K.: Anita Blake, Vampire Hunter—V5, **S2** (books 1–5), **S5** (books 6–19), H3 (UF)

Hamilton, Laurell K.: Meredith Gentry—V4, **S5,** H2 (UF)

Handeland, Lori: Nightcreature—V4, **S4,** H3 (SMR)

Handeland, Lori: Phoenix Chronicles—V4, **S4,** H2 (UF)

Harper, Nina: Succubus Series—V4, **S5,** H4 (CH)

Harris, Charlaine: Southern Vampire (Sookie Stackhouse) Mysteries— V3, **S4,** H3 (UF)

Harrison, Kim: The Hollows—V4, **S5,** H3 (UF)

Hart, Raven, and Virginia Ellis: Savannah Vampires—V5, **S5,** H3 (UF)

Henry, Mark: Amanda Feral—V5, **S4,** H5 (CH)

Herron, Rita: The Demonborn—V4, **S5,** H1 (SMR)

Hilburn, Lynda: Kismet Knight, Vampire Psychologist—V5, **S5,** H3 (UF)

Hill, Joey W.: Vampire Queen—V5, **S5+,** H1 (SMR)

Holling, Jen: MacDonell Brides—V3, **S4,** H3 (HIS, SMR)

Holly, Emma: Fitz Clare Chronicles/Upyr—V4, **S4,** H2 (HIS, SMR)

Howard, Linda, and Linda Jones: Spirit Warriors—V5, **S4,** H1 (SMR)

Ione, Larissa: Demonica—V5, **S4,** H3 (SMR)

Ivy, Alexandra: Guardians of Eternity—V4, **S4,** H3 (SMR)

James, Allyson: Dragon Series—V2, **S5,** H3 (SMR)

James, Allyson: Stormwalker—V4, **S4,** H2 (UF)

Kane, Stacia: Downside Ghosts—V5, **S4,** H1 (UF)

Kane, Stacia: Megan Chase—V4, **S4,** H3 (UF)

Kantra, Virginia: CHILDREN OF THE SEA—V4, **S4,** H2 (SMR)

Kenner, Julie: SUPERHERO CENTRAL—V2, **S3–4,** H4 (CH, SMR)

Kenyon, Sherrilyn: DARK-HUNTERS—V3, **S4,** H3 (SMR)

Kenyon, Sherrilyn: DREAM-HUNTERS—V3, **S4,** H3 (SMR)

Kessler, Jackie: HELL ON EARTH—V4, **S5,** H5 (UF)

Kittredge, Caitlin: NOCTURNE CITY—V5, **S4,** H3 (UF)

Knight, Angela: MAGEVERSE—V5, **S5,** H3 (SMR)

Knight, Deidre: GODS OF MIDNIGHT—V4, **S4,** H2 (SMR)

Kohler, Sharie: MOON CHASERS—V4, **S5,** H2 (SMR)

Krinard, Susan: FANE—V4, **S4,** H2 (HIS, SMR)

Krinard, Susan: HISTORICAL WEREWOLF SERIES—V3, **S4,** H1 (HIS, SMR)

Lane, Amy: LITTLE GODDESS—V5, **S5,** H3 (SMR)

Laurenston, Shelly: PRIDE—V4, **S5,** H5 (SMR)

Laurey, Rosemary: VAMPIRE SERIES—V3, **S4,** H2 (SMR)

Leigh, Lora: BREEDS—V4, **S5,** H1 (SMR)

Leto, Julie: PHANTOM—V3, **S4,** H2 (SMR)

Love, Kathy: THE YOUNG BROTHERS—V4, **S4,** H4 (SMR)

MacAlister, Katie: AISLING GREY, GUARDIAN—V3, **S4,** H5 (SMR)

MacAlister, Katie: DARK ONES—V2, **S5,** H5 (SMR)

MacAlister, Katie: SILVER DRAGON—V3, **S4,** H5 (SMR)

Maclaine, Jenna: CIN CRAVEN—V3, **S4,** H3 (HIS)

Maverick, Liz, Marjorie M. Liu, Patti O'Shea, Carolyn Jewel, and Jade Lee:
   CRIMSON CITY—V4, **S4,** H1 (SMR)

Mayhue, Melissa: DAUGHTERS OF THE GLEN—V3, **S4,** H3 (SMR)

McCarthy, Erin: CUTTERSVILLE GHOSTS—V1, **S5,** H4 (SMR)

McCarthy, Erin: SEVEN DEADLY SINS—V1, **S5,** H3 (SMR)

McCarthy, Erin: VEGAS VAMPIRES—V3, **S5,** H5 (SMR)

McCleave, Annette: SOUL GATHERERS—V3, **S4,** H1 (SMR)

McCray, Cheyenne: MAGIC—V5, **S5,** H2 (SMR)

Mead, Richelle: DARK SWAN—V4, **S5,** H3 (UF)

Mead, Richelle: GEORGINA KINCAID—V2, **S4,** H4 (UF)

Moning, Karen: HIGHLANDER SERIES—V3, **S4,** H2 (HIS, SMR)

Monk, Devon: ALLIE BECKSTROM—V4, **S4,** H1 (UF)

Morgan, Alexis: PALADINS OF DARKNESS—V4, **S5,** H2 (SMR)

Morgan, Alexis: TALIONS—V4, **S4,** H2 (SMR)

O'Shea, Patti: LIGHT WARRIORS—V4, **S4** (book 1 = 5+), H1 (SMR)

Palmer, Pamela: FERAL WARRIORS—V5, **S4,** H1 (SMR)

Parks, Lydia: EROTIC VAMPIRE SERIES—V5, **S5+,** H1 (SMR)

Phoenix, Adrian: THE MAKER'S SONG—V5, **S5,** H1 (UF)

Popp, Robin T.: NIGHT SLAYER—V3, **S4,** H1 (SMR)

Raye, Kimberly: DEAD END DATING—V3–4, **S2–4,** H4 (CH)

Reinke, Sara: THE BRETHREN—V5, **S4,** H1 (SMR)

Roberts, Nora: SIGN OF SEVEN TRILOGY—V4, **S4,** H4 (SMR)

Rowen, Michelle: IMMORTALITY BITES—V3, **S4,** H3 (CH)

Rowland, Diana: KARA GILLIAN—V3, **S4,** H3 (UF)

Rush, Jaime: OFFSPRING—V4, **S4,** H1 (SMR)

Russe, Savannah: DARKWING CHRONICLES—V5, **S5,** H2 (CH)

Russe, Savannah: SISTERHOOD OF THE SIGHT—V3, **S4,** H2 (SMR)

St. Giles, Jennifer: SHADOWMEN—V3, **S4,** H1 (SMR)

Sands, Lynsay: ARGENEAU VAMPIRES—V4, **S4,** H3 (SMR)

Shayne, Maggie: IMMORTAL WITCHES—V3, **S4,** H2 (HIS, SMR)

Shayne, Maggie: WINGS IN THE NIGHT—V4, **S4,** H3 (SMR)

Showalter, Gena: ALIEN HUNTRESS—V4, **S4,** H2 (SMR)

Showalter, Gena: ATLANTIS—V4, **S4,** H3 (SMR)

Showalter, Gena: LORDS OF THE UNDERWORLD—V4, **S4,** H3 (SMR)

Showalter, Gena: TALES OF AN EXTRAORDINARY GIRL—V4, **S4,** H3 (UF)

Silver, Eve: COMPACT OF SORCERERS—V5, **S5,** H2 (SMR)

Singh, Nalini: PSY-CHANGELINGS—V3, **S4,** H3 (SMR)

Sizemore, Susan: PRIMES—V4, **S4,** H2 (SMR)

Smith, Kathryn: BROTHERHOOD OF BLOOD—V3, **S5,** H2 (HIS, SMR)

Smith, Kathryn: NIGHTMARE CHRONICLES—V3, **S4,** H2 (UF)

Smith-Ready, Jeri: WVMP RADIO—V5, **S4,** H3 (UF)

Sparks, Kerrelyn: LOVE AT STAKE—V4, **S5,** H4 (CH, SMR)

Spear, Terry: WOLF SERIES—V4, **S4,** H2 (SMR)

Spencer, Jorrie: STRENGTH—V4, **S4,** H2 (SMR)

Squires, Susan: THE COMPANION—V5, **S5,** H1 (HIS, SMR)

Stone, Juliana: JAGUAR WARRIOR—V4, **S4,** H1 (SMR)

Sunny: DEMON PRINCESS CHRONICLES—V5, **S5,** H2 (UF)

Sunny: MONÉRE: CHILDREN OF THE MOON—V5, **S5,** H2 (UF)

Thompson, Ronda: WILD WULFS OF LONDON—V4, **S4,** H2 (HIS, SMR)

Thompson, Vicki Lewis: HEX SERIES—V1, **S4,** H5 (SMR)

Viehl, Lynn: THE DARKYN SERIES—V5, **S5,** H3 (SMR)

Vincent, Rachel: WERECATS—V5, **S4,** H3 (UF)

Walker, Shiloh: THE HUNTERS—V3, **S4,** H1 (SMR)

Ward, J. R.: BLACK DAGGER BROTHERHOOD—V5, **S5,** H3 (SMR)

Ward, J. R.: FALLEN ANGELS—V4, **S4,** H2 (SMR)

Warren, Christine: THE OTHERS—V4, **S4,** H4 (SMR)

Whiteside, Diane: TEXAS VAMPIRES—V4, **S5,** H2 (SMR)

Wilks, Eileen: WORLD OF THE LUPI—V4, **S4,** H3 (SMR)

Windsor, Anna: DARK CRESCENT SISTERHOOD—V4, **S5,** H3 (SMR)

Wisdom, Linda: HEX SERIES—V5, **S4,** H5 (UF)

Yarbro, Chelsea Quinn: SAINT-GERMAIN—V4, **S4,** H3 (HIS)

York, Rebecca: MOON SERIES—V4, **S4–5+,** H1 (SMR)

LEVEL OF HUMOR: 0–2 (LITTLE OR NO HUMOR)

Adams, C. T., and Cathy Clamp: TALES OF THE SAZI—V4, S3–4, **H1** (SMR)

Adams, C. T., and Cathy Clamp: THRALL—V5, S4, **H1** (UF)

Aguirre, Ann: CORINE SOLOMON—V4, S2, **H1** (UF)

Andersen, Jessica: THE FINAL PROPHECY—V5, S4, **H1** (SMR)

Armintrout, Jennifer: BLOOD TIES—V5, S4–5, **H1** (UF)

Arthur, Keri: MYTH AND MAGIC SERIES—V5, S5, **H2** (SMR)

Arthur, Keri: RILEY JENSEN, GUARDIAN—V5, S5, **H2** (UF)

Ashley, Amanda: DARK SERIES—V3, S3, **H2** (SMR)

Ashley, Amanda: NIGHT SERIES—V3, S3, **H2** (SMR)

Bacon-Smith, Camille: DAEMONS, INC.—V4, S3, **H1** (UF)

Baker, Trisha: CRIMSON—V5, S5, **H0** (UF)

Banks, L. A.: CRIMSON MOON—V4, S4, **H2** (UF)

Banks, L. A.: VAMPIRE HUNTRESS LEGEND—V4, S4, **H2** (UF)

Barbieri, Elaine: WOLF SERIES—V2, S1, **H1** (HIS, SMR)

Bast, Anya: ELEMENTAL WITCHES—V4, S5, **H2** (SMR)

Bast, Anya: THE EMBRACED—V4, S5+, **H1** (SMR)

Bickle, Laura: ANYA KALINCZYK—V3, S4, **H2** (UF)

Black, Shayla: THE DOOMSDAY BRETHREN—V4, S4, **H1** (SMR)

Blue, Lucy: BOUND IN DARKNESS—V4, S3, **H1** (HIS, SMR)

Boyd, Donna: DEVONCROIX DYNASTY—V4, S4, **H1** (UF)

Brennan, Allison: SEVEN DEADLY SINS—V4, S2 (book 1), S4 (book 2), **H1** (UF)

Burton, Jaci: DEMON HUNTER—V4, S4, **H2** (SMR)

Butler, Octavia: *Fledgling* (novel)—V4, S4, **H1** (UF)

Byrd, Rhyannon: PRIMAL INSTINCT—V5, S4, **H1** (SMR)

Caine, Rachel: OUTCAST SEASON—V4, S2, **H1** (UF)

Caine, Rachel: WEATHER WARDEN—V5, S3, **H1** (UF)

Chance, Karen: CASSANDRA PALMER—V3, S4, **H2** (UF)

Cooke, Deborah: DRAGONFIRE—V4, S4, **H2** (SMR)

Crane, Carolyn: JUSTINE JONES: DISILLUSIONIST—V3, S4, **H2** (UF)

Cunningham, Elaine: CHANGELING DETECTIVE AGENCY—V4, S3, **H2** (UF)

Day, S. J.: MARKED—V5, S5, **H2** (UF)

Dean, Cameron: CANDACE STEELE, VAMPIRE KILLER—V3, S5, **H2** (SMR, UF)

Devlin, Delilah: DARK REALM—V1, S5+, **H1** (UF)

Dodd, Christina: DARKNESS CHOSEN—V4, S4, **H2** (SMR)

Drake, Jocelynn: DARK DAYS—V4, S4, **H1** (UF)

Durgin, Doranna: THE RECKONERS—V4, S2, **H2** (UF)

Eden, Cynthia: MIDNIGHT TRILOGY—V4, S4, **H2** (SMR)

Elrod, P. N.: *Quincey Morris, Vampire* (novel)—V3, S3, **H2** (HIS)

Fallon, Linda: SHADES SERIES—V3, S4, **H2** (HIS, SMR)

Farren, Mick: RENQUIST QUARTET—V5, S3, **H1** (UF)

Feehan, Christine: THE CARPATHIANS (DARK) SERIES—V5, S5, **H1** (SMR)

Feehan, Christine: GHOSTWALKERS—V4, S4, **H2** (SMR)

Feehan, Christine: LEOPARD—V4, S4, **H1** (SMR)

Finlay, C. C.: TRAITOR TO THE CROWN—V4, S2, **H2** (HIS)

Foster, L. L.: SERVANT—V5, S4, **H2** (UF)

Frank, Jacquelyn: THE GATHERERS—V4, S4, **H1** (SMR)

Frank, Jacquelyn: SHADOWDWELLERS—V4, S5, **H1** (SMR)

Frost, P. R.: TESS NONCOIRÉ—V4, S3, **H2** (UF)

Galenorn, Yasmine: SISTERS OF THE MOON—V4, S4, **H2** (UF)

Gideon, Nancy: MOONLIGHT—V4, S4, **H1** (UF)

Gilman, Laura Anne: PARANORMAL SCENE INVESTIGATIONS—V3, S2, **H2** (UF)

Gleason, Colleen: GARDELLA VAMPIRE CHRONICLES—V4, S4, **H2** (HIS)

Green, Chris Marie: VAMPIRE BABYLON—V4, S4, **H1** (UF)

Greiman, Lois: WITCHES OF MAYFAIR—V4, S4, **H2** (HIS, SMR)

Hamilton, Laurell K.: MEREDITH GENTRY—V4, S5, **H2** (UF)

Hansen, Jamie Leigh: *Betrayal; Cursed* (no series title)—V3, S3, **H1** (SMR)

Hecht, Daniel: CREE BLACK—V3, S2, **H2** (UF)

Hendee, Barb: VAMPIRE MEMORIES—V4, S1, **H1** (UF)

Hendee, Barb, and J. C. Hendee: NOBLE DEAD SAGA—V4, S3, **H2** (HIS)

Herron, Rita: THE DEMONBORN—V4, S5, **H1** (SMR)

Hill, Joey W.: VAMPIRE QUEEN—V5, S5+, **H1** (SMR)

Holly, Emma: FITZ CLARE CHRONICLES/UPYR—V4, S4, **H2** (HIS, SMR)

Holzner, Nancy: DEADTOWN—V3, S2, **H2** (UF)

Hooper, Kay: BISHOP/SPECIAL CRIMES UNIT—V5, S3, **H2** (SMR)

Howard, Linda, and Linda Jones: SPIRIT WARRIORS—V5, S4, **H1** (SMR)

Hunter, Faith: JANE YELLOWROCK—V5, S2, **H2** (UF)

James, Allyson: STORMWALKER—V4, S4, **H2** (UF)

Kane, Stacia: DOWNSIDE GHOSTS—V5, S4, **H1** (UF)

Kantra, Virginia: CHILDREN OF THE SEA—V4, S4, **H2** (SMR)

Kenner, Julie: BLOOD LILY CHRONICLES—V4, S2, **H1** (UF)

Kittredge, Caitlin: BLACK LONDON—V4, S3, **H2** (UF)

Knight, Deidre: GODS OF MIDNIGHT—V4, S4, **H2** (SMR)

Kohler, Sharie: MOON CHASERS—V4, S5, **H2** (SMR)

Krinard, Susan: FANE—V4, S4, **H2** (HIS, SMR)

Krinard, Susan: HISTORICAL WEREWOLF SERIES—V3, S4, **H1** (HIS, SMR)

Laurey, Rosemary: VAMPIRE SERIES—V3, S4, **H2** (SMR)

Leigh, Lora: BREEDS—V4, S5, **H1** (SMR)

Leto, Julie: PHANTOM—V3, S4, **H2** (SMR)

Liu, Marjorie M.: DIRK AND STEELE—V3, S3, **H1** (SMR)

Liu, Marjorie M.: HUNTER KISS—V3, S2, **H1** (UF)

Maverick, Liz, Marjorie M. Liu, Patti O'Shea, Carolyn Jewel, and Jade Lee: CRIMSON CITY—V4, S4, **H1** (SMR)

McCleave, Annette: SOUL GATHERERS—V3, S4, **H1** (SMR)

McCray, Cheyenne: MAGIC—V5, S5, **H2** (SMR)

McGuire, Seanan: OCTOBER DAYE—V4, S1, **H2** (UF)

Moning, Karen: FEVER SERIES—V4, S3, **H1** (UF)

Moning, Karen: HIGHLANDER SERIES—V3, S4, **H2** (HIS, SMR)

Monk, Devon: ALLIE BECKSTROM—V4, S4, **H1** (UF)

Morgan, Alexis: PALADINS OF DARKNESS—V4, S5, **H2** (SMR)

Morgan, Alexis: TALIONS—V4, S4, **H2** (SMR)

Murphy, C. E.: NEGOTIATOR TRILOGY—V3, S3, **H2** (UF)

O'Shea, Patti: LIGHT WARRIORS—V4, S4 (book 1 = 5+), **H1** (SMR)

Palmer, Pamela: FERAL WARRIORS—V5, S4, **H1** (SMR)

Parks, Lydia: EROTIC VAMPIRE SERIES—V5, S5+, **H1** (SMR)

Pettersson, Vicki: SIGNS OF THE ZODIAC—V4, S3, **H1** (UF)

Phoenix, Adrian: THE MAKER'S SONG—V5, S5, **H1** (UF)

Popp, Robin T.: NIGHT SLAYER   V3, S4, **H1** (SMR)

Reinke, Sara: THE BRETHREN—V5, S4, **H1** (SMR)

Richardson, Kat: GREYWALKER—V3, S3, **H1** (UF)

Robertson, Linda: CIRCLE/PERSEPHONE ALCMEDI—V3, S3, **H2** (UF)

Rush, Jaime: OFFSPRING—V4, S4, **H1** (SMR)

Russe, Savannah: DARKWING CHRONICLES—V5, S5, **H2** (CH)

Russe, Savannah: SISTERHOOD OF THE SIGHT—V3, S4, **H2** (SMR)

St. Giles, Jennifer: SHADOWMEN—V3, S4, **H1** (SMR)

Saintcrow, Lilith: DANTE VALENTINE—V4, S3, **H1** (UF)

Saintcrow, Lilith: JILL KISMET—V5, S3, **H2** (UF)

Shayne, Maggie: IMMORTAL WITCHES—V3, S4, **H2** (HIS, SMR)

Showalter, Gena: ALIEN HUNTRESS—V4, S4, **H2** (SMR)

Silver, Eve: COMPACT OF SORCERERS—V5, S5, **H2** (SMR)

Sizemore, Susan: LAWS OF THE BLOOD—V4, S3, **H2** (SMR)

Sizemore, Susan: PRIMES—V4, S4, **H2** (SMR)

Smith, Kathryn: BROTHERHOOD OF BLOOD—V3, S5, **H2** (HIS, SMR)

Smith, Kathryn: NIGHTMARE CHRONICLES—V3, S4, **H2** (UF)

Sniegoski, Thomas E.: REMY CHANDLER—V4, S2, **H2** (UF)

Spear, Terry: WOLF SERIES—V4, S4, **H2** (SMR)

Spencer, Jorrie: STRENGTH—V4, S4, **H2** (SMR)

Squires, Susan: THE COMPANION—V5, S5, **H1** (HIS, SMR)

Stein, Jeanne C.: ANNA STRONG CHRONICLES—V4, S3, **H2** (UF)

Stone, Juliana: JAGUAR WARRIOR—V4, S4, **H1** (SMR)

Sunny: DEMON PRINCESS CHRONICLES—V5, S5, **H2** (UF)

Sunny: MONÉRE: CHILDREN OF THE MOON—V5, S5, **H2** (UF)

Thompson, Ronda: WILD WULFS OF LONDON—V4, S4, **H2** (HIS, SMR)

Troop, Alan F.: DRAGON DELASANGRE—V5, S3, **H1** (UF)

Walker, Shiloh: THE HUNTERS—V3, S4, **H1** (SMR)

Ward, J. R.: FALLEN ANGELS—V4, S4, **H2** (SMR)

Weldon, Phaedra: ZOË MARTINIQUE—V4, S2, **H2** (UF)

Wellington, David: LAURA CAXTON—V5, S3, **H0** (UF)

Whiteside, Diane: TEXAS VAMPIRES—V4, S5, **H2** (SMR)

York, Rebecca: MOON SERIES—V4, S4–5+, **H1** (SMR)

LEVEL OF HUMOR: 4–5 (LOTS OF LAUGHS)

Acosta, Marta: CASA DRACULA—V3, S4, **H4** (CH)

Armstrong, Kelley: WOMEN OF THE OTHERWORLD—V4, S4, **H4** (UF)

Austen, Jane, and Seth Grahame-Smith: *Pride and Prejudice and Zombies* (novel)—V5, S1, **H4** (CH, HIS spoof)

Bangs, Nina: Castle of Dark Dreams—V2, S5, **H5** (SMR)

Bangs, Nina: MacKenzie Vampires—V2, S3, **H5** (SMR)

Bardsley, Michele: Broken Heart Vampires—V3, S4, **H4** (SMR)

Bartlett, Gerry: Glory St. Claire—V4, S5, **H4** (CH)

Benson, Amber: Calliope Reaper-Jones—V3, S2, **H5** (CH)

Blair, Annette: Accidental Witch Trilogy—V0, S4, **H4** (SMR)

Blair, Annette: Triplet Witch Trilogy—V1, S5, **H4** (SMR)

Blair, Annette: Vintage Magic—V2, S2, **H4** (CH, COZ)

Blair, Annette: Works like Magick—V3, S4, **H4** (SMR)

Butcher, Jim: Dresden Files—V4, S3, **H4** (UF)

Carriger, Gail: The Parasol Protectorate—V4, S3, **H4** (CH, HIS)

Cassidy, Dakota: Accidental Friends—V3, S5, **H5** (CH, SMR)

Cassidy, Dakota: Demonic Romance—V2, S4, **H5** (CH, SMR)

Castle, Kendra Leigh: MacInnes Werewolves Trilogy—V3, S5, **H5** (SMR)

Child, Maureen: Fiend—V4, S4, **H5** (CH)

Child, Maureen: Queen of the Otherworld—V3, S4, **H4** (UF)

Daniels, Casey: Pepper Martin Mysteries—V3, S3, **H4** (CH)

Davidson, MaryJanice: Fred the Mermaid—V2, S4, **H4** (CH)

Davidson, MaryJanice: Queen Betsy—V4, S4, **H4** (CH)

Douglas, Carole Nelson: Delilah Street, Paranormal Investigator—V4, S4, **H4** (UF)

Fox, Andrew: Fat White Vampire—V5, S3, **H5** (UF)

Fox, Angela: Demon Slayers—V3, S5, **H5** (CH)

Garey, Terri: Nicki Styx—V2, S3, **H4** (UF)

Green, Simon R.: Secret Histories—V4, S2, **H4** (UF)

Haddock, Nancy: Oldest City Vampire—V3, S5, **H4** (UF)

Hallaway, Tate: Garnet Lacey—V3, S3, **H4** (CH)

Harper, Molly: Nice Girls—V3, S3, **H4** (CH)

Harper, Nina: Succubus Series—V4, S5, **H4** (CH)

Havens, Candace: BRONWYN THE WITCH—V3, S3, **H4** (CH)

Havens, Candace: CARUTHERS SISTERS—V5, S3, **H4** (CH, SMR)

Henry, Mark: AMANDA FERAL—V5, S4, **H5** (CH)

Huff, Tanya: SMOKE TRILOGY—V4, S3, **H4** (UF)

James, Dean: SIMON KIRBY-JONES MYSTERIES—V2, S2, **H5** (COZ)

Kenner, Julie: DEMON-HUNTING SOCCER MOM—V5, S3, **H5** (UF)

Kenner, Julie: SUPERHERO CENTRAL—V2, S3–4, **H4** (CH, SMR)

Kessler, Jackie: HELL ON EARTH—V4, S5, **H5** (UF)

Klasky, Mindy: AS YOU WISH—V1, S3, **H4** (CH, SMR)

Laurenston, Shelly: PRIDE—V4, S5, **H5** (SMR)

Lockwood, Cara: DEMON SERIES—V3, S2, **H5** (CH)

Love, Kathy: THE YOUNG BROTHERS—V4, S4, **H4** (SMR)

MacAlister, Katie: AISLING GREY, GUARDIAN—V3, S4, **H5** (SMR)

MacAlister, Katie: DARK ONES—V2, S5, **H5** (SMR)

MacAlister, Katie: SILVER DRAGON—V3, S4, **H5** (SMR)

MacInerney, Karen: TALES OF AN URBAN WEREWOLF—V2, S3, **H4** (UF)

McCarthy, Erin: CUTTERSVILLE GHOSTS—V1, S5, **H4** (SMR)

McCarthy, Erin: VEGAS VAMPIRES—V3, S5, **H5** (SMR)

Mead, Richelle: GEORGINA KINCAID—V2, S4, **H4** (UF)

Pratt, T. A.: MARLA MASON—V3, S3, **H4** (UF)

Raye, Kimberly: DEAD END DATING—V3–4, S2–4, **H4** (CH)

Roberts, Nora: SIGN OF SEVEN TRILOGY—V4, S4, **H4** (SMR)

Rowe, Stephanie: IMMORTALLY SEXY—V2, S3, **H5** (SMR)

Simmons, Wm. Mark: CHRIS CSÉJTHE: HALF/LIFE CHRONICLES—V5, S3, **H4** (UF)

Sparks, Kerrelyn: LOVE AT STAKE—V4, S5, **H4** (CH, SMR)

Strout, Anton: SIMON CANDEROUS—V4, S3, **H4** (UF)

Thompson, Vicki Lewis: HEX SERIES—V1, S4, **H5** (SMR)

Thurman, Rob: CAL LEANDROS—V5, S3, **H4** (UF)

Thurman, Rob: TRICKSTER—V4, S2, **H4** (UF)

Warren, Christine: THE OTHERS—V4, S4, **H4** (SMR)

Warren, J. D.: WORLD OF THE STORM RAVENS—V2, S2, **H4** (UF)

Wilson, F. Paul: REPAIRMAN JACK—V5, S3, **H4** (UF)

Wisdom, Linda: HEX SERIES—V5, S4, **H5** (UF)

CHAPTER 2

series descriptions

a sample entry

....

Kohler, Sharie

MOON CHASERS (SMR—V4, S5, H2)

Pocket Star: *Marked by Moonlight* (2007); *Kiss of a Dark Moon* (2008); *To Crave a Blood Moon* (2009)

Gideon and Kit March are brother-sister lycan (werewolf) executioners. Most of these werewolves are savage killers who are executed by agents of the National Organization for Defense against Evolving and Ancient Lycanthropes (NODEAL). Each book follows one of the siblings through the steps of a soul-mate romance (SMR) as he or she finds true love while battling both the werewolves and the NODEAL bad guys who are trying to kill them both.

Explanation: The author is Sharie Kohler. The series is entitled MOON CHASERS. The publisher is Pocket. The books, in chronological order, are *Marked by Moonlight*, *Kiss of a Dark Moon*, and *To Crave a Blood Moon*. The series has some heavy violence (V4), graphic sex scenes (S5), and very little humor (H2). Although the plot includes some paranormal battles, the focus is on the progression of the protagonists' romantic relationships with their soul mates (SMR).

Acevedo, Mario

FELIX GOMEZ (UF—V5, S3, H3)

The Nymphos of Rocky Flats (Eos, 2007); *X-Rated Bloodsuckers* (Eos, 2008); *The Undead Kama Sutra* (Eos, 2008); *Jailbait Zombie* (Eos, 2009); *Werewolf Smackdown* (Eos, 2010); *Mario Acevedo's Felix Gomez: Killing the Cobra—Chinatown Trollop* (graphic novel, IDW Publishing, 2010)

Don't judge this series by its titles, which imply X-rated content. In reality, the stories are more like noir detective yarns—multiple murders solved by knitting together strands of seemingly unconnected clues. The titles refer more to characters and situations than to the sensuality levels, and the sensuality that is included is mostly left to the imagination. The series follows the adventures of Felix Gomez, a vampire private detective in the present-day American West. The Araneum (Latin for "spiderweb"), the secret global network that vampires formed to protect themselves from human extermination, assigns many of his jobs. In Felix's world, vampires can tolerate most sunshine (except for sunrise) as long as they protect their skin with sun-block lotion. Two of the books involve extraterrestrials to some degree, but most of the scenes focus on Felix's adventures as he tries to solve the multiple murders he faces in each book.

Acosta, Marta

CASA DRACULA (CH—V3, S4, H4)

Happy Hour at Casa Dracula (Pocket, 2006); *Midnight Brunch* (Pocket, 2007); *The Bride of Casa Dracula* (Pocket, 2008); *Haunted Honeymoon at Casa Dracula* (Gallery, 2010)

Milagro de los Santos is a frustrated writer, taking advertising jobs to pay the rent while she works on her novels. When she accidentally shares blood with Oswald Grant, a handsome vampire, her life changes completely. Soon, she is running for her life—away from her ex-boyfriend Sebastian, who wants to use her body for various horrendous experiments, and toward a possible life with Oswald. Other possible love interests, however, do turn up, including the sexy and powerful vampire lord Ian. Oswald and his family see themselves not as vampires but as people with a "condition"—an enzyme deficiency that can be controlled only through ingesting excessive amounts of protein, specifically, blood and other red foods. The high sensuality rating is related to the bloodletting (with scalpels—they don't have fangs) that occurs during sexual scenes. Plots involve various attempts to kidnap Milagro for her blood.

Adair, Cherry

T-FLAC Night Trilogy (SMR—V4, S4, H3)

Night Fall (Ballantine, 2008); *Night Secrets* (Ballantine, 2008); *Night Shadow* (Ballantine, 2009); *Shadow Fall* (Leisure, 2010)

Simon Blackthorne, Lucas Fox, and Alex Stone lost their parents in separate violent accidents, and each spent his childhood in foster care and was mentored by Dr. Mason Knight, a powerful wizard. Each boy grows up to be a full wizard and a psi operative for T-FLAC (Terrorist Force Logistical Assault Command), an organization of wizards and humans who work to combat global terrorism. Now, each man is thirty-six years old, and each feels his wizard powers (primarily teleportation and invisibility) slipping away. The T-FLAC organization is facing a monumental, worldwide bio-terrorism threat, and the three men must solve that problem, all the while trying to figure out how to regain their powers. Along the way, each meets an attractive human woman whose touch seems to regenerate his powers. Of course, each one spends a great deal of time denying this connection. Eventually, each couple goes off into a happy future as lifemates. The adventures take place all over the world, and the violent battles often involve powerful terrorist wizards. Adair has also written the T-FLAC Edge trilogy, a similar series about three more T-FLAC psi operatives (Ballantine: *Edge of Danger*, 2006; *Edge of Fear*, 2006; and *Edge of Darkness*, 2006).

Adams, C. T., and Cathy Clamp

Tales of the Sazi (SMR—V4, S3–4, H1)

Tor: *Hunter's Moon* (2004); *Moon's Web* (2005); *Captive Moon* (2006); *Howling Moon* (2007); *Moon's Fury* (2007); *Timeless Moon* (2008); *Cold Moon Rising* (2009); *Serpent Moon* (2010)

The Sazi are the shape-shifters of the world. Centuries ago, representatives of each known werespecies came together in an attempt to defend themselves against extermination by humans. They established a council, with representatives taken from the strongest of each species, and pledged to remain hidden from humans. They also established the Wolven, the law enforcement branch of their government. The books tell the SMR stories of various Sazi couples. Most of the rambling plots revolve around rogue Sazi who try to interrupt, or end, the lives of law-abiding Sazi, but the romantic relationships are more important than the plots. Several books center on the adventures of Tony Giodone, a mob assassin and newly created werewolf, and his mate, Sue, a human.

• •

The Thrall has existed since the dawn of time. They've evolved over the millennia from the equivalent of a tapeworm to become a highly intelligent parasitic species with a unique culture and language.... They are extremely sensitive to damage to the Host. This is apparently because the primary ganglia actually *fuses* to the Host's spinal cord.... And damage to the Thrall, such as an injury to a feeding tube [fang] in the mouth or a blow to the nesting site at the base of the skull will stun the Host into a comatose-like state. . . . Anything sufficient to kill the Thrall will kill the Host. It's only recently that we've learned that the Thrall's body actually merges with and *replaces* human brain tissue. When the parasite grows too big, the hypothalamus is destroyed and the Host dies. The usual life span seems to be about three to four years.

> Dr. MacDougal explains how to injure or kill the Thrall,
> in C. T. Adams and Cathy Clamp's *Touch of Evil*

• •

Adams, C. T., and Cathy Clamp (cont.)

THRALL (UF—V5, S4, H1)

Tor: *Touch of Evil* (2006); *Touch of Madness* (2007); *Touch of Darkness* (2008)

Bucking the recent vampire-as-boyfriend trend, the vampires in this trilogy are parasites who attach themselves to human hosts. The parasite egg is carried in vampire saliva and is injected into the host through a bite. Queens, who may be either male or female, lead the vampire nests (called the Thrall). Once it has selected as a host, the parasite wears down the human's body to the point of death. Kate Reilly is a bonded courier who delivers valuable objects (e.g., gemstones, artworks) across the globe. Kate lives in Denver near her two brothers: Joe, an emergency-room physician, and Bryan, a brain-dead addict. Her best friend, Michael, was once her boyfriend but is now her priest. A vampire queen bit Kate shortly before the beginning of book 1, but she survived without becoming part of the herd. Because of that survival, she is now known as "Not Prey," and all vampires and werewolves must treat her with as much respect as they do their own leaders. At the beginning of book 1, Kate meets Tom, a handsome werewolf fireman, and they fall in love. The series takes the couple through one bloody and violent battle after another as Kate attempts to defeat the Thrall once and for all.

Kate seems to spend every other chapter in a hospital bed recovering from horrific injuries, but she's always able to recover in time for the next attack.

Adrian, Lara

THE MIDNIGHT BREED (SMR—V3, S4, H2)
Dell: *Kiss of Midnight* (2007); *Kiss of Crimson* (2007); *Midnight Awakening* (2007); *Midnight Rising* (2008); *Veil of Midnight* (2008); *Ashes of Midnight* (2009); *Shades of Midnight* (2009); *Taken by Midnight* (2010); *Deeper Than Midnight* (2011)

The vampire world is split into Breeds (heroes) and Rogues (villains), with beautiful, young human women always in danger but inevitably rescued by the good guys. Each heroine is marked (literally) by fate to be a Breedmate, with a physical mark somewhere on her body. The hero in each book has usually decided, for various reasons, to be alone. He is inevitably startled and dismayed when he discovers that the heroine is his Breedmate, and then, of course, falls deeply in love with her by the end of the book.

Aguirre, Ann

CORINE SOLOMON (UF—V4, S2, H1)
Roc: *Blue Diablo* (2009); *Hell Fire* (2010); *Shady Lady* (2011)

Aguirre won the P.E.A.R.L. Award for best new author in 2008. Corine is a handler—a psychometrist. She can touch something and know its history and, sometimes, its future. She is not the usual gun-toting, smart-mouthed UF heroine. Instead, she dresses in hippie chic; likes to eat; runs an antique shop; and has a dry, understated sense of humor. In the past, Corine and her lover, Chance, earned their living by using Corine's ability to find missing persons. Chance has his own supernatural power: his luck, which (so far) keeps him safe but not those around him, not even Corine. On their last job together, Corine was badly injured, but Chance escaped unharmed. When she recovered, Corine ran away, believing that Chance had been using her for his own profit. In book 1, Corine has hidden herself away in a small Mexican town, where she finally feels safe, but Chance finds her and convinces her to help him find his mother, who has disappeared. The plot includes demons, sorcerers, ghosts, witchcraft, and black magic. An additional love interest surfaces in book 1: Jesse Saldana, a sexy Texas police officer. In book 2, Corine and Jesse go back to Corine's tiny Georgia hometown to learn about the details of the horrific death of her mother. They soon find that a dark force has taken control of the town.

Allen, Harper

CROSSE TRIPLETS (CH, SMR—V5, S3, H3)

Silhouette Bombshell: *Vampaholic* (2006); *Dressed to Slay* (2006); *Dead Is the New Black* (2007)

As the Crosse triplets plan their weddings, their world comes tumbling down around them. First, the girls have to stake their prospective grooms when a vengeful vampire queen turns the guys into vampires and sends them out to kill their brides. Then their long-lost Russian grandfather turns up with news of the real story behind their parents' deaths and a prophecy that will affect all three of the triplets. Each book tells one sister's story as she finds her destiny and meets her true love. Although each book has one relatively detailed sex scene, the plots are more concerned with supernatural conflicts than with sexual exploits and include battles with two deranged vampire queens and an evil master vamp. The first two books have the usual love-hate relationships, multiple misunderstandings, and happy endings. The romance in the third story is not so straightforward, and its ending is more ambiguous. The stories include enough fashion references and girlfriend moments to make it CH, but the plots are definitely SMR.

Alt, Madelyn

BEWITCHING MYSTERIES (CH—V3, S2, H3)

Berkley: *The Trouble with Magic* (2006); *A Charmed Death* (2006); *Hex Marks the Spot* (2007); *No Rest for the Wiccan* (2008); *Where There's a Witch* (2009); *A Witch in Time* (2010)

This series could almost be classified as cozy, because it involves an amateur sleuth, one dead body per book, gossipy townsfolk, and a somewhat bungling police force, but this sleuth has two boyfriends, a group of girlfriends, and enough wardrobe description to push it into CH. Maggie O'Neill is an empath and a sensitive. She can sense the emotions of the living and the spirits of the dead. Maggie lives in Stony Mill, Indiana, and works at Enchantments Antiques and Fine Gifts, which is run by her friend Felicity Dow, an English witch. Maggie's love interests (limited to long, romantic kisses) are Tom Fielding, a handsome, buttoned-down police detective who is uncomfortable both with Maggie's friends and with her empathic abilities, and Marcus Quinn, a sexy, motorcycle-riding medium who wants Maggie to learn to appreciate her supernatural talents. Maggie's friends and family are also involved in each story. In each book, there is a murder, and Maggie gets herself into one dangerous situation after another as she searches for each killer.

Andersen, Jessica

THE FINAL PROPHECY (SMR—V5, S4, H1)
   Signet: *Nightkeepers* (2008); *Dawnkeepers* (2009); *Skykeepers* (2009); *Demonkeepers* (2010)

This series focuses on the Mayan end-times apocalypse prophecy of December 21, 2012. The heroes and heroines are the Nightkeepers, sworn to protect humanity by defeating the demonic forces that will unleash themselves on the earth on that critical date. Each Nightkeeper is a trained warrior with a magical talent. Book 1 provides detailed background information about the Nightkeepers, so it includes a great deal of Mayan "history." The series focuses on a series of violent battles with various dark forces as the countdown to global cataclysm draws nearer. Each book tells the SMR story of one Nightkeeper couple as they try to save the world while traveling down love's rough road. As each couple mates, a magical mark appears on their right arms to mark them as *jun tan* (beloved). The high rating for violence is based on both the brutal battles and the ritualistic bloodletting that the Nightkeepers engage in when they cast spells: slashing their palms with knives and stabbing their tongues with stingray spines—ouch! Andersen includes a glossary of Mayan terms.

Andrews, Ilona

KATE DANIELS (UF—V5, S2, H3)
   Magic Bites (Ace, 2007); *Magic Burns* (Ace, 2008); *Magic Strikes* (Ace, 2009); "Magic Mourns" in *Must Love Hellhounds* anthology (Berkley, 2009); *Magic Bleeds* (Ace, 2010)

In an alternate Atlanta, waves of magic and technology ebb and flow across the city. When magic rises, it knocks out all technology and the supernaturals' powers increase. Citizens use both horses and cars for transportation because cars (and other technology, like phones) don't run when the magic is up. Kate is a powerful magic-using mercenary with a mysterious past. She is recruited by the Order of Merciful Aid, a group run by knights and crusaders, whose purpose is to protect humanity against harm. Kate is a typical UF heroine with her sarcastic sniping, tough street cred, and excellent fighting skills. Her usual plan of attack is to "go and annoy everyone involved until somebody tries to kill you" (*Magic Strikes*). In Kate's world, there are two groups of supernatural power brokers:

- The People, run by necromancers (Masters of the Dead). They are devoted to the study of the undead, animating them as vampires who serve as nonsentient, but powerful, slaves. Their leader is Roland, who has a mysterious link to Kate's past.
- The Pride, a unification of all of the shape-shifters under Curran, Lord of the Free Beasts (aka "Beast Lord"), who becomes Kate's nemesis (and love interest).

Plots include horrendous supernatural battles, with the expected level of injuries. Kate faces dozens of deadly creatures as she fights her way through life. The weird supernatural villains are reminiscent of those in Simon R. Green's NIGHTSIDE and Rob Thurman's CAL LEANDROS.

Andrews, Toni

MERCY HOLLINGS (UF—V3, S4, H3)
Mira: *Beg for Mercy* (2007); *Angel of Mercy* (2008); *Cry Mercy* (2009)

Mercy Hollings is a hypnotherapist whose secret is that she can "press" her will on others. Her best friend is Sukey, her office manager and one of the few in on Mercy's secret. Their adventures take place on Balboa Peninsula in California. Mercy's adventures stem from various interactions among her friends and acquaintances, with a central theme involving Mercy and Sukey's investigation to discover what Mercy is, where she came from, and if there are any similar beings out there.

Armintrout, Jennifer

BLOOD TIES (UF—V5, S4–5, H1)
Mira: *The Turning* (2006); *Possession* (2007); *Ashes to Ashes* (2007); *All Soul's Night* (2008)

The blood ties of the series title are the ones that bind Dr. Carrie Ames to the two men in her life: Cyrus, the cruel and arrogant vampire who attacks and turns her, and Nathan, the emotionally crippled vampire who helps her adjust to her new life. The series takes place over a six-month period, beginning with Cyrus's attack on Carrie. In this world, the law-abiding vamps belong to the Voluntary Vampire Extinction Movement, which strictly and violently enforces laws that forbid vampires from killing humans or siring new vamps. Cyrus and his father, Jacob (aka "Soul Eater"), lead the anti-Movement group, which wants to free vamps from the Movement's rules so that they can do whatever they please. The hatred between the two groups results in many violent and bloody battles. Book 4 is rated 5 in sensuality for its graphic scenes of homoerotic sex.

Armstrong, Kelley

WOMEN OF THE OTHERWORLD (UF—V4, S3, H4)

Bitten (Plume, 2004); *Stolen* (Plume, 2004); *Dime Store Magic* (Bantam, 2004); *Industrial Magic* (Bantam, 2004); *Haunted* (Bantam, 2005); *Broken* (Bantam, 2006); *No Humans Involved* (Bantam, 2008); *Personal Demon* (Bantam, 2008); *Living with the Dead* (Bantam, 2009); *Frostbitten* (Bantam, 2009); "Chaotic" in *Dates from Hell* anthology (Avon, 2006); "Twilight" in *Many Bloody Returns* anthology (Ace, 2009); "Stalked" in *My Big Fat Supernatural Honeymoon* anthology (St. Martin's Griffin, 2007); "Zen and the Art of Vampirism" in *A Fantasy Medley* anthology (Subterranean, 2009); *Men of the Otherworld* (Bantam, 2009) includes two short stories and two novellas that fill in the back stories of male pack members; *Tales of the Underworld* (Bantam, 2010) includes stories about various Otherworld characters

The series tells the stories of a diverse group of supernatural women and their mates. The main couples are Elena and Clay (werewolves); Paige (witch) and Lucas (sorcerer); and Jeremy (werewolf) and Jaime (necromancer). Other major players are Eve and her daughter Savannah (witches). Various other supernaturals play supporting roles. Each couple's meet, hate, and fall-in-love story is told in the context of many suspenseful and danger-filled adventures. The women (and a few of the men) are put in jeopardy again and again but always make it through, sustaining some relatively serious injuries along the way. Plots include murderous, power-hungry werewolf "mutts"; mad parapsychologists; a serial-killing vampire; bloodthirsty ghouls; evil Cabals (think supernatural Mafia); and a serial-killing black-magic cult.

Arthur, Keri

RILEY JENSEN, GUARDIAN (UF—V5, S5, H2)

Dell: *Full Moon Rising* (2006); *Kissing Sin* (2007); *Tempting Evil* (2007); *Dangerous Games* (2007); *Embraced by Darkness* (2007);

The Darkest Kiss (2008); *Deadly Desire* (2009); *Bound to Shadows* (2009); *Moon Sworn* (2010)

Riley Jensen and her twin brother, Rhoan, are *dhampires* (half werewolf, half vampire) who work for Melbourne's Directorate of Other Races, an organization of paranormal beings dedicated to destroying evil nonhumans. Riley has—against her will—been subjected to medical experimentation, and as a result, her powers grow and change as the series progresses. Riley's various boyfriends range from handsome young werewolves to the sexy vampire Quinn, but Riley continues to search for her true wolf soul mate and dreams of the possibility of a family. As each full moon rises, the werecharacters' heat levels also rise—to lascivious heights. In the meantime, Riley and her Directorate coworkers defeat a variety of evil vamps, mad human geneticists, and traitorous werewolves, all of whom try to gain power in many devious and dangerous ways. Riley is not the ubiquitous mouthy, shallow UF heroine found in so many UF series. Instead, she is smart, tough, and independent. Her struggle with the two sides of her nature is compelling, as is her seemingly doomed desire for a child.

Arthur, Keri (cont.)

MYTH AND MAGIC SERIES (SMR—V5, S5, H2)
Dell: *Destiny Kills* (2008); *Mercy Burns* (2010)

Destiny McCree is a shape-shifting sea dragon that cruel scientists have captured and held captive for ten years so that they can study her as a rare animal. In book 1, she escapes and teams up with air dragon Trae Wilson. They try to rescue other captured dragons, including Destiny's mother, and fall in love along the way. Book 2 features Trae's sister, Mercy.

Ashley, Amanda (pseudonym for Madeline Baker)

Ashley writes SMR stories populated primarily by strong, dark, handsome, lonely vampires who, after many loveless centuries, are shocked and initially dismayed to find that their soul mates are beautiful, young, unfulfilled (frequently virginal), twenty-first-century Christian women who are both attracted to and repelled by their undead status but inevitably succumb to the hero's charms. Marriage is very important to Ashley's heroines, and unlike most soul-mate pairs, each couple generally holds off on full consummation until after the wedding. Ashley also writes stand-alone vampire novels.

NIGHT SERIES (SMR—V3, S3, H2)

>Zebra: *Night's Kiss* (2005); *Night's Touch* (2007); *Night's Master* (2008); *Night's Pleasure* (2009)

In the early books, a vampire-werewolf war is the focus of the plot, with werewolves generally being the bad guys. Members of the Cordova family are featured, and several characters (e.g., Mara, oldest of all the vampires) appear in minor roles in each of the novels.

DARK SERIES (SMR—V3, S3, H2)

>*Shades of Gray* (Love Spell, 1998); *After Sundown* (Zebra, 2003); *Desire after Dark* (Zebra, 2006)

This trilogy revolves around a small group of characters, as each book tells one SMR story. Mara from the NIGHT SERIES makes a brief appearance in *Desire after Dark*.

Ashley, Jennifer

SHIFTERS UNBOUND (SMR—V3, S4, H3)

>*Pride Mates* (Leisure, 2010); *Shifter Lovin'* (Berkley Sensation, 2011)

In this world, all shifters must wear silver collars that meld with their bodies. They have no civil rights and are not allowed access to most electronics (e.g., cable Internet, cable television, iPods, multiuse cell phones). In book 1, Kim Fraser is an attorney defending a young werewolf client accused of murdering his human girlfriend. Liam Morrissey is the son of the leader of the weres living on Austin's East Side. When Kim seeks help from Liam to build her case, the two are drawn into a nefarious plot by the greater Austin pack leader to get rid of the hated collars and turn the shifters loose on the human population. Ashley has also written two erotic paranormal series under the pseudonym Allyson James, both published by Berkley: DRAGON SERIES: *Dragon Heat* (2007), *The Black Dragon* (2007), and *The Dragon Master* (2008); and MORTAL SERIES: *Mortal Temptations* (2009) and *Mortal Seductions* (2009).

Ashley, Jennifer (books 1, 4, 5, 8), Joy Nash (books 3, 6, 8), and Robin Popp (books 2, 7, 8)

THE IMMORTALS (SMR—V3, S5, H3)

>Love Spell: *The Calling* (2007); *The Darkening* (2007); *The Awakening* (2007); *The Gathering* (2007); *The Redeeming* (2008);

The Crossing (2008); *The Haunting* (2008); *Immortals: The Reckoning* anthology (2009)

The series is unique in that three authors take turns writing the books, which tell the stories of five immortal brothers, the products of liaisons between five ancient Egyptian priests and five female manifestations of the goddess Isis. The brothers are immortal warriors whose mission is to help humans fight the death magic of powerful demons. The first five books tell the brothers' stories as they try to save the youngest from a demon and meet their soul mates along the way. The remaining titles tell the SMR stories of related characters.

· ·

It is a truth universally acknowledged that a zombie in possession of brains must be in want of more brains.

Opening sentence of Jane Austen and Seth Grahame-Smith's
Pride and Prejudice and Zombies

· ·

Austen, Jane, and Seth Grahame-Smith

Quirk: *Pride and Prejudice and Zombies* (2009) (CH, HIS spoof—V5, S1, H4)

As the story begins, England is facing a mysterious plague that causes the dead to return to life as flesh-eating zombies. Many families send their children to China or Japan to be trained in the martial arts so that they can defend their home estates. Both Elizabeth and Darcy happily battle their way through hordes of "unmentionables" all the way to their happy ending. Eighty-five percent of the text is Austen's, with Grahame-Smith's extremely violent zombie battles interwoven throughout. This is the first of several recent paranormal-spoof treatments of classic novels.

Bacon-Smith, Camille

DAEMONS, INC. (UF—V4, S3, H1)

DAW: *Daemon Eyes* (2007) contains the first two books of the series, *Eye of the Daemon* and *Eyes of the Empress*, which were originally published separately in the late 1990s; *A Legacy of Daemons* (2010)

Evan Davis and his partners, Brad and Lily, run a seemingly normal Philadelphia detective agency specializing in art theft and fraud, but the three are definitely not your average detectives. Brad ("Badad") and his cousin Lily ("Lirion") are actually daemon lords, trapped in human form until they complete a job that neither wants to do. Evan, Brad's half-human son, is just beginning to realize his daemon (after being bound and tortured by an enemy daemon in book 1). Although each book focuses on a mystery, usually an art theft, to be solved by the detectives, the subplots always revolve around the relationships among the three detectives, with Evan desperate for love from both Brad and Lily and the daemons unable to comprehend the meaning of love in any form. The tone of the series is dark, with Evan always in danger of mental and physical harm, both from villainous art thieves and from his own daemon relatives.

Baker, Trisha

Crimson (UF—V5, S5, H0)

Pinnacle: *Crimson Kiss* (2001); *Crimson Night* (2002); *Crimson Shadows* (2003)

In this extremely dark and violent series, Meghann O'Neill is an innocent college girl with a dark side when, in 1944, Simon Baldevar, a brutal and sadistic vampire, turns her into a vampire and puts her life under his complete control. The three books take the couple through decades of graphic sensual and violent episodes as they get together, break apart, and come together again. These episodes constitute the major action of the series, and the final book tells the tragic story of their children's lives. The books include disturbing graphic scenes of bloodlust, torture, and degradation.

Bangs, Nina

Gods of the Night (SMR—V3, S3, H3)

Leisure: *Eternal Pleasure* (2008); *Eternal Craving* (2009)

The Eleven Gods of the Night are the ultimate predators: shape-shifting dinosaurs. Their human names give clues to their beasts within (e.g., Ty is a Tyrannosaurus Rex). These strong, handsome men are incarnated in response to the ancient Mayan prediction that the world will end on December 21, 2012. Other paranormal creatures want the prophecy to come true so that they can take over the world, but the Eleven are sworn to protect humanity by defeating the villains. In addition to fighting the bad guys, each of the Eleven also finds and wins his soul mate.

Bangs, Nina (cont.)

MacKenzie Vampires (SMR—V2, S3, H5)

Master of Ecstasy (Love Spell, 2004); *Night Bites* (Love Spell, 2005); *A Taste of Darkness* (Leisure, 2006); *One Bite Stand* (Leisure, 2008)

This humorous series follows members of the MacKenzie family of vampires as they find their soul mates and fight their enemies along the way. The first book involves time travel. The final three books take place at the Woo Woo Inn, owned by the couple who get together in the first book. Several characters also appear in the Castle of Dark Dreams series, including Sparkle Stardust—a cosmic troublemaker who specializes in creating sexual chaos throughout the universe.

Castle of Dark Dreams (SMR—V2, S5, H5)

Wicked Nights (Berkley, 2005); *Wicked Pleasure* (Berkley, 2007); *Wicked Fantasy* (Berkley, 2007); *My Wicked Vampire* (Leisure, 2009)

Run by Eric, Brynn, and Conall McNair, the Castle, located in an adult theme park in Galveston, Texas, offers opportunities for sexy role-playing. Eric is a vampire, Conall is a demon, and Brynn is an immortal warrior living under a curse. All three play different characters in the daily fantasies. Books 1–3 tell their stories, focusing on each one's personal paranormal problem as well as the wooing and winning of his soul mate. Book 4 tells the SMR story of a woman who fantasizes about a vampire lover—and finds herself confronted with a real vampire. A few bad guys are thrown into each plot to keep the soul-mate relationship from proceeding too smoothly.

Banks, L. A.

Vampire Huntress Legend (UF—V4, S4, H2)

St. Martin's: *The Minion* (2003); *The Awakening* (2004); *The Hunted* (2005); *The Bitten* (2005); *The Forbidden* (2006); *The Damned* (2007); *The Forsaken* (2007); *The Wicked* (2008); *The Cursed* (2008); *The Darkness* (2008); *The Shadows* (2008); *The Thirteenth* (2009); *Dawn and Darkness* (2010)

In this African American urban fantasy, Damali Richards is a hip-hop star and a Neteru (vampire huntress), who, assisted by her team of guardians, spends her life hunting down and killing evil vampires and demons. Both

Damali and her guardians were born to their positions in life. Carlos Rivera, the man born to be Damali's mate, makes the wrong choices as a teen and becomes a drug-dealing vampire—but he retains his soul and her love. Damali, her team, and her lover travel the globe as they face danger from rogue vampires and demons from the Dark Realm. Contains urban street slang and some coarse language.

CRIMSON MOON (UF—V4, S4, H2)
St. Martin's: *Bad Blood* (2008); *Bite the Bullet* (2008); *Undead on Arrival* (2009); *Cursed to Death* (2009); *Left for Undead* (2010)

Sasha Trudeau, a highly trained special ops soldier, is also a werewolf, heavily medicated by the U.S. military to keep her wolf side from showing. On one of her operations, she meets Max Hunter, leader of the shadow wolves, a mystical Ute werewolf pack. Both have mysterious pasts that haunt them as adults. The plots revolve around the couple's attempts to control the demon werewolf population and to battle vampire gangsters, werewolf drug runners, and government spies. Native American mysticism and twenty-first-century experimental medical science are combined in a complex series of incidents, which the many alliances, councils, and military levels that are intertwined throughout the series make even more complicated. The action always moves toward the ultimate apocalyptic battle.

Barbieri, Elaine
WOLF SERIES (HIS, SMR—V2, S1, H1)
Sign of the Wolf (Dorchester, 2007); *Night of the Wolf* (Leisure, 2007); *Cry of the Wolf* (Leisure, 2008)

This series tells the stories of Letty Wolf, a woman of Kiowa heritage, and her three grown daughters. The paranormal connection here is that Letty and her daughters see an old Indian man accompanied by a howling wolf whenever death or danger is imminent. All three books take place in the Old West in the late 1800s. Letty, as well as each of her daughters, finds her true love by the end of the series.

Bardsley, Michele
BROKEN HEART VAMPIRES (SMR—V3, S4, H4)
Signet Eclipse: *I'm the Vampire, That's Why* (2006); *Don't Talk Back to Your Vampire* (2007); *Because Your Vampire Said So* (2008); *Wait Till Your*

Vampire Gets Home (2008); *Over My Dead Body* (2009); *Come Hell or High Water* (2010); *Cross Your Heart* (2010)

Set in the tiny town of Broken Heart (the town with the highest rate of divorce and the highest percentage of single parents in Oklahoma), the action begins when a diseased vampire-lycan hybrid escapes from custody and bites and nearly kills eleven of the human townspeople—all single parents. To save their lives, members of the Consortium (a vampiric organization that facilitates relations between humans and supernaturals) turn the eleven into vampires. Each book tells one newbie's story—from first adjustment to meeting and mating with his or her soul mate—as they all battle evil vamps, fierce lycans, scary dragons, and dangerous demons who want to steal their developing powers.

Bartlett, Gerry

GLORY ST. CLAIRE (CH—V4, S5, H4)

Berkley: *Real Vampires Have Curves* (2007); *Real Vampires Live Large* (2008); *Real Vampires Get Lucky* (2008); *Real Vampires Don't Diet* (2009); *Real Vampires Hate Their Thighs* (2010); *Real Vampires Have More to Love* (2010)

Gloriana "Glory" St. Clair is a former Vegas showgirl and a vampire with a Rubenesque figure. Glory settles in Austin, Texas, where she opens Vintage Vamp's Emporium, a vintage clothing store. Plots revolve around Glory and her vamp friends as they battle human vampire hunters, evil energy vampires, and paranormal drug dealers. Other characters include Glory's sire and longtime lover, Jeremiah "Jerry" Blade; her talking guard dog; her werecat neighbor; her gay vamp friends; two ghosts who haunt her shop; and several hot male vamps who would like to take Blade's place with Glory.

Bast, Anya

ELEMENTAL WITCHES (SMR—V4, S5, H2)

Berkley: *Witch Fire* (2007); *Witch Blood* (2008); *Witch Heart* (2009); *Witch Fury* (2009)

The Coven is an organization that rules the good witches of the world: witches of air, fire, water, and earth. Their time is spent battling two sets of bad guys: the Duskoff (a warlock cabal) and demons from the world of Eudae. Each book tells the SMR story of one witchy couple, with lots of kinky sex along the way. The usual gender parameters for witches and war-locks do not hold: each group contains both males (very alpha!) and females.

The Embraced (SMR—V4, S5+, H1)

Ellora's Cave: *Blood of the Rose* (2004); *Blood of the Raven* (2005); *Blood of an Angel* (2005); *Blood of the Damned* (2007)

In this erotic series, several supernatural vampiric couples spend most of their time in the bedroom, with detailed, over-the-top sex scenes, including ones with multiple partners. Villains attempt to come between them, but the lovebirds spend more time in carnality than in combat.

Benedict, Lyn (pseudonym for Lane Robins)

Shadows Inquiries (UF—V4, S3, H3)

Ace: *Sins and Shadows* (2009); *Ghosts and Echoes* (2010)

Wisecracking Sylvie Lightner has a complex set of paranormal powers, including the ability to resist many types of dark magic. She and her friend Alex run Shadows Inquiries, which Sylvie describes as "a P.I. firm without a license." Her motto (tattooed on her back) is *Cedo Nulli* ("I do not yield"), and she is a tough, streetwise survivor with a sardonic and flippant attitude toward practically everyone. Sylvie has two main enemies: *Magicus Mundi*, a group that practices dark forces of magic and sorcery, and the Internal Surveillance and Intelligence (ISI) agency, government agents who stalk her every move—think Homeland Security gone wild. Her primary contact with the ISI is Agent Michael Demalion, who was her lover until she learned that he was really an ISI spy. Knowledge of the hierarchy of Greek gods is helpful in understanding the finer points of the plot.

Benson, Amber

Calliope Reaper-Jones (CH—V3, S2, H5)

Ace: *Death's Daughter* (2009); *Cat's Claw* (2010)

This frenetically written series stars Calliope "Callie" Reaper-Jones, who is Death's daughter. In book 1, Callie's father and older sister are kidnapped, along with all of Death's key executives, and Calliope must pass a test to prove that she can take over his position and prevent her family from being made mortal. In book 2, Callie must pay a debt she owes to Cerberus, the three-headed dog she met in book 1. Other characters include her younger sister, Clio; Death's executive assistant, Jarvis (a faun); and Daniel, the devil's human protégé; as well as a host of goddesses and devil-related beings. Callie, of course, is the typical wisecracking, fashion-loving, career-minded chick-lit heroine, with her big mouth always getting her into trouble. Some segments of the story are a bit far-fetched, even for a paranormal novel, and the humorous dialogue goes over the top at times.

Bickle, Laura (pseudonym for Laura Mailloux)

ANYA KALINCZYK (UF—V3, S4, H2)

Juno-Pocket: *Embers* (2010); *Sparks* (2010)

Anya Kalinczyk is an arson investigator for the Detroit Fire Department, but she is also a member of Detroit Area Ghost Researchers (DAGR), a group of ghost busters. Anya is a psychic medium (here called a Lantern) who can absorb ghosts into her body. She is always accompanied by Spark, a ghostly, electricity-loving salamander (a mythical being who can live in or withstand fire) who is disguised as Anya's copper neck collar. Anya leads a lonely life, always feeling like an outsider. In book 1, a serial firebug—possibly supernatural—has hit Detroit, and finding him becomes Anya's sole purpose in life. Anya's love interest is Brian, a technology geek and fellow DAGR member, but in book 1 she is also attracted to her prime suspect. Book 2 finds Anya battling a power-hungry celebrity psychic. Bickle provides a fine sense of place as she describes the failing city. Bickle also writes urban fantasy under the name Alayna Williams.

Black, Jenna

MORGAN KINGSLEY, EXORCIST (UF—V4, S5+, H3)

Dell: *The Devil Inside* (2007); *The Devil You Know* (2008); *The Devil's Due* (2008); *Speak of the Devil* (2009); *The Devil's Playground* (2010)

In Morgan's world, demons are a part of everyday life. In fact, her parents belong to a group of religious fanatics who donate their bodies as hosts to demons because they believe that demons are wise, all-knowing beings. Morgan has broken with her family and has become a demon hunter and exorcist. Unfortunately for Morgan, though, she was drugged and kept unconscious long enough for her body to become the unwilling host for the demon king, Lugh, who is planning to reform the demon world against the wishes of his two powerful brothers. Now, Morgan spends her time fighting her own battles as well as those of Lugh's enemies. Stories include coarse language and over-the-top graphic sex, including phone sex, sadomasochism, and homoeroticism.

Guardians of the Night (SMR—V4, S5, H3)

Tor: *Watchers in the Night* (2006); *Secrets in the Shadows* (2007); *Shadows on the Soul* (2007); *Hungers of the Heart* (2008)

The Guardians of the Night sacrifice the superior physical and psychic strength that comes with feeding on humans because even a single human kill could leave them helplessly addicted to murder. Instead of human blood, these vampires live on a mixture of lamb's blood and milk (yuck!). Set in Philadelphia, each book tells one Guardian's story as he fights off Killers (evil vampires) and finds his soul mate. Problematically for the lover of vampire romances, these heroes come across as a bit wimpy, because their Guardian membership severely curtails their major vampire strengths and abilities. Inevitably, they must rely on the superpowers of a friendly Killer or two to assist them in their struggles.

Black, Shayla

The Doomsday Brethren (SMR—V4, S4, H1)

Pocket: *Tempt Me with Darkness* (2008); *Seduce Me in Shadow* (2009); *Possess Me at Midnight* (2009); *Entice Me at Twilight* (2010); *Embrace Me at Dawn* (2011)

This series is all about the ups and downs of the complicated soul-mate relationships among a small group of English wizards who call themselves the Doomsday Brethren. Their mission is to protect the *Doomsday Diary* and to defeat the powerful sociopathic wizard Mathias before he and his undead army can take over the world. The series tells the stories of couples just beginning their soul-mate relationships, couples who lose their mates either permanently or temporarily, and couples who (rarely) maintain their soul-mate relationships and live happily ever after.

Blackwell, Juliet (pseudonym for Hailey Lind)

Witchcraft Mysteries (CH—V3, S3, H3)

Signet: *Secondhand Spirits* (2009); *A Cast-Off Coven* (2010)

Lily Ivory is an undercover witch who owns a vintage clothing store in San Francisco. The men in her life include Aidan Rhodes, an attractive and powerful witch; Max Carmichael, a "myth-busting" journalist who does not believe in magic of any kind; and Inspector Romero of the San Francisco Police Department, who seems to accept Lily's magical side. Other characters include Lily's familiar, Oscar, a gargoyle-like creature who frequently takes the form of a Vietnamese pig, and Bronwyn, a Wiccan, who is Lily's business partner. Book 1 finds Lily opening her new store and outwitting an evil Mexican spirit as she searches for a missing child and solves a client's murder. Ratings are based on book 1. Book 2 finds Lily investigating a ghostly—or possibly demonic—presence in the bell tower of the San Francisco School of the Arts.

Blair, Annette

ACCIDENTAL WITCH TRILOGY (SMR—V0, S4, H4)
Berkley: *The Kitchen Witch* (2004); *My Favorite Witch* (2006); *The Scot, the Witch and the Wardrobe* (2006)

This series is extremely light on paranormal magic. In the first book, the only witch mentioned is a friend of the heroine, but she does nothing that is magical in any way. In the second book, the heroine is the witch from the first book, but the most witchy thing she does is recite a few rhyming spells that may or may not have any effect on ensuing events. The third book focuses on four sisters—all witches and friends of the heroines of the first two books, and there are a few magical episodes. The series follows each couple through the usual SMR progression, with lightweight, humorous plot lines and no real villains or bad guys to interfere.

TRIPLET WITCH TRILOGY (SMR—V1, S5, H4)
Berkley: *Sex and the Psychic Witch* (2007); *Gone with the Witch* (2008); *Never Been Witched* (2009)

The triplet witches were introduced in *The Scot, the Witch and the Wardrobe* (ACCIDENTAL WITCH TRILOGY). Each beautiful sister has a particular psychic ability, and each gets herself into an SMR situation. Dialogue is light and fluffy. Nonviolent plots deal with ghosts haunting a castle, mysterious crying babies, and a handsome man who doesn't believe in magic (but soon changes his mind).

VINTAGE MAGIC (CH, COZ—V2, S2, H4)
Berkley: *A Veiled Deception* (2009); *Larceny and Lace* (2009); *Death by Diamonds* (2010); *Skirting Grace* (2011)

This series has many cozy elements: an amateur sleuth, relatively bloodless murders, and not much sex, but there are more than enough fashion references to make it chick lit. Madeira "Maddy" Cutler is a New York fashion designer who longs for small-town life. In book 1, she goes home to Mystic Falls, Connecticut, for her sister's wedding and immediately becomes involved in a murder mystery. Maddy soon learns that she has the gift of learning the history of an item just by touching it. Soon, she has visions and begins to see the spirits of the dead. Eventually, she opens a vintage clothing shop that comes with its own ghost. Her two love interests are her on-again, off-again boyfriend (Nick) and the town's police detective (Lytton Werner), Maddy's childhood nemesis.

- -

> "Your eyes are violet," she said.
>
> "They're dragon-elli eyes. . . . All my brothers have eyes this color."
>
> "It's in the genes, then?"
>
> "No, that is my man lance in my jeans. I am sorry if it distracts you."
>
> Bastian has a homonym-challenged moment with
> McKenna, in Annette Blair's *Naked Dragon*

- -

WORKS LIKE MAGICK (SMR—V3, S4, H4)

Berkley: *Naked Dragon* (2010); *Bedeviled Angel* (2010)

Bastian Dragonelli is a dragon in human form who comes to earth to clear the way for his brother dragons to travel to safety from their embattled homeland. McKenna Greylock owns a Victorian house in Salem, Massachusetts, and she is turning it into a bed and breakfast inn so that she has enough income to prevent foreclosure. Vivica, the local witch, knows Bastian's secret and sends him to McKenna as a handyman. Because Bastian doesn't know the language, he takes everything quite literally, which is the source of much of the humor. There are also lots of "man lance" one-liners. The villains are a sleazy land developer, who wants to tear down McKenna's home and build condos, and a supernatural enemy who has followed Bastian from his homeland. Ratings are based on book 1 because book 2 had not yet been released at the time of this writing.

Blue, Lucy

BOUND IN DARKNESS (HIS, SMR—V4, S3, H1)

> Pocket: *My Demon's Kiss* (2004); *The Devil's Knight* (2006); *Dark Angel* (2006)

In this medieval trilogy, a small group of vampires, including some knights, searches for a magical chalice that will turn them back into humans. Along the way, they all meet their soul mates. The villain is Lucan Kivar, an ancient, murderous vampire who has sired, or is at least related to, these vampires. Lucan wants the chalice for his own evil purposes.

Boyd, Donna (pseudonym for Donna Ball)

DEVONCROIX DYNASTY (UF—V4, S4, H1)

> HarperTorch: *The Passion* (1999); *The Promise* (2006)

The unusual approach to werewolves here is that they are mightier than humans in all ways—and proud of it! Although they live under wraps, so to speak, they have secretly created the world's greatest industries, financial empires, inventions, technological products, and works of art and literature. Each book moves between the present and the past in flashbacks to tell the story of the Devoncroix pack, specifically the lives of Alexander and Denis—brothers and rivals; Elise and Tessa, their mates; and Matise, Brinna, and Nicholas, the next generation. The villains are the Siberian-based Dark Brotherhood, which wants to rid the world entirely of pathetic, useless humans and let werewolves rule supreme. The author tells the story through formal dialogue and narration, with many realistic discussions of the "historical facts" surrounding the development of werewolves from earliest times.

Brennan, Allison

SEVEN DEADLY SINS (UF—V4, H1)

> "Deliver Us from Evil," in *What You Can't See* anthology (prequel—Pocket, 2007); *Original Sin* (Ballantine, 2010); *Carnal Sin* (Ballantine, 2010)

The series follows the consequences of an incident in book 1 in which a coven of dark witches, led by Fiona O'Donnell, unleashes incarnate forms of the demons who control the seven deadly sins. Moira, Fiona's eldest daughter, was raised to be her mother's "mediator" between her witches and the underworld. When Moira learned of Fiona's plans, she ran away; joined a mysterious, cultlike Catholic group; and quit practicing magic. Now, Moira must wrest control of the demons from Fiona before the dark side takes control of the world. In book 1, Moira's search leads her to a small California town where she meets Rafe, an ex-seminarian. Together with another couple (Anthony, a demonologist, and his girlfriend, Skye, the town sheriff), they attempt to stop Fiona, who is aided by Moira's sister, Serena. Book 2 continues their adventures as they take down more of the demons that have been unleashed.

Briggs, Patricia

The all-inclusive series title is WORLD OF THE MARROK (the Marrok is the head of the werewolf clan that is the focus of the series), but there are two subseries, each focusing on one half of the clan: the city werewolves (MERCY THOMPSON) and the country werewolves (ALPHA AND OMEGA).

MERCY THOMPSON (UF—V3, S4, H3)

Moon Called (Ace, 2006); *Blood Bound* (Ace, 2007); *Iron Kissed* (Ace, 2008); *Bone Crossed* (Ace, 2009); *Silver Borne* (Ace, 2010); *Mercy Thompson Homecoming* (graphic novel, Del Rey, 2009); "The Star of David" in *Wolfsbane and Mistletoe* anthology (Ace, 2008); *River Marked* (Ace, 2011)

Living in the Pacific Northwest, Mercedes "Mercy" Thompson is a Native American "walker" who can shift at will into coyote form. In a feminist twist, she owns her own garage where she repairs German cars. In this world, paranormal beings are gradually making themselves known to the public, beginning with the lesser creatures (e.g., brownies, elves, garden sprites) and gradually moving to the greater beings (e.g., werewolves). Mercy's love interests, who include two alpha werewolves (Sam, her childhood sweetheart, and Adam, the local pack leader), complicate her life. The books contain no graphic sexual scenes, but there are a number of bloodlust scenes, particularly in the later books, which contribute to the high sensuality rating.

ALPHA AND OMEGA (SMR, UF—V3, S3, H3)

"Alpha and Omega" in *On the Prowl* anthology (a prequel to the series Berkley, 2007); "Seeing Eye" in *Strange Brew* anthology (St. Martin's, 2009); *Cry Wolf* (Ace, 2008); *Hunting Ground* (Ace, 2009)

Readers should begin with "Alpha and Omega," where Briggs introduces Anna and Charles in an SMR story. The two novels continue the couple's story in a UF manner. Anna is an Omega werewolf who spent years of abuse in a dysfunctional pack. In the short story, Charles, the executioner for his father's pack, rescues Anna and becomes her mate. *Cry Wolf* begins with their move to Charles's Montana home, where the two become embroiled in a battle with a powerful witch. *Hunting Ground* takes place just weeks later, when the couple heads to Seattle for a meeting with the leaders of the European werewolves and where attempts are made to kidnap Anna.

Brook, Meljean

THE GUARDIANS (SMR—V4, S4, H3)

Berkley: "Falling for Anthony" in *Hot Spell* anthology (2006); *Demon Angel* (2007); "Paradise" in *Wild Thing* anthology (2007); *Demon Moon* (2007); *Demon Night* (2008); "Thicker Than Blood" in *First Blood* anthology (2008); *Demon Bound* (2008); *Demon Forged* (2009); "Blind Spot" in *Must Love Hellhounds* anthology (2009); *Demon Blood* (2010)

Protagonists in this series are primarily Guardians (i.e., Guardian Angels), who are responsible for protecting humankind from the demons. Set primarily in San Francisco, this series is best enjoyed if the reader has some knowledge of demonic mythology (e.g., myths about hellhounds, nosferatu, nephilim, guardian angels, and various types of demons). The mythology in book 1 is particularly complex. Each book tells the SMR story of one Guardian couple as they battle the bad guys and come to terms with their own relationship. In general, the soul-mate pair has so many second (and third and fourth) thoughts about their relationship that sexual tension is at peak levels throughout each book. The author's website (http://meljeanbrook.com/the -guardian-series/primer) provides a primer on plots, characters, creatures, and rules.

Burton, Jaci

DEMON HUNTER (SMR—V4, S4, H2)

Dell: *Surviving Demon Island* (2006); *Hunting the Demon* (2007); *The Darkest Touch* (2008); *Taken by Sin* (2009)

The Realm of Light is an ancient organization that controls the gates between heaven and hell to maintain the balance between good and evil in the world. Its purpose is to keep evil demons from entering the human world. Within the realm are the Keepers (men who are gifted with a special sight to recognize demons) and Hunters (trained human warriors who hunt down and execute demons). The demon world has its own hierarchy: the Sons of Darkness, led by the twelve Dark Lords. The plots consist of never-ending battles in various parts of the world, but the battles are not as important as the romances. In each book, one couple makes it all the way through the soul-mate relationship, and several others begin the journey. Each book ends with a cliff-hanger.

. . . .

I'm not stupid. I've got eyes. I see some things everyone else tries to pretend aren't there. This vampire craze sweeping the nation. Why the hell shouldn't there be some genuine vampires in it? Did you know that violent crimes have increased nearly forty percent in the last three years, Mr. Dresden? Murder alone has almost doubled, particularly in heavy urban areas and isolated rural areas. Abductions and disappearances have gone up nearly three hundred percent. . . . So what if the supernatural world is making a comeback? What if that accounts for some of what is going on?

The teenage werewolf Billy Borden's take on the
perpetrators of crime, in Jim Butcher's *Fool Moon*

. . . .

Butcher, Jim

Dresden Files (UF—V4, S3, H4)

Storm Front (Roc, 2000); *Fool Moon* (Roc, 2001); *Grave Peril* (Roc, 2001); *Summer Knight* (Roc, 2002); *Death Masks* (Roc, 2003); *Blood Rites* (Roc, 2004); *Dead Beat* (Roc, 2006); "Something Borrowed" in *My Big Fat Supernatural Wedding* anthology (St. Martin's Griffin, 2006); *Proven Guilty* (Roc, 2007); *White Night* (Roc, 2008); "It's My Birthday, Too" in *Many Bloody Returns* anthology (Ace, 2009); "Heorot" in *My Big Fat Supernatural Honeymoon* anthology (St. Martin's Griffin, 2007); *Small Favor* (Roc, 2009); "Day Off" in *Blood Lite* anthology (Pocket, 2008); "Last Call" in *Strange Brew* anthology (St. Martin's Griffin, 2009); *Turn Coat* (Roc, 2009); "Even Hand" in *Dark and Stormy Knights* anthology (St. Martin's Griffin, 2010); "The Warrior" in *Mean Streets* anthology (Roc, 2009); *Side Jobs: Stories from the Dresden Files* (Roc, 2010)

Think Philip Marlowe meets a grown-up Harry Potter. Harry Blackstone Copperfield Dresden is both an independent private investigator and the only practicing professional wizard in Chicago. He lives in a basement apartment with Mister, his thirty-pound cat, and Bob, a sex-crazed ghost who lives in his own skull. Harry has an ironic sense of humor, an empty bank account, a tragic past, and a conscience that puts him at odds with both the bad guys and the (supposedly) good guys. His life is filled with dangerous jobs, beautiful women, and treachery—both human and supernatural—around every corner. The books were made into a television series (Syfy, 2007–2008), which is available on DVD. Butcher has also written *Backup* (Subterranean, 2008), a spin-off novella about Harry Dresden's world, featuring Thomas Raith, Harry's vampire half brother. Del Rey has published some of Harry's adventures as graphic novels.

Butler, Octavia

> Grand Central: *Fledgling* (2007) (UF—V4, S4, H1)

In this stand-alone novel, Shori Matthews awakens in a cave, badly injured and with no memory of her identity or her previous life. Gradually, she realizes that she is a vampire (called Ina in this story) and that she has traits and abilities that are unheard of among her people (e.g., dark skin, ability to be awake in the daytime and walk in the sunlight). When Wright Hamlin, a construction worker who becomes Shori's first "symbiont" (personal blood donor), rescues Shori, the couple attempts to solve the mystery of her life. They eventually locate Shori's relatives, who assist them in bringing the murderers to justice. The sensuality rating of 4 is not for graphic sex but for the numerous blood-taking scenes between Shori and her male and female symbionts.

Byrd, Rhyannon

PRIMAL INSTINCT (SMR—V5, S4, H1)

> HQN: *Edge of Hunger* (2009); *Edge of Danger* (2009); *Edge of Desire* (2009); *Touch of Seduction* (2010); *Touch of Surrender* (2010)

This series tells the SMR stories of several couples belonging to two groups of good-guy shape-shifters (the Merrick and the Watchmen) as they battle two very different enemies (the Casus and the Collective) (see table 3). The Merrick exist in human form until their supernatural inner self awakens when an evil Casus comes after them. At that point, their need for blood and sex kicks in, and they develop their Merrick form and strength so that they can eliminate the Casus. Several of the characters have various psychic abilities in addition to their shifter talents. The men are all alphas, and the women, though feisty and independent, are relatively submissive when it comes to sex. Extreme distrust exists among the characters most of the time. In addi-

TABLE 3   Shape-Shifter Groups in Primal Instinct

GROUP	FORMS	PURPOSE	SOURCE OF STRENGTH
The Merrick	Human men and women, can shift to humanoid Merrick form, with talons, fangs, and super strength	To protect humans from the Casus	Eat human food but need sex and human blood to feed their Merrick strength; talismans (called Dark Markers) provide additional protection
The Watchmen	Human men and women who work for the Consortium; can shift to various animal forms	To monitor super-natural activity; to train and provide backup for the Merrick	Extensive training in various fighting techniques; strongest in their animal forms
The Casus	Murderous spirits, or "shades," can possess a human body and can shift to super-strong humanoid shape with wolflike head, fangs, and claws	To kill all Merrick and steal their talis-mans; to bring more Casus through the portal	Need sex and blood from humans to feed their strength; also derive strength from killing humans and Merrick
The Collective	Human (or maybe something else) fanatics who hate supernatural beings	To kill all super-naturals	Training; possible supernatural abilities

tion, the hero and heroine in each story have high levels of self-loathing, so the levels of angst and sexual tension are always extremely high. In later books, a schism forms in the Collective, further complicating the situation.

Caine, Rachel (pseudonym for Roxanne Longstreet Conrad)

WEATHER WARDEN (UF—V5, S3, H1)

Roc: *Ill Wind* (2003); *Heat Stroke* (2004); *Chill Factor* (2005); *Windfall* (2005); *Firestorm* (2006); *Thin Air* (2007); *Gale Force* (2008); *Cape Storm* (2009); *Total Eclipse* (2010)

Joanne Baldwin is a Weather Warden, one of a small supernatural group that controls the forces of the earth's air and water. Other Wardens control fire and earth. Together they try to keep the earth's elements in balance at the cost of as few human lives as possible. The Wardens derive some of their power from djins (think genies), who serve as slaves to the strongest of the Wardens and who assist the Wardens in their elemental struggles. Unfortunately, some of the Wardens have accepted the help of dark demonic forces to gain more power. Joanne and her love interest, David (a djin), spend most of their time battling demonically possessed Wardens, power-hungry humans, and Wardens gone bad. The long-term plot of the series unwinds on a tight continuum over several weeks, with only days separating the action from book to book. Occasionally, the weather science segments can be a bit technical (think Weather Channel on overload).

Caine, Rachel (cont.)

OUTCAST SEASON (UF—V4, S2, H1)
Roc: *Undone* (2009); *Unknown* (2010)

In this WEATHER WARDEN–related world, Cassiel was once a powerful djin, but she refused a task set by her leader and was cast out, forced to continue her life in human form with a fraction of her previous power. Her first earthly assignment is to serve as an assistant to Manny Rocha, an Earth Warden in Albuquerque, New Mexico, where she finds herself attracted to Manny's brother, Luis. The series plot centers around a malevolent force from Cassiel's past that has now manifested itself on the earth and is taking power from human children as it tries to erase all of the djins from the earth. Cassiel and Luis must track down this force and eliminate it to save both the djins and the human race.

Carey, Mike

FELIX CASTOR (UF—V5, S3, H3)
The Devil You Know (Grand Central, 2007); *Vicious Circle* (Grand Central, 2008); *Dead Men's Boots* (Grand Central, 2009); *Thicker Than Water* (Orbit, 2009); *The Naming of Beasts* (Orbit, 2009)

Felix could be Harry Dresden's English cousin, both being big-city investigators with magical powers and a tendency to get into trouble. In Felix's world, the dead are rising in increasing numbers. As an exorcist-spiritualist, Felix makes a meager living by binding supernatural spirits to the music he plays on his tin whistle and then sending them off to another place. Where they go is a mystery that haunts Felix every day. Elegantly and humorously written, each book puts Felix into a variety of seemingly unrelated situations and follows him as he pulls together disparate clues and solves the mystery, getting horrifically beaten and battered every step of the way. Felix's friends include a witch, a succubus, a zombie, and a demon-possessed man. One oddity of the series: werewolves (and other types of shifters) are creepy creatures formed when a spirit enters the body of an animal and reshapes it in its (sort-of) human image. Carey also writes Marvel's *X-Men* comics.

Carriger, Gail

The Parasol Protectorate (CH, HIS—V4, S3, H4)

Orbit: *Soulless* (2009); *Changeless* (2010); *Blameless* (2010)

In an alternate London in the late 1800s, Alexia Tarabotti is a twenty-six-year-old, freethinking spinster. Her most unusual characteristic is that she has no soul. As a result, her touch causes supernatural creatures to become briefly human. In Alexia's world, England has both a human and a supernatural populace, with werewolves and vampires taking their places alongside humans in high society. Even Queen Victoria has supernaturals among her advisers. Book 1 follows Alexia's hate-to-love relationship with Lord Conall Maccon, the werewolf who heads up London's supernatural law enforcement agency, the Bureau of Unnatural Registry. Villains are scientists who want to perform deadly experiments on the supernaturals. In book 2, Conall and Alexia enjoy their newly married life, but just as they solve a major mystery, a complication develops in their personal relationship that may drive them permanently apart. In book 3, Alexia tries to prove her innocence while Conall has a hard time coping with life without her. Steam-driven and spring-loaded tools, weapons, and transportation enhance the lives of the characters, including Alexia's parasol with its spring-loaded, hidden weaponry. This combination of Victorian London and steam technology is known as steampunk—a science fiction subgenre.

Cassidy, Dakota

Accidental Friends (CH, SMR—V3, S5, H5)

Berkley: *The Accidental Werewolf* (2008); *Accidentally Dead* (2008); *The Accidental Human* (2009); *Accidentally Demonic* (2010)

The emphasis is on humor and sex in this contemporary series about three friends in New York City. In book 1, Marty, a devoted cosmetics saleswoman, is accidentally turned into a werewolf. In book 2, Nina, a dental assistant,

. . . .

> Joke all you like, but they [paranormal romance novels] have been helpful, now haven't they? I mean, you wouldn't have known about the sun . . . and then you would have burned to a crisp the first time you went outside. . . . Make fun all you like, but some of the people that write these romance novels are right on the money. . . . Where they come up with some of this and call it fiction is beyond me. If they only knew how accurate they really are, huh?
>
> Wanda tries to help Nina deal with her accidental
vampirism with the help of romance "reference" books,
in Dakota Cassidy's Accidentally Dead

. . . .

has the unfortunate on-the-job experience of being accidentally bitten by a vampire patient. In book 3, Wanda is diagnosed with a terminal illness but is saved by her friends. In book 4, Wanda's sister, Casey, is accidentally possessed.

Cassidy, Dakota (cont.)

DEMONIC ROMANCE (CH, SMR—V2, S4, H5)

Berkley: *Kiss and Hell* (2009); *My Way to Hell* (2010)

Delaney Markham sees and hears dead people—all the time, wherever she goes. She meets her true love, Clyde Atwell, when he turns up as a spirit during one of her séances and then appears in solid demonic form in her bedroom—and refuses to leave. The plot involves a satanic contract made with one of Delaney's relatives, which Delaney unknowingly inherits after that relative's death. The wisecracking, sarcastic dialogue provides the humor. At the end of book 1, Delaney's ghostly skills transfer to her brother, Kellen. Book 2 focuses on Kellen's romantic experiences with Delaney's best friend, Marcella, who is also a demon.

Castle, Kendra Leigh

MACINNES WEREWOLVES TRILOGY (SMR—V3, S5, H5)

Sourcebooks Casablanca: *Call of the Highland Moon* (2008); *Dark Highland Fire* (2008); *Wild Highland Magic* (2009)

For generations, the MacInnes werewolves of the Scottish highlands have been guarding the Lia Fáil, the stone portal between Earth and the Drakkyn realm, a land of dangerous demons and dragons. Gideon, Gabriel, and Catrionna MacInnes battle rogue werewolves, vicious vampires, powerful dragon royalty, and Drakkyn curses, but they inevitably survive and find their soul mates.

Chance, Karen

CASSANDRA PALMER (UF—V3, S4, H2)

> Roc: *Touch the Dark* (2006); *Claimed by Shadow* (2007); *Embrace the Night* (2008); *Curse the Dawn* (2009)

In this fantasy series, Cassandra "Cassie" Palmer is a clairvoyant with a mysterious past who finds that she is the new Pythia, a direct descendant of the priestess at Apollo's oracle in Delphi. Various factions want her dead to extinguish her power, including the evil vampire Rasputin (yes, that Rasputin). Vampires, shape-shifters, ghosts, witches, pixies, sybils, mages, and various other fae make up the cast of characters, along with an occasional human servant. This society has plenty of layers and lots of rules. The stories include almost too much historical information, mostly based on fact. Plots are relatively simple, but intermittent time-travel episodes add complexity because Cassie often inhabits someone else's body while Billy, her ghostly familiar, inhabits hers.

· ·

> He seemed to be enjoying the special version of steak tartare that Radu's chef had worked up for the main course. He'd already finished the helping Geoffrey had served us, and now used the end of his knife to spear another of the tiny cows that were wandering around the central serving dish. The rest of the miniature herd scattered, lowing, to hide under the spinach leaves that rimmed the plate.
>
> A typical dinner at Radu the vampire's
> house, in Karen Chance's *Midnight's Daughter*

· ·

DORINA BASARAB, DHAMPIR (UF—V3, S4, H3)

> Onyx: *Midnight's Daughter* (2008); *Death's Mistress* (2010)

Dorina "Dory" Basarab is the daughter of the vampire Mircea (from the CASSANDRA PALMER series), and she is a *dhampir*—half human, half vampire. Dory is a streetwise, tough young woman who has always lived on the fringes of society. She is an expert fighter and has killed many vampires. The first book deals with Dorina's search for her evil Uncle Vlad (Dracula), who is Mircea's younger brother. This is an offshoot of the CASSANDRA PALMER series and includes many characters from that series. Ratings are based on book 1 because book 2 had not yet been released at the time of this writing.

Child, Maureen

FIEND (CH—V4, S4, H5)
NAL Trade: *More Than Fiends* (2007); *A Fiend in Need* (2008)

Cassidy "Cassie" Burke is the wisecracking single mom of a teenager (Thea) and the owner of a small cleaning service in coastal Southern California. Book 1 opens on Cassie's thirty-second birthday, when she meets Jasmine, a strange old woman who says that Cassie has come into her hereditary position as the town's demon duster (i.e., one who hunts down demons and rips out their hearts, thereby turning their bodies to dust). Cassie's demon-dusting adventures begin immediately and make up the general plot line of the remaining books. Complicating Cassie's life are her relationships with several handsome men who are vying for her affections: Logan Miller, a cop who has returned after sixteen years and wants to get reacquainted with Cassie and Thea, the daughter he never knew he had; Devlin Cole, a "good" demon who owns a fancy sex club; and Brady (book 2), a faery who seeks sanctuary—and a bit more—from Cassie.

QUEEN OF THE OTHERWORLD (UF—V3, S4, H4)
Signet: *Bedeviled* (2009); *Beguiled* (2009)

Maggie Donovan is an artist who lives next door to her sister, Nora, and her niece, Eileen, in small-town coastal California. Her life is normal, if lonely, until she accidentally kills a demon and absorbs some faery dust. This serves as a catalyst for the development of Maggie's dormant faery qualities. Maggie soon learns that she is destined to battle Mab, the faery queen, for control of the Otherworld throne. Culhane, a seemingly helpful, handsome faery warrior whose motives are suspect, and Bezel, the pixie who must train her for her big battle, complicate Maggie's life. In addition to her problems with troublesome demons who keep attacking her on the street, Maggie's biggest problem has to do with Culhane: does he really love her, or is he just using her to get control of the Otherworld crown?

Clamp, Cathy. *See* Adams, C. T., and Cathy Clamp

Cole, Kresley

IMMORTALS AFTER DARK (SMR—V4, S5, H3)

Pocket: *A Hunger like No Other* (2006); *No Rest for the Wicked* (2006); *Wicked Deeds on a Winter's Night* (2007); *Dark Deeds at Night's Edge* (2008); *Dark Desires after Dusk* (2008); *Kiss of a Demon King* (2009); *Deep Kiss of Winter* (2009); *Pleasure of a Dark Prince* (2010); *Demon from the Dark* (2010)

Stories revolve around a coven of valkyries and a set of lycan brothers, with a few vampires, phantoms, and demons mixed in. Each book tells the story of one couple as they make every attempt to avoid falling in love (but do anyway), try very hard to avoid sex (but fail), and eventually give in to the fact that they are really soul mates. Sexual tension runs rampant. Plots involve everything from an evil demon enslavement to a supernatural treasure hunt to the search for a magic sword. Appearing in all the books is the eccentric Nïx, the oldest and most powerful of the valkyries. She adds to the humor and confusion with her loopy, metaphorical predictions of future events. *A Hunger like No Other* won the RITA Award for best paranormal romance (2007).

Cooke, Deborah (pseudonym for Claire Delacroix)

DRAGONFIRE (SMR—V4, S4, H2)

Signet: *Kiss of Fire* (2008); *Kiss of Fury* (2008); *Kiss of Fate* (2009); *Winter Kiss* (2009); *Whisper Kiss* (2010); *Darkfire Kiss* (2011)

For millennia, the Pyr (shape-shifting dragon warriors) have commanded the four elements (earth, water, air, and fire) and guarded the earth's treasures, including its human inhabitants. The series tracks the conflicts between the Pyr and the evil Slayer dragons, who want to eliminate both the humans and the Pyr. Each book begins with a total lunar eclipse during which the Wyvern (a female Pyr prophetess) announces the next Pyr to experience "dragonfire"—the phenomenon that indicates that a given Pyr will be linked with his life partner, a human female. When the two touch each other, sparks literally fly—thus *dragonfire*. Unfortunately, each time a dragonfire relationship is foretold, all dragon shifters feel it—both the Pyr and the Slayers—and the Slayers do everything they can to stop the couple from conceiving a child, because that child would grow up to be their enemy.

Crane, Carolyn

JUSTINE JONES: DISILLUSIONIST (UF—V3, S4, H2)

    Spectra: *Mind Games* (2010); *Double Cross* (2010)

Crane takes a fresh approach to retribution in this series set in Midcity, which could be any large, Rust Belt urban area. In this world, people with magic (who would be called mages in other series) are called highcaps, each with a particular magical ability and each tending to misuse his or her power. One highcap (Sterling Packard) has the ability to understand any person's psychological structure. Packard has assembled a team of humans with crippling psychological problems (e.g., alcoholism, gambling compulsion, depression, rage, extreme angst), and he uses them as psychological vigilantes to punish various villains who have somehow escaped unscathed from the judicial system. Team members (called disillusionists) are taught to channel their bad feelings into the villains' psyches. As the bad guys and gals absorb more and more of each disillusionist's fears and anxieties, the team members feel much better, but the villains feel much worse, to the point that their lives eventually collapse and they must rebuild their essence from the beginning. Thus, the villains are punished—but nonviolently—and turned into good citizens who have learned from their past mistakes. What a concept! No need for prisons or trials or executions or criminal lawyers! The heroine is Justine Jones, an über-hypochondriac, whose tattered life is spent in emergency rooms waiting for her brain to explode, as her mother's did, from a severe vascular condition. She meets Packard, who promises to rid her permanently of her health-related fears, but he doesn't tell her the whole truth because he has secrets and fears of his own. When Justine joins Packard's team, the two, of course, begin a love-hate relationship. Justine has two other love interests: her normal, human boyfriend, Cubby, and Otto Sanchez, the hunky police chief, seemingly a good guy who is trying to stop a crime wave in Midcity. Supporting characters are the other disillusionist team members, each with his or her own problems and sad life story. In book 2, serial killers threaten Packard, the mayor, and other city leaders.

Cunningham, Elaine

CHANGELING DETECTIVE AGENCY (UF—V4, S3, H2)

    Tor: *Shadows in the Darkness* (2004); *Shadows in the Starlight* (2006)

Gwen Gelman is forced to leave her job with the Providence, Rhode Island, Police Department after an undercover vice job goes bad and she is blamed for her partner's death. Gwen starts her own detective agency, specializing in domestic cases involving runaways. As she investigates her cases, she uncovers information about her own mysterious past and begins to understand that she has certain strange abilities—that she is different, perhaps not human. But what is she? How did her parents really die? Is there a supernatural connection? Which of her friends and acquaintances can she really trust? Although Gwen solves her primary case in each book, her own personal mystery unravels in very short strands from book to book. Book 2 follows book 1 by just a day or so.

Damsgaard, Shirley

OPHELIA AND ABBY MYSTERIES (COZ—V3, S2, H3)

Avon: *Witch Way to Murder* (2005); *Charmed to Death* (2006); *The Trouble with Witches* (2006); *Witch Hunt* (2007); *The Witch Is Dead* (2007); *The Witch's Grave* (2008); *The Seventh Witch* (2010)

Thirtysomething Ophelia Jensen, a librarian in small-town Iowa, and Abigail "Abby" McDonald, her grandmother, are witches with psychic powers, a fact that they keep secret from their neighbors. Abby has been a practicing witch all her life, but Ophelia has been reluctant to surrender to her powers because they failed her several years ago when she was unable to prevent the brutal murder of her best friend. Gradually, Ophelia begins to trust her magic, as she and Abby become embroiled in a series of mysteries and murders—one per book. Frequently, a handsome man serves as a temporary romantic interest for Ophelia (just a few kisses), but she always ends each book alone and independent. The series has mostly COZ elements (amateur sleuth in a small town with quirky neighbors and relatively bloodless murders), but its heroine does have some UF characteristics: independence, angst, and sarcasm.

Daniels, Casey

PEPPER MARTIN MYSTERIES (CH—V3, S3, H1)

Don of the Dead (Avon, 2006); *The Chick and the Dead* (Avon, 2007); *Tombs of Endearment* (Avon, 2007); *Night of the Loving Dead* (Berkley, 2009); *Dead Man Talking* (Berkley, 2009); *Tomb with a View* (Berkley, 2010)

Fashion-savvy Pepper works as a tour guide in Garden View Cemetery in Cleveland. After falling and hitting her head on a gravestone, she suddenly gains the ability to see and talk with ghosts. Soon, Pepper becomes a private investigator for her ghostly companions, investigating the mysteries surrounding their deaths. Her adventures generally include one or both of her two boyfriends: Quinn Harrison, a "just-the-facts" Cleveland police detective who doesn't believe in ghosts, and Dan Callahan, a research scientist who studies the brain waves of people with supernatural traits (like seeing the dead).

Davidson, MaryJanice

QUEEN BETSY (CH—V4, S4, H4)

Undead and Unwed (Berkley, 2004); *Undead and Unemployed* (Berkley, 2004); "Biting in Plain Sight" in *Bite* anthology (Jove, 2004); *Undead and Unappreciated* (Berkley, 2005); *Undead and Unreturnable* (Berkley, 2006); *Undead and Unpopular* (Berkley, 2007); *Undead and Uneasy* (Berkley, 2007); *Undead and Unworthy* (Berkley, 2008); "Dead Girls Don't Dance," from *Cravings* anthology (Jove, 2004); *Undead and Unwelcome* (Berkley, 2009); *Undead and Unfinished* (Berkley, 2010)

Elizabeth "Betsy" Taylor is a former model turned vampire, whose special nonvampiric characteristics (e.g., not sun sensitive, not allergic to human food, not repulsed by religious objects) make her the prophesied queen of the vampires. Her love interest is her tall, dark, and handsome vampire king, Eric Sinclair. Supporting characters include Betsy's wealthy African American friend Jessica; her gay doctor friend Marc; her half sister, Laura (the devil's daughter); police detective and former flame Nick; and Eric's sire and assistant, Tina. Together, they solve various supernatural mysteries while causing many of their own problems through carelessness and lack of foresight. The series follows Betsy as she familiarizes herself with vampire life, comes to grips with her queenly role, and establishes a romantic relationship with Eric. All the while, Betsy continues to build her collection of designer clothes and, especially, shoes. The tone of the series is generally humorous, but the vampire battles are quite violent, with frequent beheadings and dismemberments. The first six books take Betsy from initial vampirehood to marriage. In "A Note to the Reader" at the beginning of *Undead and Unworthy* (book 7), Davidson says that books 7–9 should be considered "a trilogy within a series," with their own story arc that includes the evolving relationship between Betsy and Laura.

FRED THE MERMAID (CH—V2, S4, H4)

Jove: *Sleeping with the Fishes* (2006); *Swimming without a Net* (2007); *Fish out of Water* (2008)

Fredericka, called "Fred," is a marine biologist and a half-human mermaid with two boyfriends: Thomas, a marine biologist, and Artur, a merman and prince of the Undersea Folk. Her best friend, Jonah, a wisecracking metrosexual, adds to the humor. Plots revolve around evil human corporate polluters, a rebellion among the Undersea Folk, and various misunderstandings among the characters. The big question is, of course, which man Fred will choose.

Day, Alyssa

WARRIORS OF POSEIDON (SMR—V3, S4, H3)

Berkley: *Atlantis Rising* (2007); "Wild Hearts in Atlantis" in *Wild Thing* anthology (2007); *Atlantis Awakening* (2007); *Atlantis Unleashed* (2009); *Atlantis Unmasked* (2009); *Atlantis Redeemed* (2010)

More than eleven thousand years ago, just before Atlantis sank into the sea, a group of warriors met with Poseidon's high priest and were divided into seven groups of seven. Each group was assigned to protect humankind from the forces of evil. In the modern-day world, evil translates into powerful vampires who have come out to the world and have taken over America's political system through violence and trickery. Each book tells the story of one of these warriors as he fights the evil vamps and—guess what?—meets up with his twenty-first-century, human soul mate.

Day, S. J. (Sylvia)

MARKED (UF—V5, S5, H2)

Tor: *Eve of Darkness* (2009); *Eve of Destruction* (2009); *Eve of Chaos* (2009)

When Evangeline "Eve" Hollis goes to a job interview, she receives something unexpected—the mark of Cain branded on her arm. Ten years earlier, Eve had an affair with Alec Cain, and she is now being punished for being a temptation to him—that is her only sin. A girl just can't win! Eve's life has now changed forever. She has become a Mark, the lowest level of the heavenly bureaucracy, with superhuman strength and stamina. When a human or an Infernal (nonhuman) sinner receives a death sentence from God, the

· ·

> Relating it to the human judicial system might make it easier to understand. Every sinner has a trial in absentia and the Lord presides over every case. Christ acts as the public defender. . . . If there's a conviction, one of the seraphim send the order down to a firm to hunt the Infernal. . . . Think of it as the bail bond agency. An archangel becomes responsible for bringing them in—like a bail bondsman. They don't actually do any hunting. The Marks do the dirty work and they collect a bounty, just as a bounty hunter would, only in this case the prize is indulgences. Earn enough and you'll work off your penance.
>
> Abel explains the heavenly justice system
> to Eve, in S. J. Day's *Eve of Darkness*

· ·

punishment is assigned to a Mark, who must hunt down and kill that being (see quotation above). Eve's handler (and the one who marked her) is Reed Abel, Cain's hated brother. Yes, that Cain and that Abel—the two infamous biblical brothers, who are now low-level angels. They still hate each other, and they both want Eve. The series was published over a three-month period, and the story line is just about that tight. Each book is filled to the brim with violent battles and graphic sex.

Dean, Cameron

CANDACE STEELE, VAMPIRE KILLER (SMR, UF—V3, S5, H2)

> Ballantine: *Passionate Thirst* (2006); *Luscious Craving* (2006); *Eternal Hunger* (2006)

This is a UF series with an SMR touch. In this trilogy, Candace Steele works security at a Las Vegas casino, and she hunts down and executes blood-lusting vampires. As a result of her "close" relationship with her on-again, off-again vampire boyfriend, Ash, Candace can easily detect these dangerous vampires in the casino crowds. In the story arc for the trilogy, the Board (a group of really bad, powerful vamps) takes control of important humans (e.g., politicians, millionaires) to gain worldwide power, and Ash and Candace struggle to beat them down. *Spoiler alert!* No happy SMR ending for this couple.

Del Franco, Mark

CONNOR GREY (UF—V3, S1, H3)

Ace: *Unshapely Things* (2007); *Unquiet Dreams* (2008); *Unfallen Dead* (2009); *Unperfect Souls* (2010)

Connor is a Druid whose powers were almost totally destroyed in an incident with an evil elf, a nuclear power plant, and a ring of power. Don't ask! The elf figures into many of the plots and subplots. Now that Connor is relatively powerless, he lives a solitary life in the Weird (the ghetto of the supernatural section of Boston) and does police consultant work to earn a living. His few friends include Joe, a flit (small fairylike creature); Briallen, a powerful Druid; Murdock, Connor's human Boston Police Department partner; and Meryl, an archivist working for the Guild (the government agency that tries to keep the supernatural world under control). Stories include human characters and many different types of supernaturals. Plots revolve around paranormal politics, so the reader must keep track of a large and complex cast of characters connected to a variety of social and political structures of the supernatural world.

LAURA BLACKSTONE (UF—V4, S2–3, H3)

Ace: *Skin Deep* (2009); *Face Off* (2010)

Laura Blackstone is an undercover agent with multiple identities (e.g., varying names, jobs, facial features, hair and eye color, mannerisms). She is a Druid who can "glamour" herself to take on any appearance. In her Laura persona, she is a public-relations director for the Fey Guild, which combats magic-based criminal activity and acts as a buffer between humans and fey (supernaturals). In book 1, Laura and two of her personae must track down a rogue fairy who has killed a policeman and plans to assassinate government officials. Her love interest is Jono Sinclair, a half-fey Washington, D.C., SWAT team member. In book 2, Laura gets into a struggle involving both anti-fey humans and internal fey power conflicts.

Devlin, Delilah

DARK REALM (UF—V1, S5+, H1)

Avon Red: *Into the Darkness* (2007); *Seduced by Darkness* (2008); *Darkness Burning* (2009)

Set in New Orleans, this series follows humans and vampires (both good and bad) on a series of exceedingly erotic sexual adventures. In general, the story line is a bare frame on which to hang endless scenes of graphic sex, including homoerotic scenes, each one more extreme than the last.

Dodd, Christina

DARKNESS CHOSEN (SMR—V4, S4, H2)

Signet: *Scent of Darkness* (2007); *Touch of Darkness* (2007); *Into the Shadow* (2008); *Into the Flame* (2008)

Each of the sons of the Wilder family has the ability to shape-shift into an animal form: wolf, hawk, panther, and cougar. The series involves a family prophesy (or is it a curse?), a dangerous enemy from the Old World past, and four beautiful women (one soul mate for each book and brother).

THE CHOSEN ONES (SMR—V3, S4, H3)

Signet: *Storm of Visions* (2009); *Storm of Shadows* (2009); *Chains of Ice* (2010); *Chains of Fire* (2010)

Two groups square off in a battle for power: the Chosen and the Others. The members of both groups were abandoned as infants and adopted by an adult from one of the groups. Each has a special birthmark, and each develops some type of mental or physical power. The Chosen are the good guys; the Others fight for the devil. Each book tells one Chosen couple's story as they fight against the Others and fall in love. One of the Chosen is a young member of the Wilder family from Dodd's DARKNESS CHOSEN series.

Douglas, Carole Nelson

DELILAH STREET, PARANORMAL INVESTIGATOR (UF—V4, S4, H4)

Dancing with Werewolves (Juno, 2007); *Brimstone Kiss* (Juno, 2008); *Vampire Sunrise* (Pocket, 2009); *Silver Zombie* (Pocket, 2010)

The lead character combines the strength and sassiness of Laurell K. Hamilton's Anita Blake with the magical mirror walking of Alice (the one from Wonderland). Paranormal investigator (and former television reporter) Delilah faces supernatural bad guys and solves paranormal mysteries in 2013 Las Vegas, more than a decade after the Millennium Revelation—when the world learned that supernatural creatures are real. Delilah's faithful, magical wolfhound, Quicksilver, backs her up in her battles. Also by her side is her hot Latino boyfriend, Ric Montoya ("Cadaver Kid"), who can locate and raise dead bodies. Other colorful characters include Snow, a casino-owning rock star who may be the devil himself; Hector, a flesh-eating ghoul who is Delilah's eccentric landlord; and a variety of CinSims (from *cinema simulacrums*), seemingly real people who are actually the result of melding silver-screen stars with zombies.

Drake, Jocelynn
DARK DAYS (UF—V4, S4, H1)
Eos: "The Dead, the Damned, and the Forgotten" in *Unbound* anthology (2009); *Nightwalker* (2008); *Dayhunter* (2009); *Dawnbreaker* (2009); *Pray for Dawn* (2010); *Wait for Dusk* (2010)

Mira ("Fire Starter") is a nightwalker (vampire) in Savannah, Georgia. For hundreds of years, the Coven (the nightwalkers' governing body) has used Mira as their enforcer because of her strength and her mastery of fire. Now the malevolent "naturi" are after Mira because they need her special powers to open the gate between their world and the human world. The naturi are ancient guardians of the earth who were banished because they believe that the only way to protect the earth is to kill all humans and nightwalkers. Another problem for Mira is Danaus, a sexy vampire hunter. Will he kill her, or can she trust him to help her battle the naturi? In addition to the naturi plot line, Mira also has to contend with her discovery that her nightwalker mentors, who taught her everything she knows, have been lying to her for as long as she's known them. The first three books are told from Mira's point of view. *Pray for Dawn* is told from Danaus's point of view, and Mira is portrayed in a much more objective—and unsympathetic—manner. *Wait for Dusk* goes back to Mira's story.

Durgin, Doranna
THE RECKONERS (UF—V4, S2, H2)
The Reckoners (Tor, 2010); "Deep River Reckoning," short story available in e-book form (Blue Hound Visions, 2010); *Storm of Reckoning* (Tor, 2011)

Lisa McGarrity ("Garrie") leads a team of ghost busters in San Jose. She is a powerful reckoner, who can communicate and influence all kinds of spirits. Her team members are Lucia, a spiritual empath; Drew, a historian; and

Quinn, a brainy (and handsome) researcher, who is also Lisa's onetime boy-friend. In a humorous twist, the team always carries a supply of plastic bag-gies (containing an herbal mixture) in which they trap the ghosts they cap-ture. In book 1, Trevarr, a hunky demon hunter from another realm, needs a reckoner—namely Garrie—to help him rid a historic mansion of demonic spirits who are trying to maintain a portal to the human world. Trevarr and Garrie, of course, are attracted to each other almost immediately as they battle the demons and rescue some humans as well as a few innocent ghosts. Trevarr's bond-partner, Sklayne, who appears as a red cat, adds humor to the story. Their adventures continue in the following story and book.

Eden, Cynthia
MIDNIGHT TRILOGY (SMR—V4, S4, H2)
Brava: *Hotter after Midnight* (2008); *Midnight Sins* (2008); *Midnight's Master* (2009)

In this series, Atlanta teems with supernaturals: vampires, shifters, and demons. This trilogy tells the SMR stories of three couples (human female and shifter male, succubus and human male, human female and demon male) as they try to keep Atlanta safe from various preternatural serial killers.

Elias, Amelia
GUARDIANS' LEAGUE (SMR—V3, S4, H3)
Samhain: *Hunted* (2006); *Outcast* (2006); *Chosen* (2008)

In this world, the good vampires belong to the Guardians' League, and the bad vampires—hunted down and killed by the League—are called Outcasts. *Dhampyrs* (half human, half vampire) also play a part in the plots, particularly as "bondmates" (aka soul mates), who must make a conscious decision to spend their lives either as humans or as vampires—or die if they refuse to make that choice. In each book, a vampire and a human female are attracted instantly to each other, and the story follows their always-rocky romantic path as they have many second thoughts but eventually become full bond-mates. Plot intrusions include the vampire-hating Knights Templar (descen-dants of the original group from the Crusades), who want all vampires dead, and the Outcasts, who want the League to leave them alone to their blood-lust and murder of humans. Naturally, each new bondmate is a prime target for the bad guys' hate.

Elrod, P. N. (Patricia Nead)

VAMPIRE FILES (UF—V4, S3, H3)

Bloodlist (Ace, 1990); *Lifeblood* (Ace, 1990); *Bloodcircle* (Ace, 1990); *Art in the Blood* (Ace, 1991); *Fire in the Blood* (Ace, 1991); *Blood on the Water* (Ace, 1992); *A Chill in the Blood* (Ace, 1999); *Dark Sleep* (Ace, 1999); *Lady Crymsyn* (Ace, 2001); *Cold Streets* (Ace, 2003); *Song in the Dark* (Ace, 2005); *Dark Road Rising* (Ace, 2009); "Hecate's Golden Eye" in *Strange Brew* anthology (St. Martin's Griffin, 2009). Two compilations have been published: *The Vampire Files*, vol. 1 (Ace, 2003), contains books 1–3; *The Vampire Files*, vol. 2 (Ace, 2006), contains books 4–6.

Jack Fleming (Elrod took Jack's last name from Ian Fleming), a New York reporter, takes a trip to Chicago, where he is killed by a mobster and rises as a vampire because he had exchanged blood in the past with his vampire lover, who has gone missing. Jack teams up with a private investigator, and they begin solving crimes, some of which involve people related to Jack's mysterious past. The action takes place in the 1930s just a few years after the demise of Al Capone's gang.

Baen: *Quincey Morris, Vampire* (2001) (HIS—V3, S3, H2)

This stand-alone novel by Elrod tells the story of Quincey Morris, the Texan who died in Bram Stoker's *Dracula*. Morris soon rises from the dead—to his great surprise—and finds Dracula waiting for him, as a mentor, no less. Dracula explains that Morris is a different breed of vampire—not a killer of humans. Morris eventually travels to England and reveals himself to his human vampire-hunting friends. He also meets and falls in love with a beautiful woman. Dr. Van Helsing, as one would expect, does not welcome Morris in his undead state.

Fallon, Linda (pseudonym for Linda Winstead Jones)

SHADES SERIES (HIS, SMR—V3, S4, H2)

Zebra: *Shades of Midnight* (2003); *Shades of Winter* (2003); *Shades of Scarlet* (2003)

The primary characters in this series are Lucien Thorpe, who can see and communicate with ghosts, and Eve Abernathy, the girl he left at the altar two years ago when he got caught up in a ghostly adventure and lost track of the date. They follow their rocky road to happiness throughout the series, which takes place in the 1880s. Meanwhile, their friends pair off, one couple per book. While falling in love with each other, the friends solve several ghostly crimes in small-town Georgia. *Shades of Midnight* won the RITA Award for best paranormal romance (2004).

Farren, Mick

RENQUIST QUARTET (UF—V5, S3, H1)

Tor: *The Time of Feasting* (1996); *Darklost* (2000); *More Than Mortal* (2001); *Underland* (2003)

Farren, a rock musician, takes Bram Stoker's vampire world and mixes in some Jules Verne and H. P. Lovecraft. The series follows Victor Renquist, centuries-old leader of a nosferatu colony, from New York to Los Angeles to England to the underworld as he battles a fanatic vampire hunter, a cult leader attempting to summon an ancient evil spirit, primitive vampires trying to take power from the reborn wizard Merlin, alien beings, and renegade Nazis. Internal clan strife also comes into play. One of the continuing plot points is that, every seven years, nosferatu go on feeding frenzies. In between, the colony survives primarily on stolen hospital blood. Farren drops several literary and cultural icons into his plots (e.g., Kurt Carfax, a bad-boy vampire rock star [Kurt Cobain]; a passing reference to Saint-Germain, Chelsea Quinn Yarbro's aristocratic vampire hero). Lots of vampire-shaded world "history" is included in the stories—generally in dream sequences.

Feehan, Christine

THE CARPATHIANS (DARK) SERIES (SMR—V5, S5, H1)

Dark Prince (Love Spell, 1999); *Dark Desire* (Leisure, 2006); *Dark Gold* (Love Spell, 2007); *Dark Magic* (Leisure, 2008); *Dark Challenge* (Leisure, 2009); *Dark Fire* (Love Spell, 2001); *Dark Legend* (Leisure, 2002); *Dark Guardian* (Leisure, 2002); *Dark Symphony* (Jove, 2003); "Dark Descent" in *The Only One* anthology (Leisure, 2003); *Dark Melody* (Leisure, 2003); *Dark Destiny* (Leisure, 2004); "Dark Hunger" in *Hot Blooded* anthology (Jove, 2004); *Dark Secret* (Jove, 2005); *Dark Demon* (Jove, 2006); "Dark Dream" in *Dark Dreamers* anthology (Leisure, 2006); *Dark Celebration: A Carpathian Reunion* (Jove, 2007); *Dark Possession* (Berkley, 2007); *Dark Curse* (Jove, 2009); *Dark Slayer* (Berkley, 2009)

The Carpathians are an ancient race with many vampiric abilities. Although they feed on human blood, they don't kill their human prey, and they generally live undetected among humans. Despite their gifts, the Carpathians are on the verge of extinction because no female Carpathians have been born in more than five hundred years. In the absence of their female "lifemates," male Carpathians lose the ability to feel emotions and to see colors. The only feeling left to them is the thrill of making a kill. Once a male has killed, he loses his soul and "turns," becoming a monster vampire. Males are forced to make a stark choice: either become a killer vampire or "greet the dawn" (i.e., commit suicide). However, when they do find lifemates, their emotions and their ability to see colors are restored to them, and their souls are saved. Each book tells of a Carpathian male's search for his lifemate, complicated by various bad guys—both human and supernatural.

DRAKE SISTERS (SMR—V3, S5, H3)

Magic in the Wind (Berkley, 2005); *The Twilight before Christmas* (Pocket Star, 2003); *Oceans of Fire* (Jove, 2005); *Dangerous Tides* (Jove, 2006); *Safe Harbor* (Jove, 2007); *Turbulent Sea* (Jove, 2008); *Hidden Currents* (Jove, 2009)

Each of the seven Drake sisters—witches all—has a particular magical power (e.g., communicating with dolphins, healing, controlling wind and rain). Set in coastal Northern California, each book tells one sister's story as she finds her soul mate and battles various evildoers—from human serial killers to psychotic slashers to evil supernatural beings.

GHOSTWALKERS (SMR—V4, S4, H2)

Jove: *Shadow Game* (2003); *Mind Game* (2004); *Night Game* (2005); *Conspiracy Game* (2006); *Deadly Game* (2007); *Predatory Game* (2008); *Murder Game* (2008); *Street Game* (2010)

The premise is similar to Lora Leigh's BREEDS series in that a scientist tampers with genetics to create soldiers with heightened paranormal powers. These soldiers, however, are enhanced humans, not shape-shifters. Dr. Peter Whitney first experiments with a group of psychically talented female orphans that includes his adopted daughter, Lily. He uses various experimental drugs and genetic strategies to enhance their abilities, resulting in mental and emotional problems for many of the girls, thus causing him to halt the program. After sending the girls away for adoption by unknowing families, Dr. Whitney begins to experiment on trained military men with known psychic abilities. Now, ten years later, a rogue military group learns of his latest experimental group and tries to steal his data to sell to foreign governments. The series follows the group of psychic men—who call themselves GhostWalkers—as they stop the traitors and help Lily locate the girls so that she can show them how to cope with their enhanced abilities. In each book, a GhostWalker searches for and finds one of the orphan girls, and the two live out the SMR experience while battling a variety of villains. In the later books, the GhostWalker men have become urban warriors. Controlled by a shadowy government agency, they hunt down terrorists of all kinds around the world, but they still find plenty of angst-ridden time to pursue and win their soul mates.

Feehan, Christine (cont.)
Leopard Series (SMR—V4, S4, H1)
> *Fever* (Berkley, 2006, reprint; contains "The Awakening" and *Wild Rain*); *Burning Wild* (Jove, 2009); *Wild Fire* (Jove, 2010)

This series tells the stories of a group of shape-shifting leopards, with locales ranging from the jungles of Borneo and Panama to the wide-open country of the American West. Each male shifter meets and romances his soul mate as they both fight off a series of predators, both human and supernatural. Angst levels are high as a result of self-doubt, distrust, and miscommunications between each pair of lovers. The series has been republished in a variety of media, including print, audio, and e-book.

Finlay, C. C.
Traitor to the Crown (HIS—V4, S2, H2)
> Del Rey: *The Patriot Witch* (2009); *A Spell for the Revolution* (2009); *The Demon Redcoat* (2009)

Proctor Brown and Deborah Walcott, along with their small coven of good colonial witches and warlocks, fight off the Covenant, an evil English coven whose goal is to make sure that the Redcoats win the American Revolution. All of the famous colonial heroes (e.g., George Washington, Paul Revere) are woven into the plot lines.

Foster, L. L. (pseudonym for Lori Foster)
Servant (UF—V5, S4, H2)
> *The Awakening* (Berkley, 2007); *The Acceptance* (Jove, 2008); *The Kindred* (Jove, 2009)

. . . .

Caught in an illimitable quandary, the pain intensified to egregious pro-
portions. She stumbled, fell against a wall. . . . From what she prevised,
only one summons would offer erudition. God help her if she chose the
wrong one. Hating herself, Gaby gave over to the deepest encroachment
of consecrated instruction. Driven forward, following a compulsion, she
traversed to a dark alley. The pain blistered and popped—then settled
into a fizzling ache.

Gaby gets God's signal that evil is afoot in the city
(note the level of the vocabulary), in L. L. Foster's *The Acceptance*

. . . .

This dark series fully meets the definition for urban fantasy: a smart, independent, angst-ridden heroine battling evil in a dark and dangerous urban
environment. Gabrielle "Gaby" Cody is a paladin—a warrior servant of
God—whose destiny is to hunt down and destroy all evil. When she feels
God's call for justice (evidenced by severe physical pain), her body is so
attuned that she proceeds directly to the evil situation and ends it, generally
by killing the perpetrator. Her love interest is Luther Cross, a by-the-book
police detective who does not believe in the supernatural. Together, they
bring to justice one psychopathic serial killer per book, including a deranged
cancer research doctor, a psychotic killer of prostitutes, and a lunatic vampire wannabe. As a sideline, Gaby writes and illustrates a graphic novel series
called *Servant*, which is based on her own life. The author's (and Gaby's)
vocabulary is several notches above the level of most paranormal romances
(e.g., *dehiscent burst, perspicacious eyes, deific duties, endogenous perception, omni-
potent numen, tutelary power, atramentous gravity, banausic nature*), which can
be somewhat distracting, because Gaby herself states that her schooling
ended at the eighth grade.

Fox, Andrew

FAT WHITE VAMPIRE (UF—V5, S3, H5)

Ballantine: *Fat White Vampire Blues* (2003); *Bride of the Fat White
Vampire* (2004)

In this homage to John Kennedy Toole's *Confederacy of Dunces*, vampire Jules
Duchon is a bumbling 450-pound cab driver in New Orleans, the fattest city
in the nation. Jules gets bigger and bigger because he preys on the underclass,
who feed themselves a rich diet of po'boys and fried food. In book 1, when

a young African American vampire (Malice X) burns down Jules's house and tries to run him out of town, Jules seeks help from his ex-lover, Maureen, an obese vampire stripper, and his ex-sidekick, Doodlebug, a California vampire guru who is a transvestite. In book 2, Jules battles depression and tries to find meaning in a loveless life as he is bullied into assisting an exclusive vampire group in finding the person responsible for maiming several of their young members. Odd characters and cultural references (e.g., 1930s pulp fiction, superhero comic books) turn up on every page, and scenes move from humor to violence to tragedy in quick succession, all interwoven with evocative portraits of pre-Katrina New Orleans neighborhoods and frequent condemnations of the evils of strip malls and retail chains.

Fox, Angela

DEMON SLAYERS (CH—V3, S5, H5)

Love Spell: *The Accidental Demon Slayer* (2008); *The Dangerous Book for Demon Slayers* (2009); *A Tale of Two Demon Slayers* (2010)

This frenetically funny series focuses on wisecracking Lizzie Brown, a preschool teacher and demon slayer; Pirate, her talking dog; Grandma Gertie, a geriatric, biker witch; and Lizzie's handsome boyfriend, Dimitri Kallinikos, a shape-shifting griffin. Their adventures include a variety of supernatural bad guys, from powerful werewolves to succubi to plain old everyday demons. The dialogue is full of sniping sarcasm, particularly when the Red Skull biker witches (Gertie's girlfriends) get involved in the action.

Frank, Jacquelyn

NIGHTWALKERS (SMR—V4, S5, H3)

Zebra: *Jacob* (2006); *Gideon* (2007); *Elijah* (2007); *Damien* (2008); *Noah* (2008)

Books 1, 2, 3, and 5 each take a demon through the process of finding his soul mate. Book 4 does the same for a vampire prince. These demons are muscular, handsome, wealthy men who appear to be human males in their thirties, even though some of them are up to nine hundred years old. They are definitely not the evil demons of mythology. The villains are the Necromancers—humans who summon the demons, force them to change into demon form, torture them for information about their friends, and then kill them. Three of the heroines (books 1, 2, 5) are human women (virgins, of course) who become Druids when they mate with their demon soul mates.

Two of the heroines (books 3 and 4) are lycanthrope royalty (werewolves). There's plenty of graphic sex for all.

SHADOWDWELLERS (SMR—V4, S5, H1)
Zebra: *Ecstasy* (2009); *Rapture* (2009); *Pleasure* (2009)

The main characters are part of the NIGHTWALKERS milieu, and much of the action takes place away from the human world. The Shadowdwellers move among their three worlds: Realscape (their real world), Shadowscape (a lightless dimension just a step out of phase with Realscape), and Dreamscape (the land of sleep and dreams). Besides the Shadowdwellers, the other residents of Shadowscape are comatose humans. The Shadowdwellers are extremely light sensitive (think instant combustion!) and must spend most of their time either in the dark or in moonlight. Each book tells one couple's SMR story in the context of a burgeoning revolution against the royalty of the Shadowdwellers.

THE GATHERERS (SMR—V4, S4, H1)
Zebra: *Hunting Julian* (2010); *Stealing Kathryn* (2010)

In this series, the Beneath is a realm below Earth inhabited by a race that lives on energy. Positive energy—mainly in the form of orgasmic sex—feeds the colonies, whereas negative energy—rage, for example—can cause earthquakes and confusion. Each colony has a male Gatherer, who goes to Earth to find women with his particular type of energy. When the Gatherer finds a potential candidate, he shows the woman his colony in a dream. When she awakens, they discuss the dream, and he asks her to leave her Earth life forever and go there with him. Women are rare in this culture, having mostly died out during a gender-specific plague. Because they are few, women are highly valued, both as energy sources and as mothers of future generations. A council called the Ampliphi, which has (as any paranormal romance reader would expect) some rotten apples in its membership, rules each colony. Other dangers come from the *okrill* and *tamblyn*, dangerous animals that roam the colonies at certain times of the day and night. In book 1, Julian, a Gatherer who specializes in sexual energy, is forced to take a human woman without her consent. This, of course, is bad enough, but then he discovers that she is his *kindra* (soul mate), and the complications get even worse. Book 2 is a beauty and the beast story in which a human woman (Kathryn) is stolen by the malformed monster, Adrian, who thrives on the negative emotions of nightmares. Kathryn eventually transforms Adrian with her love as they become *kindra* and provide plenty of energy for the inhabitants of the Beneath.

Frost, Jeaniene

NIGHT HUNTRESS (UF—V5, S4, H3)

"Reckoning" in *Unbound* anthology (Eos, 2009); *Halfway to the Grave* (Avon, 2007); *One Foot in the Grave* (Avon, 2008); *At Grave's End* (Avon, 2008); *Destined for an Early Grave* (Avon, 2009); "Happily Never After" in *Weddings from Hell* anthology (Harper, 2008); *This Side of the Grave* (Avon, 2011)

Catherine ("Cat") is an Ohio farm girl who is the product of her human mother's rape by a newly turned vampire. To avenge her mother, Cat spends her teen years seeking out and killing predatory vampires in local bars. One night she meets Bones, a master vampire who defeats her and tricks her into assisting him on his own vampire-killing hunts. Love blossoms between them, but, of course, their love life does not run smoothly, especially when her vampire-hating mother finds out about their relationship. After a major scandal that involves killing the villainous Ohio governor, Cat and Bones are separated for several years when Cat is forced to become a preternatural agent for the U.S. government. By book 2, Cat has turned into a tough Anita Blake, vampire-killing clone, going into battle with multiple silver knives and swords strapped to her arms and legs. Verbal sparring among the characters adds humor to the stories. Although there are a few graphic sex scenes and some coarse language, the emphasis is more on violent vampire action and less on sensuality. *One Foot in the Grave* won an honorable mention for the P.E.A.R.L. Award for best overall paranormal romance (2008).

NIGHT HUNTRESS WORLD (UF—V5, S4, H3)

Avon: *First Drop of Crimson* (2010); *Eternal Kiss of Darkness* (2010)

This is an SMR extension of NIGHT HUNTRESS, with main characters who are friends or family of Cat and Bones. In each book, a couple falls in love as they get involved in supernatural adventures.

Frost, P. R.

TESS NONCOIRÉ (UF—V4, S3, H2)

DAW: *Hounding the Moon* (2007); *Moon in the Mirror* (2008); *Faery Moon* (2009)

Tess is a warrior of the Sisterhood of the Celestial Blades. Along with her imp sidekick, Scrap, Tess fights demonic invasions into the human world. Scrap has the ability to turn himself into a weapon for her to use, from a small dagger to the powerful Celestial Blade. Tess's love interests are Dill, the ghost of her late husband; Guilford Van der Hoyden-Smyth ("Gollum"), a cerebral professor whose family has long studied the warriors; and Donovan Estevez, a handsome mystery man who may or may not be human. Prior to book 1, Tess stumbled into the warriors' citadel after coming down with imp flu just after Dill's seemingly accidental death in a fire. She was cured by the sisters and trained to be a warrior, but Tess's inability to keep from questioning the strict rules of the sisterhood caused her to be thrown out of the citadel. Now, she is a rogue warrior who must protect humanity on her own, with Scrap's assistance, of course. In her ordinary human life, Tess is a best-selling fantasy author who spends much of her time attending sci-fi and fantasy conventions. Tess battles a variety of villains, including a vengeful Windago demon, an army of vicious garden gnomes, a power-hungry rogue witch, and Donovan's demonic foster father. Tess also assists a coven of witches who suddenly reappear after their disappearance decades ago and helps a group of fairies held against their will. Tess's actions can be somewhat illogical at times, and the reader may wonder at a few plot inconsistencies (e.g., we are led to believe in the first two books that the warriors are all women, but in book 3, a male warrior turns up). Most of Tess's adventures take place in the human world, but many of Scrap's exploits take him to other realms.

Galenorn, Yasmine

SISTERS OF THE MOON (UF—V4, S4, H2)

Berkley: *Witchling* (2006); *Changeling* (2007); *Darkling* (2008); *Dragon Wytch* (2008); *Night Huntress* (2009); *Demon Mistress* (2009); *Bone Magic* (2010); "Silver Etched" in *Inked* anthology (2010); *Harvest Hunting* (2010)

This hodgepodge of urban fantasy, soul-mate romance, and chick lit probably comes closest to urban fantasy. The three D'Artigo sisters are half human, half fairy. In addition, one is a newbie vampire. They have been sent from Otherworld to Earthworld (Seattle) to police the portals between the two worlds. The stories generally focus on a search for nine spirit seals that control all of the portals. The primary villain, Shadow Wing, wants to control the seals so that his demons can control both worlds. He sends a series of demonic monsters to take down the sisters as they try to find the seals.

Garey, Terri

Nicki Styx (UF—V2, S3, H4)

Dead Girls Are Easy (Avon, 2007); *A Match Made in Hell* (Avon, 2008); "Ghouls Night Out" in *Weddings from Hell* anthology (Harper, 2008); *You're the One That I Haunt* (Avon, 2009); *Silent Night, Haunted Night* (Avon, 2009)

After a near-death experience in which she was told to go back and do good, Nicki, the owner of a vintage clothing store in Atlanta, finds that she can see and hear the ghosts of dead women—most of whom are looking for her help. Nicki's love interest, Joe Bascombe, is the handsome, down-to-earth emergency-room doctor who brought her back to life. Her gay business partner, Evan, provides sardonic repartee to raise the humor level. Adventures involve a variety of supernaturals, including many needy ghosts, an evil voodoo spirit, and bad boy Samael "Sammy" Divine—the devil himself, who has designs on Nicki. To complicate matters further, Nicki discovers that Joe is married to a woman who may be her twin sister. Although the series has some chick-lit elements (e.g., lots of fashion descriptions, breezy tone—particularly from Evan), the heroine has enough attitude and angst to make it an urban fantasy.

Gideon, Nancy

Moonlight (UF—V4, S4, H1)

Pocket: *Masked by Moonlight* (2010); *Chased by Moonlight* (2010); *Captured by Moonlight* (2010)

Charlotte ("Cee Cee") Caissie is a New Orleans homicide detective who is still trying to get her life in balance after several tragedies in her past. Max Savoie is a mob enforcer, seemingly indentured to the big boss, Jimmy Legere. Max is also a shape-shifter who can become a huge beast or a wolf. Book 1 explores the developing romance between the two as a series of brutal murders sets New Orleans on edge. In this world, supernatural creatures are unknown by mortals, and shifters exist in secretive clans. The next books follow the development of the couple's romance as they try to maintain their relationship in the face of their widely different lifestyles and moral codes, particularly when Max moves up to a top position with the mob. In book 2, Max is a murder suspect, and Cee Cee must prove his innocence. In book 3, Max's mysterious past catches up with him and threatens his life with Cee Cee.

Gilman, Laura Anne

RETRIEVERS (UF—V5, S3, H3)

Luna: *Staying Dead* (2004); *Curse the Dark* (2005); *Bring It On* (2006); *Burning Bridges* (2007); *Free Fall* (2008); *Blood from Stone* (2010)

Like Simon R. Green's John Taylor (NIGHTSIDE), Genevieve Valere (aka "the Wren") is a Retriever of lost things. Wren is a powerful witch-mage-psychometrist (or Talent) who can find almost anything that has been lost or stolen, and that is how she and her partner (and love interest), Sergei Didier, make their living. Six very different groups are trying unsuccessfully to coexist in New York City:

> *Mage Council:* a corrupt, arrogant coalition of Talents who believe that they are in charge of the magical world
>
> *Lonejacks:* independent Talents like Wren, who are averse to alliances with anyone
>
> *Wizzarts:* crazed Talents who have fried their brains by overusing their power
>
> *Silence:* a group of mostly men who believe their duty is to right the wrongs of the world—but they get to define what is "right" and what is "wrong"
>
> *Fatae:* supernatural beings of all sorts (e.g., fairies, gnomes, demons) who are looked down on by the Council and hated by many humans and by the Silence
>
> *Nulls:* humans with no magical abilities, some of whom have become vigilantes, striking out against the Fatae and the Lonejacks

The Talents pull energy from the world around them (e.g., electrical circuits, thunderstorms) to fuel their magic. The story arc for the series follows Wren's and Sergei's attempts to discover the truth behind the murders and kidnappings of many Fatae and Talents while successfully completing retrieval jobs and, less successfully, maintaining their ever-more-complicated relationship.

PARANORMAL SCENE INVESTIGATIONS (UF—V3, S2, H2)

Luna: *Hard Magic* (2010); *Pack of Lies* (2011)

Set in the same magical New York City world as Gilman's RETRIEVERS, this series tells the stories of members of Private, Unaffiliated Paranormal

Investigations (P.U.P.I), a team of five twentysomething Talents who work as forensic magicians, using their own magical abilities to solve crimes caused by the dark magic of others. Told from the viewpoint of team member Bonnie Torres, book 1 focuses on the formation of the team and their preparation for their first case, the murder of two Chicago Council members. Ian Stosser and Ben Venec, both powerful Talents with mysterious pasts, lead P.U.P.I. Bonnie immediately feels a sensual connection with Venec, but the relationship is unconsummated—actually not even fully realized—in book 1. Although there are several confrontations with the villains, the battles are waged with current, so there is not much blood. Ratings are based on book 1 because book 2 had not yet been released at the time of this writing.

Gleason, Colleen

GARDELLA VAMPIRE CHRONICLES (HIS—V4, S4, H2)

Signet: *The Rest Falls Away* (2007); *Rises the Night* (2007); *The Bleeding Dusk* (2008); *When Twilight Burns* (2008); *As Shadows Fade* (2009)

In the Gardella family, one person in each generation is called to accept the family legacy: slaying evil vampires. Victoria Gardella Grantworth is the chosen one of her generation in late-nineteenth-century England. The first part of the first book reads more like a typical Regency romance, with Victoria attending balls and fending off suitors, with, of course, the added twist of staking a vampire every now and again. The tone quickly changes at the close of the first book, however, as Victoria's "career" leads to a heart-wrenching tragedy in her personal life. The rest of the series follows Victoria on a much darker path and features various battles with Lilith, the vampire queen, and an ongoing love triangle with Max Pesaro and Sebastian Vioget, two others caught up in the world of vampire slaying.

Green, Chris Marie

VAMPIRE BABYLON (UF—V4, S4, H1)

Night Rising (Ace, 2007); *Midnight Reign* (Ace, 2008); *Break of Dawn* (Ace, 2008); *A Drop of Red* (Ace, 2009); *The Path of Razors* (Ace, 2009); *Deep in the Woods* (Brava, 2010); "Double the Bite" in *First Blood* anthology (Berkley, 2008)

Green imagines that the tragic deaths of young Hollywood stars are not what they seem—that these stars didn't really die. Instead, they made deals with the Underground, a vampire community, to receive immortality. They "die" and then return decades later, still at their peak of beauty and talent. Dawn Madison gets drawn into this intrigue when she arrives in Los Angeles looking for her missing father. Dawn is a self-confessed slut, seeking acceptance and love through a series of one-night stands. She has always lived in the shadow of her beautiful starlet mother, Eva, who was murdered (or was she?) when Dawn was an infant. Dawn begins working for her father's employer, Jonah Limpet, a mysterious, reclusive man (or spirit, or something else) who runs a paranormal investigative agency. The villains are members of various undergrounds in Los Angeles and London. Dawn's love interests are Jonah and Matt Lonigan, a mysterious man who claims to be a vampire hunter. Later books explain Jonah's identity and powers, both of which complicate the love story. The dialogue is quite melodramatic and there are many fierce battles between Dawn's group and the vamps.

. . . .

> Many of the sleek and gleaming vehicles darting through the Nightside had to be new to Joanna; shapes and sizes and even concepts that had never known the light of day; some of them powered from sources best not thought about too much, if you wanted to sleep at night. Taxis that ran on debased holy water, limousines that ran on fresh blood, ambulances that ran on distilled suffering. You can turn a profit from anything, in the Nightside. I had to take Joanna by the arm as she drifted unrealisingly too close to the edge of the pavement.
> "Careful!" I said loudly in her ear. "Some of those things aren't really cars. And some of them are hungry."
>
> John Taylor takes Joanna Barrett on her first trip to the
> Nightside, in Simon R. Green's *Something from the Nightside*

. . . .

Green, Simon R.

NIGHTSIDE (UF—V5, S1, H3)

Something from the Nightside (Ace, 2003); *Agents of Light and Darkness* (Ace, 2003); *Nightingale's Lament* (Ace, 2004); *Hex and the City* (Ace, 2005); *Paths Not Taken* (Ace, 2005); *Sharper Than a Serpent's Tooth* (Ace, 2006); *Hell to Pay* (Ace, 2006); *The Unnatural Inquirer* (Ace, 2008); *Just Another Judgement Day* (Ace, 2009); "The Difference a Day Makes" in *Mean Streets* anthology (Roc, 2009); *The Good, the Bad, and the Uncanny* (Ace, 2010); *A Hard Day's Night* (Ace, 2011)

In this dark series, John Taylor is a private investigator who uses the special gift he was born with to find things (both concrete and abstract) for people. John's father was human; his mother was not—and he's not sure exactly what she was, because she left soon after he was born in the Nightside, a dark and creepy area in the center of London where it's always three o'clock in the morning and every imaginable type of inhuman monster roams the streets. All of John's life, people in the Nightside have been trying to kill him, and he doesn't know why. John is a sucker for a sad story—especially from a woman—and he spends his life in the Nightside trying to stay alive while helping his clients find the property and/or people they have lost.

Green, Simon R. (cont.)

SECRET HISTORIES (UF—V4, S2, H4)

Roc: *The Man with the Golden Torc* (2008); *Daemons Are Forever* (2009); *The Spy Who Haunted Me* (2009); *From Hell with Love* (2010)

Super spy Eddie Drood (aka "Shaman Bond") has Dudley Do-Right's integrity, James Bond's high-tech gadgets, and Superman's invincibility. Each Drood family member wears a golden torc (collar) that turns into impregnable armor as needed. For centuries, the Drood (think Druid) family has fought to protect humankind from the dark forces, but now Eddie has discovered that the family has its own dark secrets. Set in England, this series boasts a wide variety of villains, all of whom are trying to bring down the Droods. Eddie and his girlfriend, the wild witch of the woods Molly Metcalf, battle evil monsters in nearly every scene. The reader occasionally feels trapped in a rather violent video game (particularly in book 1), with bizarre supernatural creatures constantly attacking from all sides. The humor is dry and understated—that elegant Brit wit.

Greiman, Lois

WITCHES OF MAYFAIR (HIS, SMR—V4, S4, H2)

Avon: *Under Your Spell* (2008); *Seduced by Your Spell* (2009); *Charming the Devil* (2010)

The series follows the SMR stories of members of a coven of English witches as they fight against various evil members of the Ton. These are Regency romances with plenty of simmering undercurrents before each hero and heroine *finally* get together.

Gustainis, Justin

QUINCEY MORRIS, SUPERNATURAL INVESTIGATOR (UF—V3, S3, H3)

   Solaris: *Black Magic Woman* (2008); *Evil Ways* (2008); *Sympathy for the Devil* (2010)

Quincey Morris is the great-grandson of the rich young Texan of the same name who lost his life in the final battle with Count Dracula in Bram Stoker's novel. The modern-day Quincey investigates many strange and dangerous supernatural problems with his partner, white witch Elizabeth Chastain. The author includes plenty of genre-related in-jokes that add humor to the stories. In *Evil Ways*, Quincey even sets up a meeting with Harry Dresden (DRESDEN FILES). Plots generally have two teams working on a supernatural crime, each taking a different path toward the solution of a crime and then meeting near the end to double-team the bad guys.

Haddock, Nancy

OLDEST CITY VAMPIRE (UF—V3, S5, H4)

   Berkley: *La Vida Vampire* (2008); *Last Vampire Standing* (2009)

Francesca Marinelli is a vampire who was trapped underground for more than two hundred years and rediscovered during the renovation of a Victorian mansion in St. Augustine, Florida. She's well suited for a job as an Old Ghost Town tour guide. Unfortunately, vampire hunters are on her trail. Her hot boyfriend, preternatural crimes special investigator Deke Saber, gets involved, too.

Hallaway, Tate (pseudonym for Lyda Morehouse)

GARNET LACEY (CH—V3, S3, H4)

   Tall, Dark and Dead (Berkley, 2006); *Dead Sexy* (Berkley, 2007); *Romancing the Dead* (Berkley, 2008); *Dead If I Do* (Berkley, 2009); "Fire and Ice" in *Many Bloody Returns* anthology (Ace, 2009); *Honeymoon of the Dead* (Berkley, 2010)

Garnet is the manager of a bookstore in Madison, Wisconsin, and she's a witch who is possessed by the evil goddess Lilith. Her boyfriend, Sebastian von Straum, is a vampire created through alchemy rather than blood exchange, which means that he can eat regular food (in addition to regular blood feedings), and he can day-walk. Garnet's ex-boyfriend, ne'er-do-well Daniel Parrish (a "normal" vampire), shows up at intervals to complicate her life. The series takes Garnet through adventures with militant Vatican hunters who murder her coven; a voodoo priestess who creates zombies and possesses one of her friends; and Sebastian's conniving son, Matyas, who betrays them while claiming that he just wants to get his family back together. Despite all the criminal activity, the stories are relatively humorous. Although Garnet and Sebastian are a couple throughout the series, they do not have the typical soul-mate relationship, in that Garnet is attracted to other men and Sebastian still has feelings for his dead wife.

- -

My original plan was actually to never have to do sex on paper. I wanted every touch, every caress, to be so amazing that I didn't have to resort to writing actual intercourse. But six books into the series, we did the dirty deed on paper, and because I'd spent five books building up to it, I couldn't skimp on the scene. Or felt I couldn't. Besides, I'd written books where every crime, every bit of necessary violence was kept on full camera, no flinching. So that when it came to sex, and I wanted the camera to do that 1940s pan to the sky, I couldn't do it. What did it say about me as a person that I hadn't paled at showing murder and mayhem in every book, but the first real sex scene had me panicked. Actually, it just proved that I think like an American. Violence is dandy, but God forbid you show sex on stage. Let alone enjoyable sex between two people that know and like, and maybe love, each other.

Laurell K. Hamilton explains why Anita's story gets sexy
after book 5, in the afterword to her *The Laughing Corpse*

- -

Hamilton, Laurell K.

ANITA BLAKE, VAMPIRE HUNTER (UF—V5, S2 [books 1–5],
S5 [books 6+], H3)

"Those Who Seek Forgiveness" in *Strange Candy* anthology (Berkley, 2007) and *The Living Dead* anthology (Night Shade, 2008); *Guilty Pleasures* (Jove, 2002); *The Laughing Corpse* (Jove, 2002); *Circus of the Damned* (Jove, 2002); *Lunatic Café* (Jove, 2002); *Bloody Bones* (Jove, 2002); *The Killing Dance* (Jove, 2002); *Burnt Offerings* (Jove, 2002); *Blue Moon* (Jove, 2002); *Obsidian Butterfly* (Jove, 2002); "The Girl Who Was

Infatuated with Death" in *Strange Candy* anthology (Berkley, 2007) and *Bite* anthology (Jove, 2004); *Narcissus in Chains* (Jove, 2002); *Cerulean Sins* (Jove, 2004); *Incubus Dreams* (Jove, 2005); *Micah* (Jove, 2006); *Danse Macabre* (Berkley, 2006); *The Harlequin* (Berkley, 2007); *Blood Noir* (Jove, 2009); *Skin Trade* (Berkley, 2009); *Flirt* (Berkley, 2010); *Bullet* (Berkley, 2010). Also available is a book of essays: *Ardeur: Unauthorized Essays on Laurell K. Hamilton's Anita Blake, Vampire Hunter Series* (BenBella, 2010). Marvel Comics has published graphic novels based on the series.

The protagonist is a female animator (raiser of the dead) and vampire executioner who lives in St. Louis. Throughout the series, Anita's metaphysical powers continue to grow. Her outlook on life changes dramatically as she goes from hating vampires and fearing lycanthropes to trusting them, befriending them, and eventually loving some of them. Sexual content varies greatly across volumes. In the first five books, Anita develops friendships with Jean-Claude, master vampire, and Richard Zeeman, head of the local werewolf pack, but she remains celibate. Beginning with book 6 (*The Killing Dance*), those two relationships, and others, become sexual. Beginning with book 10 (*Narcissus in Chains*), there is an increasing focus on Anita's infection with the *ardeur* (a supernatural hunger requiring her to feed it via direct or vicarious sexual energy), which dramatically increases the number and level of graphic sex scenes with multiple supernatural sexual partners. In the later books of the series, as plots become less and less important, the only mystery is which paranormal hunk(s) will satisfy Anita's *ardeur*?

MEREDITH GENTRY (UF—V4, S5, H2)

Ballantine: *Kiss of Shadows* (2002); *Caress of Twilight* (2003); *Seduced by Moonlight* (2004); *Stroke of Midnight* (2006); *Mistral's Kiss* (2007); *A Lick of Frost* (2008); *Swallowing Darkness* (2009); *Divine Misdemeanors* (2010)

Meredith "Merry" Gentry is a clone of Anita Blake—except she is a fairy princess (no wings) and a private detective instead of a vampire executioner. The two series share many traits: the physical appearance of the heroine, frequent scenes of graphic sex, expansion of magical powers through sex, multiple sexual partners for the heroine, and very long (i.e., ankle-length) hair on many of the men. Because Merry is an heir to the throne, her life is frequently in danger, and a group of handsome warriors guards her. The current queen wants Merry pregnant as soon as possible (by one of her guards— *any* one of them)—a setup for the frequent graphic sex scenes.

Handeland, Lori

NIGHTCREATURE (SMR—V4, S4, H3)

St. Martin's: *Blue Moon* (2004); *Hunter's Moon* (2005); *Dark Moon* (2005); *Crescent Moon* (2006); *Midnight Moon* (2006); *Rising Moon* (2006); *Hidden Moon* (2007); *Thunder Moon* (2008)

Werewolves (most of them, anyway) are definitely the bad guys here. Think *X-Files* set in Red Riding Hood's woods. Plot lines for early books combine mystical Ojibwe mythology and Nazi legends as the Jäger-Sucher (hunter-searchers employed in secret by the U.S. government) spend their time in the forests of Wisconsin, killing and disposing of dangerous and powerful werewolves. Later books expand the villainy list to other types of shifters and move the action to places like New Orleans and Haiti, where voodoo reigns. Each book tells one couple's story as they meet, battle supernatural enemies, and become soul mates. *Blue Moon* won the RITA Award for best paranormal romance (2005).

PHOENIX CHRONICLES (UF—V4, S4, H2)

St. Martin's: *Any Given Doomsday* (2008); *Doomsday Can Wait* (2009); *Apocalypse Happens* (2009); *Chaos Bites* (2010)

Elizabeth "Lizzie" Phoenix is a seer (psychic empath), one of the sacred few on the earth who have the psychic powers to fight the evil forces that constantly try to wipe out the human race. Lizzie is an Anita Blake clone in the sense that she expands her powers through sexual acts, has two supernatural boyfriends, and is an executioner of malevolent paranormal monsters. The boyfriends are Jimmy Sanducci, a half-human and half-vampire demon killer, and Sawyer, a powerful Navajo sorcerer and skin walker. The story arc for the series builds toward a doomsday scenario as Lizzie and her troops kill the monsters, one by one.

Hansen, Jamie Leigh

Tor: *Betrayal* (2008); *Cursed* (2008) (SMR—V3, S3, H1)

Although there is no name for this series, both novels share a milieu. Plots revolve around fallen angels, demons, mysterious dreams, and ancient curses. Complex story lines and heavy use of flashbacks result in occasional chaos for the reader. In each book, one couple achieves soul-mate status.

Harper, Molly

Nice Girls (CH—V3, S3, H4)

Pocket Star: *Nice Girls Don't Have Fangs* (2009); *Nice Girls Don't Date Dead Men* (2009); *Nice Girls Don't Live Forever* (2010)

Jane Jameson is a children's librarian in Half-Moon Hollow, Kentucky, until she is mistaken for a deer, shot dead, and then wakes up as a vampire. Unfortunately, Jane's relatives don't want a vampire in the family, so they're not too sympathetic. In book 1, someone is stalking Jane and seems to want her dead. In book 2, Jane deals with the werewolf relatives of her best friend's bride. Meanwhile, Jane's sire (and love interest), Gabriel Nightengale, refuses to commit. The books are unrelentingly humorous—both characters and dialogue. Jane's mother is the typical ditzy Southern mama—wanting her daughter to forget all this silly vampire business, settle down, and marry a nice human (picked out by Mom, of course).

* * *

Airports belong to Satan. Once upon a time, flying was elegant and daring, and people dressed up for flights. Now all airport operations are under the aegis of Hell, under the direction of Moloch . . . of the Land of Tears. While his record with lost luggage is breathtaking and eliminating food on U.S. carriers was inspired, his greatest achievement was the hub system. Satan had praised him and elevated him to Prince of Hell for that innovation, guaranteeing millions more stranded travelers unable to make their connecting flights.

Lily, a succubus, rants on the trials of air travel,
in Nina Harper's *Succubus in the City*

* * *

Harper, Nina

Succubus Series (CH V4, S5, H4)

Del Rey: *Succubus in the City* (2008); *Succubus Takes Manhattan* (2008)

Lily is a successful fashion magazine editor, a succubus, and a handmaid to Satan. She lives in Manhattan and spends lots of time with her girlfriends, who are also members of Satan's Chosen (think *Sex and the City* gone to hell). In the story arc for the series, human religious fanatics are out to get Lily and her friends. In her fight against them, Lily has help from her two boyfriends: Marten, a demonic magician, and Nathan, a Yale-educated specialist in Eastern languages who has become a private investigator.

· ·

I'd been waiting for the vampire for years when he walked into the bar.

Ever since vampires came out of the coffin (as they laughingly put it) four years ago, I'd hoped that one would come to Bon Temps. We had all the other minorities in our little town—why not the newest, the legally recognized undead? . . .

But I was waiting for my own vampire. . . . And he sat down at one of my tables. . . .

I knew immediately what he was. It amazed me when no one else turned around to stare. They couldn't tell! But to me, his skin had a little glow, and I just knew.

I could have danced for joy.

That fateful moment when Sookie meets Vampire
Bill at Merlotte's, in Charlaine Harris's *Dead until Dark*

· ·

Harris, Charlaine

SOUTHERN VAMPIRE (SOOKIE STACKHOUSE) MYSTERIES (UF—V3, S4, H3)

Ace: *Dead until Dark* (2008); *Living Dead in Dallas* (2009); *Club Dead* (2003); *Dead to the World* (2005); *Dead as a Doornail* (2006); *Definitely Dead* (2007); *All Together Dead* (2008); *From Dead to Worse* (2009); *Dead and Gone* (2009); *Dead in the Family* (2010); *A Touch of Dead* (2009) contains all of the Sookie Stackhouse short stories; "Dracula Night" in *Many Bloody Returns* anthology (2009); *The Sookie Stackhouse Companion*, a nonfiction guide to the series (2011)

In this villageous, rather than urban, fantasy series, free-spirited, mindreading Sookie is just a cocktail waitress in a small-town northern Louisiana bar until Vampire Bill sits down at one of her tables. Vampires have revealed themselves to the world because the Japanese invented synthetic blood, removing the need for humans as a food source. The series maintains Sookie as the primary character, but each of her adventures focuses on a slightly different group of friends, family, and lovers as she battles serial killers, human religious fanatics, bad vamps, and many other evil supernatural beings. The HBO series *True Blood* (available on DVD) is based on this series.

HARPER CONNELLY MYSTERIES (UF—V3, S2 [books 1–2], S3 [books 3–4], H3)

Berkley: *Grave Sight* (2006); *Grave Surprise* (2007); *An Ice Cold Grave* (2008); *Grave Secret* (2009)

Harper's paranormal gift—or curse—is her ability to locate dead people and to communicate with their spirits. This ability began after she was struck by lightning when she was a teenager. Harper and her beloved stepbrother, Tolliver Lang, establish a consultant business, hiring out Harper's services to law enforcement agencies across the country. Adventures ensue, because there is always someone who doesn't want the body found. Throughout most of the first three books, the sensuality level is 2 (simmering sexual tension, but no action), but it heats up slightly to 3 at the end of book 2.

Harrison, Kim

THE HOLLOWS (UF—V4, S5, H3)

"Two Ghosts for Sister Rachel" in *Holidays Are Hell* anthology (a prequel to the series; Harper, 2007); *Dead Witch Walking* (Eos, 2008); *The Good, the Bad, and the Undead* (Eos, 2008); "Undead in the Garden of Good and Evil" in *Dates from Hell* anthology (Avon, 2006); *Every Which Way but Dead* (Eos, 2008); *A Fistful of Charms* (Eos, 2008); "Dirty Magic" in *Hotter Than Hell* anthology (Harper, 2008); *For a Few Demons More* (Eos, 2007); *The Outlaw Demon Wails* (Eos, 2008); *White Witch Black Curse* (Eos, 2009); "Ley Line Drifter" in *Unbound* anthology (Eos, 2009); *Black Magic Sanction* (Eos, 2010); *Pale Demon* (Eos, 2011)

Rachel Morgan is a powerful earth witch in Cincinnati, a city divided into the human side north of the Ohio River and the Hollows (the supernatural, or Inderlander, side) south of the river. Forty years ago, a virus that spread through biogenetically engineered tomatoes wiped out a quarter of the world's human population, leaving the world almost equally divided between humans and supernatural beings. This resulted in the supernaturals' decision to go public and demand equal power. Currently, animosity runs deep between the two groups. Two agencies police the masses: the Federal Inderland Bureau (FIB), run by the humans, and Inderland Security (IS), run by the supernaturals. Rachel starts out as an IS bounty hunter, but quits to make it on her own. Her partners include her roommate, Ivy, a bisexual vampire who yearns for Rachel to be her scion (causing a number of sensual bloodlust scenes), and Jenks, a male pixie, who lives in Rachel's garden with his wife and fifty-four children. Other ongoing characters include Nick, her ne'er-do-well human boyfriend; Kisten, Rachel's vampire lover; Trent, a mysterious and dangerous man from her past; David, her werewolf friend and pack alpha; Algaliarept ("Al"), the demon who's out to drag Rachel back to the ever-after as his slave; and Ceri, Al's former slave. Plots include demon, vampire, and werewolf attacks as Rachel battles the bad guys and gets closer and closer to losing her soul each time she is tempted to use black (demon) magic. Many close parallels to early ANITA BLAKE.

Hart, Raven (pseudonym for Susan Goggins) (all four books) and Virginia Ellis (cowriter for books 1 and 2)

SAVANNAH VAMPIRES (UF—V5, S5, H3)
> Ballantine: *The Vampire's Seduction* (2006); *The Vampire's Secret* (2007); *The Vampire's Kiss* (2007); *The Vampire's Betrayal* (2008); *The Vampire's Revenge* (2009)

William Cuyler Thorne is an ancient vampire who relocated from Europe to the United States in colonial times; Jack McShane was a soldier when William turned him after he nearly died in a Civil War battle. Now the two are in Savannah, Georgia, where William is a Southern aristocrat and Jack is a wisecracking, Nascar-loving auto mechanic. At the series' beginning (2005), the two have had a peaceful and profitable life, but William's old enemies from Europe, including his evil sire, Reedrek, want to cash in on his success. Told from varying points of view—sometimes in the form of letters—the series resolves mysteries about William's past and Jack's future. Is William's human wife really dead, or has she lived on as a vampire? Will Jack continue his romance with Consuela, a police officer who may or may not have some preternatural traits? Can life go on peacefully in Savannah? Sensuality and violence are intertwined in many dark scenes of vampiric bloodlust. Each novel ends with a cliff-hanger, so the reader must follow the series in sequence to get all of the answers.

Havens, Candace

BRONWYN THE WITCH (CH—V3, S3, H4)
> Berkley: *Charmed and Dangerous* (2007); *Charmed and Ready* (2008); *Charmed and Deadly* (2007)

Bronwyn ("Bron") is a powerful witch with international connections. She provides protection services for such VIPs as a prime minister, a sheik, and a rock star. Because she has killed many evil warlocks and demons over the years, someone is always out to kill her and threaten her friends. Bron's love interests are Sam, a doctor, and Azir, a Dubai businessman. Havens has written a related novel, *Like a Charm* (Berkley, 2008), which includes characters from Bronwyn's world.

CARUTHERS SISTERS (CH, SMR—V5, S3, H4)
Berkley: *The Demon King and I* (2008); *Dragons Prefer Blondes* (2009)

The four wealthy and beautiful Caruthers sisters are Guardian Keys. In their world, each supernatural group lives in its own realm, with portals to connect them to one another and to the human-populated earth. Each sister protects humans from a specific supernatural group by regulating traffic through the portals: Gillian, demons; Alexandra, dragons; Mira, fairies; and Clair, sea nymphs. Between red-carpet appearances and charity balls, the girls battle villains and find true love. Romance is an integral part of each plot, but the fashion references tip the stories into CH as well.

Hecht, Daniel

CREE BLACK (UF—V3, S2, H2)
Bloomsbury USA: *City of Masks* (2004); *Land of Echoes* (2005); *Bones of the Barbary Coast* (2006)

This series has the two main UF ingredients: a sense of place and an independent female heroine. The author's goal is to write fifty CREE BLACK supernatural mystery novels—one set in each U.S. state. The first three are set in Louisiana (New Orleans), New Mexico (Gallup area), and California (San Francisco), respectively. Each plot is deeply implanted into the geography, history, and culture of its setting as the story follows Lucretia ("Cree") on her parapsychological, murder-mystery solving adventures. Cree has a partner (and love interest), Edgar, and a research assistant, Joyce, but Cree works mostly on her own. In each book, Cree's Seattle-based Psi Research Associates agency is hired to look into a mysterious situation with paranormal overtones. In the first three books, she deals with family ghosts, a ghostly possession, and werewolf-themed criminal activities. Each book includes a plethora of historical and cultural background information and plenty of technical psychospeak. The spooky, goose-bumps factor is high, especially in book 1.

Hendee, Barb

VAMPIRE MEMORIES (UF—V4, S1, H1)

Roc: *Blood Memories* (2009); *Hunting Memories* (2009); *Memories of Envy* (2010)

In book 1, Edward, a vampire worn down by countless years of darkness, commits suicide by walking into the sun. His spectacular death draws unwelcome attention from human vampire executioners, so Edward's vampire friends, Eliesha and her ward, William, must go on the run. After making a connection with one of the human executioners (Wade) and with two vampires from her past (Julian, a killer, and Philip, a friend), Eliesha finds her own kind of freedom. In book 2, Eliesha, Philip, and Wade try to make a new life for themselves as they search for other American vampires while always on the alert for attacks from Julian. In book 3, they become involved with Simone, a sinister female vampire who was turned in the 1920s. The stories include flashbacks to earlier parts of the vampires' lives, sometimes centuries ago.

Hendee, Barb, and J. C. Hendee

NOBLE DEAD SAGA (HIS—V4, S3, H2)

SERIES 1: Roc: *Dhampir* (2003); *Thief of Lives* (2004); *Sister of the Dead* (2005); *Traitor to the Blood* (2007); *Rebel Fay* (2008); *Child of a Dead God* (2009)

SERIES 2: Roc: *In Shade and Shadow* (2009); *Through Stone and Sea* (2010); *Of Truth and Beasts* (2011)

Series 1 follows the adventures of Margiere and her partner and lover, Leesil, a half-human elf, as they travel from village to village in medieval Europe as make-believe vampire killers but soon discover that Margiere is, in fact, a *dhampir* (half human, half vampire) and really is a vampire killer, with special gifts of strength and stamina. They travel with their elfin dog, Chap, who has special vampire-tracking abilities. Their lives become complicated when they meet Welstiel Massing, a mysterious stranger who first alerts Margiere to her powers and to her vampire-hunting mission in life, and then turns up regularly to cause trouble during their further adventures. The series follows Margiere and Leesil on a long series of dangerous adventures involving vampires, elves, and other mysterious supernatural creatures as they search for the truth about their past lives. Although the series takes place in medieval times, it has many UF characteristics. Series 2 follows the adventures of Margiere's friend, the sage Wynn Hygeorht, as she searches for missing vampire texts.

Henry, Mark

AMANDA FERAL (CH—V5, S4, H5)
Kensington: *Happy Hour of the Damned* (2008); *Road Trip of the Living Dead* (2009); *Battle of the Network Zombies* (2010)

Amanda is a ghoul—a flesh eater—who (along with her "ghoul-friend" Wendy and their vamp friend Gil) romps through Seattle from club to club, snacking on human body parts as she goes (ewwww!). Think *Sex and the City* meets *Night of the Living Dead.* Plots involve the usual supernatural power struggles. The humor—very, very dark—is nonstop, both situational and verbal. The graphic feeding scenes are a gross-out, and the verbal sniping is coarse and seemingly endless.

Herron, Rita

THE DEMONBORN (SMR—V4, S5, H1)
Forever: *Insatiable Desire* (2008); *Dark Hunger* (2009); *Forbidden Passion* (2010)

This trilogy follows three brothers (Vincent, Quinton, and Dante Valtrez) who were separated in childhood. Their late mother was an angel of light. Their bad-boy father, Zion, is a satanic demon who murdered their mother and is now about to rise from the grave to become the new leader of hell's legions. The brothers must find each other and unite to stop their father, finding their soul mates along the way.

Hilburn, Lynda

KISMET KNIGHT, VAMPIRE PSYCHOLOGIST (UF—V5, S5, H3)
Medallion Press: *The Vampire Shrink* (2007); *Dark Harvest* (2008)

Denver psychologist Kismet Knight has a thriving practice counseling goths and wanna-be vampires, but after she gets involved with the preternatural underworld, she adds real vampires to her patient list. In no time at all, Devereux, the handsome and very powerful leader of the Denver vampires, becomes her lover. Adventures ensue as evil vampires cause trouble for the loving couple. Many scenes intertwine sensuality and violence.

Hill, Joey W.

VAMPIRE QUEEN **(SMR—V5, S5+, H1)**

Berkley: *The Vampire Queen's Servant* (2007); *The Mark of the Vampire Queen* (2008); *A Vampire's Claim* (2009); *Beloved Vampire* (2009); *Vampire Mistress* (2010); *Vampire Trinity* (2010)

The first two books in this series tell the graphically erotic SMR story of Lady Elyssa "Lyssa" Yamato Amaterasu Wentworth, a thousand-year-old vampire queen, and Jacob Green, her human servant, who appears to be the reincarnation of a man who has given his life for her twice in the past. Book 1 introduces the two and sets the sexually explicit tone for their developing relationship; book 2 carries the relationship through to its inevitable conclusion. Book 1 has no real plot, just scene after scene of explicit sex between the two, including scenes of sadomasochism. Book 2 continues the sensuality and adds threesomes (and more), rape, and more sadomasochism. Toward the end of book 2, there is a brief battle among the good vamps, the bad vamps, and some vampire hunters, but in general, graphic sex is the focus—not the plot. The remaining books tell the SMR stories of various characters from the VAMPIRE QUEEN world.

Holling, Jen

MACDONELL BRIDES **(HIS, SMR—V3, S4, H3)**

Pocket: *My Devilish Scotsman* (2005); *My Shadow Warrior* (2005); *My Wicked Highlander* (2005); *My Immortal Promise* (2008); *My Immortal Protector* (2008)

This historical romance series follows the women of the MacDonell family —all witches—who live the Scottish highlands in the 1600s. Each book takes one of the women from love at first sight to happily ever after with her soul mate, along with many adventures involving human enemies (e.g., crazy ex-wife, witch hunter) and supernatural dangers (e.g., bad witches, vampires) in between love scenes.

Holly, Emma

FITZ CLARE CHRONICLES/UPYR **(HIS, SMR—V4, S4, H2)**

"Luisa's Desire" in *Fantasy* anthology (Jove, 2002); *Catching Midnight* (Jove, 2003); *Hunting Midnight* (Berkley, 2003); "Night Owl" in *Hot Blooded* anthology (Jove, 2004); *Courting Midnight* (Berkley, 2005);

Kissing Midnight (Berkley, 2009); *Breaking Midnight* (Berkley, 2009); *Saving Midnight* (Berkley, 2009); *Devil at Midnight* (Berkley, 2010); *Angel at Dawn* (Berkley, 2011)

In book 1, the Fitz Clare family gets involved with the Upyr—shape-shifting vampires—in 1349, when Aimery Fitz Clare falls in love with Gillian, a Upyr female. The books cover a range of time, from the 1300s through the 1930s. In each book, a member or friend of the Fitz Clares finds a soul mate, but a variety of villains and circumstances block the road to romance at every turn. *Kissing Midnight*, *Breaking Midnight*, and *Saving Midnight* form a trilogy telling Edmund's story. *Devil at Midnight* and *Angel at Dawn* are the first two books of a trilogy featuring Christian Durand.

Holzner, Nancy

DEADTOWN (UF—V3, S2, H2)

Ace: *Deadtown* (2010); *Hellforged* (2010)

Victory "Vicky" Vaughn is a Cerddorion—a shape-shifter—who specializes in killing demons. She lives in Deadtown, a quarantined section of Boston set aside for paranormal residents, who have very few civil rights in Massachusetts and none at all in the other forty-nine states. Vicky can shape-shift into any sentient being, but her shifts are limited to three per month. Vicky's two love interests are the werewolf Alexander Kane, a workaholic and activist lawyer, and Daniel Costello, a human Boston Police Department homicide detective. A decade ago, the demon that killed her father marked Vicky, and she has had to live with the effects of that mark ever since. In book 1, Vicky faces down that demon, nicknamed the Destroyer. Ratings are based on book 1 because book 2 had not yet been released at the time of this writing.

Hooper, Kay

BISHOP/SPECIAL CRIMES UNIT (four sets of trilogies) (SMR—V5, S3, H2)

SHADOWS TRILOGY: Bantam: *Stealing Shadows* (2000); *Hiding in the Shadows* (2000); *Out of the Shadows* (2000)

EVIL TRILOGY: Bantam: *Touching Evil* (2001); *Whisper of Evil* (2002); *Sense of Evil* (2004)

FEAR TRILOGY: Bantam: *Hunting Fear* (2005); *Chill of Fear* (2006); *Sleeping with Fear* (2007)

BLOOD TRILOGY: Bantam: *Blood Dreams* (2008); *Blood Sins* (2009); *Blood Ties* (2010)

Although the books are divided into four trilogies, all of the books follow Noah Bishop and his Special Crimes Unit (SCU), a special unit within the FBI in which team members have powerful psychic skills. In each book, a serial killer begins his rampage in small-town America. The local law enforcement authorities call in the FBI. When SCU investigators arrive on the scene, they team up with the locals to catch the bad guy—but not before more violent deaths occur. In the midst of each adventure, a relationship develops between an SCU team member and one of the locals, generally because the local has some psychic powers of his or her own. Although plot is more important here than in most SMR stories, the relationships do play crucial roles. In many cases, the local goes on to join the SCU and turns up as a supporting character in later books. The first three trilogies contain stand-alone plot lines for each book. BLOOD TRILOGY is different in that it has a story arc that builds through the three books, and it includes Haven—Noah Bishop's new civilian organization of gifted investigators.

Howard, Linda, and Linda Jones

SPIRIT WARRIORS (SMR—V5, S4, H1)

Ballantine: *Blood Born* (2010); *Warrior Rising* (2011)

In this world, Spirit Warriors are the spirits of soldiers who have fought and died over the course of centuries for just causes. The premise is that the warriors never really die; they continue to exist, but on a different plane. When evil forces threaten Earth, the warriors can return in their human bodies and continue the fight. If they are killed again, they go back to the spirit plane and wait to be called again. The only way the warriors can return to Earth in their corporeal forms is through their conduits—human descendants who must invite them back. Added to the mix are vampires, mostly good guys, except for the growing army of Rogues who want to subjugate humans and take over the world. Each book carries the Rogue-Warrior-vampire conflict further forward, with a couple forming a soul-mate bond along the way.

Huff, Tanya

VICTORIA NELSON/BLOOD SERIES (UF—V4, S3, H3)

DAW: *Blood Price* (2007); *Blood Trail* (2007); *Blood Lines* (2007); *Blood Pact* (2007); *Blood Debt* (2007); *Blood Bank* (2008) includes all of the

V<small>ICTORIA</small> N<small>ELSON</small> short stories; *The Blood Books*, vol. 1 (2006) contains *Blood Price* and *Blood Trail*; *The Blood Books*, vol. 2 (2006) contains *Blood Lines* and *Blood Pact*; *The Blood Books*, vol. 3 (2006) contains *Blood Debt* and *Blood Bank*

Vicki's declining vision (incurable and progressive retinitis pigmentosa) forced her to leave her beloved career as a Toronto homicide detective and start her own private investigation agency. Vicki is a blunt and outspoken modern woman whose motto is "Begin as you mean to go on." She's also the pivotal point in a love triangle that includes Mike Celluci, her irascible, no-nonsense former partner, and vampire Henry Fitzroy, romance author and bastard son of King Henry VIII. Each book is a supernatural thriller in which the trio solves a mystery in or near Toronto. The villains include demons, an ancient Egyptian mummy-wizard, werewolf killers, mad scientists, and a vengeful ghost. The series was written in the 1990s but was rereleased in 2006 in conjunction with the Lifetime television series *Blood Ties*.

S<small>MOKE</small> T<small>RILOGY</small> (UF—V4, S3, H4)

DAW: *Smoke and Shadows* (2005); *Smoke and Mirrors* (2006); *Smoke and Ashes* (2007)

The protagonist, Tony Foster, is the former lover of Henry Fitzroy from the B<small>LOOD</small> S<small>ERIES</small>. Set in Vancouver, the series tells Tony's story as he works as a production assistant for a second-rate vampire television show, where he tries to overcome his unrequited crush on Lee, the handsome—and seemingly very straight—costar of the show. Tony is also a newbie wizard. The bantering dialogue is the source of much of the dry and ironic humor. Plots include an evil sorcerer, a malevolent ghostly spirit, and a demonic convergence.

Hunter, Faith

J<small>ANE</small> Y<small>ELLOWROCK</small> (UF—V5, S2, H2)

Roc Fantasy. *Skinwalker* (2009); *Blood Cross* (2010); *Mercy Blade* (2011)

Imagine early Anita Blake as a skinwalker. Jane is a renowned vampire killer, hired by the New Orleans Vampire Council to take care of some "problem" vamps. She is seemingly the last of her kind: a Cherokee skinwalker who can assume the shape and characteristics of various animals, but principally a panther. Several possible love interests/nemeses emerge in book 1: Rick, a Cajun biker (or is he?); George, blood servant to the most powerful local vampire clan; and Leo, the head of that clan. Jane is loaded with weapons (in her hair, strapped to her arms and thighs, and more) and fights fiercely and usually successfully, but she still manages to sustain horrific, life-threatening injuries on a fairly regular basis. Jane's relationship with her beast within gives a mystical cast to the stories, particularly when the beast helps her remember parts of her childhood years, which have been wiped from her memory.

Huston, Charlie

JOE PITT CASEBOOKS (UF—V5, S2, H2)

Del Rey: *Already Dead* (2005); *No Dominion* (2006); *Half the Blood of Brooklyn* (2007); *Every Last Drop* (2008); *My Dead Body* (2009)

You can't get more urban than this dark series, in which "vampyrism" is caused by a "vyrus," and the vampyres don't have fangs but do ingest human blood. Joe Pitt is a streetwise maverick fighting on the side of justice, but besieged at every turn by the warring vampyre clans who have divided up Manhattan. Table 4 profiles the different clans in the series.

TABLE 4   Warring Vampyre Clans in Joe Pitt Casebooks

CLAN NAME	MEMBERS	LOCATED	BELIEFS
The Coalition	The Vampyre elite, who hold themselves above the other clans	Midtown	Keep Vampyrism undercover but get all the power you can, however you can
The Society	Politically correct, culturally diverse left wingers	East Village	Unite all of the clans and bring Vampyrism into the open
The Enclave	Fanatical true believers; stripping Vampyrism down to basics	SoHo	Exist on as little human blood as possible—on the edge of starvation
The Dusters	Renegade biker gang	Lower East Side	Muscle for hire
The Hood	African Americans	Harlem	Power to the "brothers"

Joe's adventures always involve his need to move into one or more of the areas "owned" by the clans, and he is constantly getting beat up by one group or another, losing body parts along the way. Joe has a beautiful, redheaded human girlfriend (Evie), who is battling AIDS, and he tries hard to keep his violent vampyre lifestyle a secret from her. Their seemingly doomed love story forms the framework for the series. The plots involve enough brutal violence to be classified as horror, but the characters are better developed than the usual horror novel.

Ione, Larissa

DEMONICA (SMR—V5, S4, H3)

Forever: *Pleasure Unbound* (2008); *Desire Unchained* (2009); *Passion Unleashed* (2009); *Ecstasy Unveiled* (2010); *Sin Undone* (2010)

The series follows the adventures of a group of demon brothers as they fight for the good of the world and find their soul mates along the way. The brothers run the Underworld General Hospital (UGH) beneath the streets of New York City to care for members of the supernatural world, particularly demons—who come in dozens of colors, shapes, sizes, personalities, and violence levels. The series follows the havoc created by the bad-seed brother, whose actions eventually lead to an Armageddon-like battle between good and evil. Characters include human demon slayers, fallen angels, vampires, and many types of demons. Each book begins with a glossary of demonic terms, and *Passion Unleashed* ends with a forty-page addendum titled "Demonica: A Demon Compendium," which describes in detail the types of demons, the hospital, and the key players in the DEMONICA world, and ends with a short-story prequel. The books should be read in sequence, but the reader may wish to read the "Demon Compendium" and the prequel first.

Ivy, Alexandra

GUARDIANS OF ETERNITY (SMR—V4, S4, H3)

Zebra: *When Darkness Comes* (2007); *Embrace the Darkness* (2007); *Darkness Everlasting* (2008); *Darkness Revealed* (2009); *Darkness Unleashed* (2009); *Beyond the Darkness* (2010)

The series follows members of a Chicago vampire clan through the SMR process. In the early books, the heroes are vampires, generally the clan leaders. Later books include werewolves as heroes. Heroines seem, at first, to be human, but each has a different supernatural trait. Plots center around various violent acts against the soul mates (e.g., an evil spell cast by wicked witches, attempted murders and kidnappings by various evil vamps and shifters). One plot line that runs through several later books is the werewolves' search for four purebred female siblings who were stolen from their nursery twenty years ago, with each sister becoming the heroine of one of the books. Each hero is aggressively alpha, and each heroine is ultra feisty. Levet, a pint-sized gargoyle, provides comic relief.

James, Allyson

DRAGON SERIES (SMR—V2, S5, H3)
> Berkley: *Dragon Heat* (2007); *The Black Dragon* (2007); *The Dragon Master* (2008)

Set in San Francisco, the action revolves around members of an Asian American family with supernatural powers and a group of dragons who can shape-shift into handsome human men. Each book tells the story of one family member and one dragon as they become soul mates and battle various supernatural beings, including a powerful witch, an evil white dragon, and a dangerous mage.

STORMWALKER (UF—V4, S4, H2)
> Berkley Sensation: *Stormwalker* (2010); *Firewalker* (2010); *Shadowwalker* (2011)

Janet Begay is a twentysomething Navaho stormwalker. She can pull power from storms and use it as an aid or a weapon. Unfortunately, Janet isn't always able to control the immense amounts of power that come from the most violent storms. In book 1, Janet returns to her New Mexico homeland, where she buys and renovates an old hotel while she searches for a missing young woman. When Janet gets into trouble with the local sheriff (who was the missing girl's fiancé), Janet's former boyfriend, Mick, shows up to rescue her. Mick is a mysterious, probably nonhuman, man who helped Janet understand her powers, but they broke up five years earlier, after he began disappearing for days at a time without letting her know where he was. Mick is a tall, dark, and handsome fire-wielder—and may be something more. For years, Janet has known that her mother is a dangerous supernatural spirit who wants to use her in some monstrous way. Now that Janet is back home, Mom sees this as an opportunity to grab Janet and use her to open a vortex that connects the mortal world to the Beneath. A shape-shifting coyote and a wisecracking magic mirror add to the action and the humor. In book 2, Mick is in danger and Janet must save him.

James, Dean

SIMON KIRBY-JONES MYSTERIES (COZ—V2, S2, H5)

Kensington: *Posted to Death* (2002); *Faked to Death* (2004); *Decorated to Death* (2005); *Baked to Death* (2006)

This mystery series has a twist—think Hercule Poirot meets Will from *Will and Grace* meets Dracula. Dr. Simon Kirby-Jones is an amateur sleuth, a medieval scholar, a romance novelist, and a gay vampire. Medication totally controls his vampiric traits (e.g., sun sensitivity, bloodlust), so for all intents and purposes, he appears to be a normal, if extremely strong, young man. (Garlic, though, can be deadly!) Simon has moved from the American South to Snupperton Mumsley, a village in the English countryside, where he lives a relatively peaceful life—until dead bodies start turning up. He makes friends with the quirky locals and begins a relationship (just a few light kisses, nothing more) with Sir Giles Blitherington, the young master of the town's first family. Humorous dialogue provides comic relief.

Kane, Stacia

MEGAN CHASE (UF—V4, S4, H3)

Personal Demons (Juno, 2008); *Demon Inside* (Pocket, 2009); *Demon Possessed* (Pocket, 2010)

Dr. Megan Chase is a practicing psychologist, a psychic, and the host of a radio show on which she is portrayed as a demon slayer (i.e., one who helps people overcome their personal demons). But the real demons of the world misinterpret her nickname and think she's out to kill them. In book 1, Megan discovers that she is the only person in the world who does not have a personal demon. Megan's adventures are linked to her mysterious past, particularly an incident that took place when she was sixteen years old (explained in book 2). Villains are demons who either want to destroy Megan or possess her. Megan's sexy (and very alpha) demon lover, Greyson Dante, wants to protect her from the bad demons, but Megan is not sure how far to trust him.

• •

> I have no need for faith. . . . I do not need faith because I know the Truth.
> I do not need to believe. Belief is unnecessary when fact is Truth. I do not
> pray to a god. Prayer implies faith and gods do not exist. Only energy
> exists, and this is Truth. The Church shows me the Truth and protects me. If
> I hold to these Truths I will enter the City of Eternity, and there I will stay.
>
> Credo of the Church of Real Truth,
>
> in Stacia Kane's *Unholy Ghosts*

• •

Kane, Stacia (cont.)

Downside Ghosts (UF—V5, S4, H1)

Del Rey: *Unholy Ghosts* (2009); *Unholy Magic* (2010);
City of Ghosts (2010)

Caesura ("Chess") Putnam lives in a world in which the underclass (who live in the Downside) live and talk as if they lived in Dickensian London, whereas the upper class live and talk just like modern-day Americans. In 1997, the Church of Real Truth—then a small, Puritanesque religious group—managed to save the day when all of the world's dead rose as ghosts and killed thousands of people. Now, the people believe in no god and have no faith; they believe only the "Truth" of the Church. In book 1, Chess is forced to take on a risky assignment from Bump, her local drug dealer, because she owes him a lot of money for her daily drugs. Yes, Chess is a junkie, using vast quantities of pills and powders to get through every day. She uses her drugs to blot out memories of extensive abuse during a childhood spent in horrible foster homes. Although her drug use sometimes muddles her mind, Chess is a powerful witch and has a successful career working for the Church as a debunker, investigating citizens' claims that ghosts are haunting their homes. Book 1 provides Chess with two possible love interests: Terrible, Bump's thuggish enforcer, and Lex, the right-hand man for Slobag, a rival drug dealer. This all sounds terribly dark and seedy, and it is—but Kane tells Chess's story sympathetically, and the constant action moves the plots right along. Books 2 and 3 find Chess in search of two different serial killers, each of whom may be a ghost—or something worse.

Kantra, Virginia

Children of the Sea (SMR—V4, S4, H2)

Berkley: "Sea Crossing" in *Shifter* anthology (2008); *Sea Witch* (2008);
Sea Fever (2008); *Sea Lord* (2009); *Immortal Sea* (2010)

Years ago, a human male (Bart Hunter) married a selkie female (Alice) and had three children—two boys and one girl. When the eldest boy (Dylan) reached puberty and "changed" into his selkie state, Alice left home and took him to the selkie sanctuary, where she died in an accident. The remaining boy (Caleb) and girl (Lucy) were raised by their father as humans, whereas the selkies raised Dylan. A selkie prophecy says that a female selkie directly related to Alice (who was really Atargatis, one of the selkies' ancient ones) will bring good fortune to the selkies and help them defeat the demons. The series tells the stories of the Hunter siblings as they meet their soul mates and battle the evil demons who want to kill any female of Atargatis's line.

Kenner, Julie

SUPERHERO CENTRAL (CH, SMR—V2, S3–4, H4)

Aphrodite's Kiss (Dorchester, 2001); *Aphrodite's Passion* (Love Spell, 2002); *Aphrodite's Secret* (Love Spell, 2003); *Aphrodite's Flame* (Love Spell, 2004); "Seeking Single Superhero" in *A Mother's Way* anthology (Love Spell, 2002); "A Step in the Right Direction" in *These Boots Were Made for Stomping* anthology (Love Spell, 2008)

The series revolves around an extended family of self-described superheroes and superheroines in contemporary Southern California whose ancestors are the gods and goddesses of Greek mythology. Most of them are good guys and gals, but there are, of course, a few black sheep in the family, and they are at the root of all of the conflict. Each supernatural meets and mates with a mortal.

DEMON-HUNTING SOCCER MOM (UF—V5, S3, H5)

Berkley: *Carpe Demon* (2005); *California Demon* (2006); *Demons Are Forever* (2007); *Deja Demon* (2009); *Demon Ex Machina* (2009)

Imagine Buffy as a thirtysomething suburban mom. Here's the history: As an orphan child found wandering the streets of Rome, Kate Conner was trained by the Vatican to be a demon hunter. When she and her husband/partner, Eric (also a hunter), moved to Southern California fourteen years ago to await the birth of their daughter, Allie, they both retired. After Eric's death five years ago, Kate married Stuart, an attorney, and they have a two-year-old son. Now, after fourteen demon-free years, they're baaaaaack! Kate has to dig her weapons out of the attic and go back to hunting—without letting Stuart in on the secret. To complicate matters even further, a high school chemistry teacher (David) turns out to be a rogue hunter who knew Eric—or maybe he really is Eric! Each book closely follows on the previous book's adventures, often with just minutes in between. Although all of the books are humorous, they can also be quite dark, particularly books 4 and 5.

Kenner, Julie (cont.)

BLOOD LILY CHRONICLES (UF—V4, S2, H1)
Berkley: *Tainted* (2009); *Torn* (2009); *Turned* (2009)

Just before book 1 begins, Lily Carlyle violently confronts her younger sister's rapist, which results in both their deaths. Now, Lily has a second chance at life. As she rises from the dead, Lily is confronted by Clarence, an elflike man who insists that Lily can achieve redemption by keeping the nine gates of hell closed so that demons cannot get through to the earth. A complication is that Lily has risen with a new body and a new name, that of a murdered girl. As she assumes Alice's life, Lily meets Deacon, a sexy bad boy who insists that he wants to be her friend (and more), but whose dark side worries Lily. Eventually, Lily becomes a double agent, working between the forces of light and dark. Naturally, the series concludes with a final apocalyptic battle that decides the future of humankind.

Kenyon, Sherrilyn

DARK-HUNTERS (SMR—V3, S4, H3)
St. Martin's: *Fantasy Lover* (2006); *Night Pleasures* (2002); *Night Embrace* (2006); *Dance with the Devil* (2003); *Kiss of the Night* (2004); *Night Play* (2004); *Seize the Night* (2004); *Sins of the Night* (2005); *Unleash the Night* (2005); *Dark Side of the Moon* (2006); *Devil May Cry* (2008); "Shadow of the Moon" in *Dead after Dark* anthology (2008); *Acheron* (2009); *One Silent Night* (2008); *Bad Moon Rising* (2009); *No Mercy* (2010); *The Dark-Hunter Companion* (2007), a nonfiction companion book to the series in which Kenyon explains and analyzes the DARK-HUNTERS world

Kenyon's fantastical world imagines a contemporary New Orleans teeming with a paranormal menagerie. Warring groups are the Dark-Hunters (ancient warriors created by the goddess Artemis to hunt and destroy Daimons) and Daimons, or Apollites (killer vampires whom Apollo originally created as a super race but punished with vampirism after they killed his mistress and son). An abundance of shape-shifters and demons also enter both the battles and the romances. Kenyon provides the usual handsome male nonhumans, but her twist is that some of her human heroines are unusual for romance novels (e.g., *Night Play*'s boutique owner, Bride McTierney, wears a size 18).

An overview of the series' entire Dark-Hunter and Daimon history is presented in *Night Embrace* (pp. 211–12). *Acheron* won the P.E.A.R.L. Award for best fantasy or magical romance and best overall romance (2008).

DREAM-HUNTERS (SMR—V3, S4, H3)

St. Martin's: *The Dream-Hunter* (2007); *Upon the Midnight Clear* (2007); *Dream Chaser* (2008); *Dream Warrior* (2009)

This world overlaps the DARK-HUNTERS world, with protagonists who are gods and goddesses of dreams. Each one meets and mates with a human.

Kessler, Jackie

HELL ON EARTH (UF—V4, S5, H5)

Hell's Belles (Zebra, 2007); *The Road to Hell* (Zebra, 2007); *Hotter Than Hell* (Kensington, 2008); "A Hell of a Time" in *Eternal Lover* anthology (Kensington, 2009); "When Hell Comes Calling" in *Lilith Unbound* anthology (Popcorn Press, 2008); "Hell Is Where the Heart Is" in *A Red Hot Valentine's Day* anthology (Avon Red, 2009)

As this series begins, Jezebel ("Jesse") is a demon—more specifically, a succubus. When King Lucifer gets transferred out of hell, Jezebel is reassigned to a new job, which she hates, so she goes on the run. To hide from her scary pursuers, she becomes a human, relocates to New York City, takes a job as an exotic dancer (i.e., stripper), and begins a romance with Paul, a New York City Police Department undercover cop. The first two books tell their story; the third book tells the sad story of Daunuan ("Daun"), an incubus who is unlucky in love. Demonic creatures complicate all of the protagonists' lives throughout the series.

Kittredge, Caitlin

NOCTURNE CITY (UF—V5, S4, H3)

St. Martin's: *Night Life* (2008); *Pure Blood* (2008); *Second Skin* (2009); *Witch Craft* (2009); *Daemon's Mark* (2010)

Luna Wilder is a Nocturne City homicide detective and an Insoli—a werewolf without a pack to protect her. She is a typical UF heroine: lots of attitude, plenty of profanity, and a total lack of respect for authority—not helpful traits for the sole female detective at the Twenty-Fourth Precinct. Luna's on-again, off-again boyfriend is Dmitri Sandovsky, pack leader of the

Redbacks. Luna battles a variety of villains, including dangerous demons, powerful feuding witches, and a murderous—but attractive—wendigo as she keeps tracking down the bad guys, breaking all the rules as she goes, and trying to keep from being suspended from her job (yet again).

Kittredge, Caitlin (cont.)

BLACK LONDON (UF—V4, S3, H2)

St. Martin's: *Street Magic* (2009); *Demon Bound* (2009); *Bone Gods* (2011)

The paranormal section of London—the Black—is reminiscent of Simon R. Green's NIGHTSIDE. In the Black, the time is always just about midnight, and the supernatural creatures gather at the Lament Pub. The heroine of the series is "Pete" Caldecott, a detective for Scotland Yard. (You'll have to wait until the end of book 1 to discover Pete's actual first name.) Sixteen years ago, Pete and her friend Jack Winter, a powerful mage, had a fateful demon-summoning experience that ended tragically. In book 1, Pete must solve a series of child kidnappings, and Jack reappears, seemingly from the dead, with magically retrieved information about the crimes. Together, Pete and Jack head into the Black, where they battle villainous sorcerers and a powerful ghost who wants to live again. Book 2 deals with a bargain Jack made thirteen years ago with the demon Belial. That debt, which Jack has kept secret from Pete, must now be paid off, with horrible consequences for Jack. Although books 1 and 2 are both written in the third person, book 1 tells the story through Pete's thoughts and actions, and book 2 follows Jack.

Klasky, Mindy

AS YOU WISH (CH, SMR—V1, S3, H4)

Mira: *How Not to Make a Wish* (2010); *When Good Wishes Go Bad* (2010); *To Wish or Not to Wish* (2010)

In each book, the heroine is in the middle of a crisis—generally boyfriend related—when she receives an old brass lamp as a gift. When she touches the lamp, a genie pops out, offering her four wishes. Although the genie grants each wish, the result is not as the heroine had imagined. Nevertheless, each woman winds up with her soul mate. After her four wishes are granted, the heroine must pass on the lamp to another deserving person, and that is the catalyst for the next book.

Knight, Angela

MAGEVERSE (SMR—V5, S5, H3)

Master of the Night (Berkley, 2004); "Galahad" in *Bite* anthology (Jove, 2004); "Seduction's Gift" in *Hot Blooded* anthology (Jove, 2004); *Master of the Moon* (Berkley, 2005); *Master of Wolves* (Berkley, 2006); *Master of Swords* (Berkley, 2006); *Master of Dragons* (Berkley, 2007); "Moon Dance" in *Over the Moon* anthology (Berkley, 2007); "Vampire's Ball" in *Hot for the Holidays* anthology (Jove, 2009); *Master of Fire* (Berkley Sensation, 2010); *Master of Smoke* (Berkley, 2011)

All of the famous Arthurian characters live on in the twenty-first century in this series. Sir Gawain rides a Harley; King Arthur wears a Grateful Dead T-shirt; and Llyr, the fairy king, has to use a credit card instead of a bag of gold to pay for his motel room. Demons, dragons, and shape-shifters are also part of the mix. In book 1, a horde of vicious, energy-sucking vampires is unleashed on the world, and the remaining books involve tracking them down. Each book tells one couple's SMR story.

Knight, Deidre

GODS OF MIDNIGHT (SMR—V4, S4, H2)

Signet: *Red Fire* (2008); *Red Kiss* (2009); *Red Demon* (2010); *Red Mortal* (2011)

At the Battle of Thermopylae, the Persians defeated Sparta, with some demon help on their side. King Leonidas and his six top warriors all die in the fighting, but when they reach the banks of the river Styx, they are commandeered by Ares, god of war, to go back into the world as immortal battlers of demons and fighters of wars. In the twenty-first century, this translates into defeating powerful conniving demons who are harming the human population. Also involved is the fulfillment of an ancient prophecy. Each book tells one warrior's story as he battles the bad guys in modern-day America and finds his soul mate along the way.

Kohler, Sharie

MOON CHASERS (SMR—V4, S5, H2)

Pocket Star: *Marked by Moonlight* (2007); *Kiss of a Dark Moon* (2008); *To Crave a Blood Moon* (2009); *My Soul to Keep* (2010)

Gideon and Kit March are brother-sister lycan (werewolf) executioners. Most of these werewolves are savage killers who are executed by agents of the National Organization for Defense against Evolving and Ancient Lycanthropes (NODEAL). Books 1 and 2 follow each sibling through the steps of a soul-mate romance as he or she battles both the evil werewolves and the NODEAL bad guys who are trying to kill them both. Book 3 tells the story of Kit's brother-in-law, Sebastian, as he escapes from a dungeon and finds true love.

Krinard, Susan

FANE (HIS, SMR—V4, S4, H2)

> *Forest Lord* (San Val, 2002); *Lord of the Beasts* (Harlequin, 2008); *Lord of Legends* (Harlequin, 2009)

Dr. Dolittle meets Greenpeace in this series set in nineteenth-century England, where the Fane, a race of magical shape-shifters, meet and mate with the local gentry. The Fane are sidhe, Irish fae who can take human shape, converse with animals, and exhibit other magical talents. They are vegetarians and fight fiercely for animal rights. In each book, one or two villains threaten the protagonists' relationship, with the first half of each book devoted to building up the stories behind the threats and the last half following the bumpy road to the inevitable happy ending.

Lane, Amy

LITTLE GODDESS (SMR—V5, S5, H3)

> iUniverse: *Vulnerable* (2005); *Wounded* (2006); *Bound* (2007); *Rampant* (2010)

This is an SMR series with a twist: multiple soul mates, or "beloveds." Cory Kirkpatrick is a nineteen-year-old goth girl working the night shift at the local Chevron station, where she meets some of the sidhe (fairies from Irish folklore), vampires, and shape-shifters who inhabit the hills near Sacramento. Cory soon falls for one (and then more) of these preternatural beings and begins to develop powers of her own. Cory and her men spend a lot of time in bed, largely because sex feeds their powers (à la Anita Blake and Meredith Gentry), and the sex can be male-female, male-male, or female-male-male. They are an extremely emotional lot—plenty of angst and tears from both men and women. Stories focus primarily on the relationships between Cory and her lovers. Villains are other supernaturals who want to interrupt the lives of the good guys in various evil ways.

Laurenston, Shelly

PRIDE (SMR—V4, S5, H5)

Brava: *The Mane Event* (2007); *The Beast in Him* (2008); *The Mane Attraction* (2008); *The Mane Squeeze* (2009)

In this series, the action revolves around several streetwise shifter groups (i.e., lions, tigers, wolves, bears, wild dogs, hyenas) on the urban East Coast. The dialogue is raunchy, the sex is hot, and the humorous sniping among the characters is never ending. Each book follows a pair of the characters from first sight to soul-mate status, with lots of hardcore graphic sex and coarse language. Laurenston has also written two similar series: MAGNUS PACK (modern-day shifters) and DRAGON KIN (medieval soul mates).

Laurey, Rosemary

VAMPIRE SERIES (SMR—V3, S4, H2)

Zebra: *Kiss Me Forever* and *Love Me Forever*, books 1 and 2 under one cover (2004); *Be Mine Forever* (2005); *Keep Me Forever* (2006); *Midnight Lover* (2007)

The series focuses on a small group of mostly male British vampires as they meet the twenty-first-century American women (two of whom are ghouls) who become their soul mates. In *Keep Me Forever*, a female vampire finds that her true love is a shape-shifter. Some books take place in England and some in the United States. Each story focuses on the primary romantic relationship, with negligible plots involving various villains (both human and supernatural) who put the female soul mate in mortal danger. In several cases, the female soul mate dies violently and then is brought back to vampire "life" by her lover, so there are many scenes involving the training of the newbie vamp. The roller-coaster plots have several semiclimactic scenes resolving individual plot points followed by a final resolution of all of the conflict, which then allows the couple to go off into their happy future.

Laurie, Victoria

PSYCHIC EYE MYSTERIES (CH—V3, S3, H3)

Signet: *Abby Cooper, Psychic Eye* (2004); *Better Read Than Dead* (2005); *A Vision of Murder* (2005); *Killer Insight* (2006); *Crime Seen* (2007); *Death Perception* (2008); *Doom with a View* (2009); *A Glimpse of Evil* (2010)

Abigail "Abby" Cooper is a psychic who lives in the Detroit metropolitan area. Along with her boyfriend Dutch Rivers, an FBI agent, she solves problems and investigates mysteries—both human and supernatural. No vampires or werewolves—just a ghost or two. One distracting note: there are many small but annoying proofreading errors in all of the books (e.g., *palpable* for *palatable*, *seem* for *seen*, *who's* for *whose*).

Laurie, Victoria (cont.)

GHOST HUNTER MYSTERIES (CH—V2, S2, H3)

Signet: *What's a Ghoul to Do?* (2007); *Demons Are a Ghoul's Best Friend* (2008); *Ghouls Just Haunt to Have Fun* (2009); *Ghouls Gone Wild* (2010); *Ghouls, Ghouls, Ghouls* (2010)

M. J. Holliday and her gay partner Gilley Gillespie are ghost busters. M. J. is a medium who can see and speak to ghosts, and Gilley is a computer-savvy tech guy. A third major character is Dr. Steven Sable, a rich and handsome surgeon who starts out as a client and ends up as an investor and a boyfriend for M. J. Plots revolve around M. J.'s ghost-busting cases. A new love interest turns up in book 4.

Leigh, Lora

BREEDS (SMR—V4, S5, H1)

FELINE BREEDS: *Tempting the Beast* (Ellora's Cave, 2008); *The Man Within* (Ellora's Cave, 2008); *Kiss of Heat* (Ellora's Cave, 2005); "The Breed Next Door" in *Hot Spell* anthology (Berkley Sensation, 2006); *Megan's Mark* (Berkley, 2006); *Harmony's Way* (Berkley, 2006); *Tanner's Scheme* (Berkley, 2007); *Dawn's Awakening* (Berkley, 2008); "A Jaguar's Kiss" in *Shifter* anthology (Berkley, 2008); *Mercury's War* (Berkley, 2008); "Christmas Heat" in *The Magical Christmas Cat* anthology (Berkley, 2008); *Bengal's Heart* (Berkley, 2009); *Lion's Heat* (Berkley, 2010); "A Christmas Kiss" in *Hot for the Holidays* anthology (Jove, 2009)

WOLF BREEDS: "Wolfe's Hope" in *Primal Heat* anthology (prequel; Ellora's Cave, 2004); *Jacob's Faith* (Ellora's Cave, 2004); *Aiden's Charity* (Ellora's Cave, 2007); *Elizabeth's Wolf* (Ellora's Cave, 2005); "In a Wolf's Embrace" in *Beyond the Dark* anthology (Jove, 2009); *Styx's Storm* (Berkley, 2010)

COYOTE BREEDS: *Soul Deep* (Ellora's Cave, 2007); *Coyote's Mate* (Berkley, 2009)

Ascertaining the reading order for this series is complicated. For the combined chronology for the entire BREEDS series, visit the author's website, at

They were created, they weren't born. They were trained, they weren't raised. They were taught to kill, and now they'll use their training to ensure their freedom.

They are Breeds. Genetically altered with the DNA of the predators of the earth. The wolf, the lion, the cougar, the Bengal: the killers of the world. They were to be the army of a fanatical society intent on building their own personal army.

Until the world learned of their existence. Until the Council lost control of their creations, and their creations began to change the world.

Now, they're loose. Banding together, creating their own communities, their own society, and their own safety, and fighting to hide the one secret that could see them destroyed.

The secret of mating heat. The chemical, the biological, the emotional reaction of one Breed to the man or woman meant to be his or hers forever. A reaction that binds physically. A creation that alters more than just the physical responses or heightens the sensuality. Nature has turned mating heat into the Breeds' Achilles' heel. It's their strength, and yet their weakness. And Mother Nature hasn't finished playing yet.

Man has attempted to mess with her creations. Now, she's going to show man exactly how she can refine them.

Killers will become lovers, lawyers, statesmen, and heroes. And through it all, they will cleave to one mate, one heart, and create a dynasty.

Lora Leigh's premise for the Breeds series, in the
foreword to her "A Jaguar's Kiss," in *Shifter*

www.loraleigh.com (click on "Breed Chronology" in the list at the left of the screen). The books are presented here in order by breed. The order given does not match the order in which the books were published, nor does it match the order given on Amazon.com. According to the author, the books were spread among three different publishers and some were published out of order.

All of the BREEDS books revolve around the actions of the evil Genetics Council, which operated secret labs in which twisted scientists created genetic beings constructed from a mix of human DNA and animal DNA. Their purpose was to create ruthless, disposable soldiers called Breeds. When the scientists found that they could not totally control the Breeds, they tried to destroy them all. The series begins after some of the breeds escape and go public, creating uproar among the populace and engendering a variety of responses from government officials. Each book tells the story of one couple's journey from first meeting to soul-mate status, with explicit sex as their major activity. Plots include attempts by various scientists and hunters to recapture individual Breeds and mean-spirited attempts to completely dehumanize the Breeds' lives. Many characters appear in multiple books. Most of the Breeds appear to be more ethical, moral, and intelligent than the humans. In general, each soul-mate couple includes one very alpha male, one strong but somewhat subservient female, and lots of graphic sex, which always includes one incredible male sexual characteristic that occurs only when a male Breed makes love to his one and only soul mate.

Leto, Julie

PHANTOM (SMR—V3, S4, H2)

Signet Eclipse: *Phantom Pleasures* (2008); *Phantom's Touch* (2008); *Kiss of the Phantom* (2009)

In the eighteenth century, an evil sorcerer curses six brothers and dooms them to spend eternity trapped inside magical inanimate objects (e.g., a painting, a mirror, a sword). Each book tells the story of one brother as he is freed from his confinement by his soul mate—a twenty-first-century American woman—and battles with the powerful forces who want to steal the magic for themselves.

Levitt, John

DOG DAYS (UF—V4, S3, H3)

Ace Fantasy: *Dog Days* (2007); *New Tricks* (2008); *Unleashed* (2009)

Mason is a magic practitioner with powers that would be stronger if he put forth some effort. He and his dog, Lou, live in San Francisco, where Mason makes his living as a freelance jazz guitarist and does occasional work for Victor, the chief magical enforcer for the Bay Area. Lou is an Ifrit, a small magical animal that chooses a person with magical powers to live with and protect. Lou and other Ifrits play major roles in all of the stories. Along with Victor and Eli, his mentor, Mason gets involved in a series of adventures involving practitioners who use magic for harmful reasons. Mason has a few love interests but nothing permanent.

Lewis, J. F. (Jeremy)

VOID CITY (UF—V5, S3, H3)

Pocket: *Staked* (2009); *ReVamped* (2009); *Crossed* (2010)

In Void City, Eric, a powerful vampire, owns a strip club and tries to balance his relationships with a number of women: his daughter, his aging ex-fiancée, his current girlfriend, her bewitching sister, and many others. Plots involve many brutal physical, mental, and emotional battles with various vamps, werewolves, and demons. Complicating matters is Eric's memory problem, which dates back to his mysterious rise from the dead.

Liu, Marjorie M.

DIRK AND STEELE (SMR—V3, S3, H1)

Tiger Eye (Love Spell, 2005); *Shadow Touch* (Love Spell, 2006); *The Red Heart of Jade* (Love Spell, 2006); *Eye of Heaven* (Leisure, 2006); *Soul Song* (Leisure, 2007); *The Last Twilight* (Leisure, 2008); *The Wild Road* (Leisure, 2008); *The Fire King* (Leisure, 2009); *In the Dark of Dreams* (Avon, 2010)

Dirk and Steele is an international detective agency whose employees have been shunned by human society because of their paranormal skills (e.g., mind reading, shape-shifting, healing). They travel the world solving crimes involving a variety of villains. Each book tells the story of one detective as he solves a crime and finds a soul mate. The stories have action-filled, complex plots, a notch above most soul-mate romances.

HUNTER KISS (UF—V3, S2, H1)

"Hunter Kiss" in *Wild Thing* anthology (Berkley, 2007); *The Iron Hunt* (Ace, 2008); *Darkness Calls* (Ace, 2009); "Armor of Roses" in *Inked* anthology (Berkley, 2010); *A Wild Light* (Ace, 2010)

In this dark world, Maxine Kiss, called Hunter by the demons and zombies that she executes, is the latest, and perhaps the last, in a long line of female Hunters. The twist here is that during the daytime, Maxine is covered with tattoos that serve as impenetrable armor, protecting her from any harm. After sunset, the tattoos strip off to form five small demons that fight for her. Maxine's companion is her lover, Grant, a former priest whose golden flute has supernatural musical powers. Demonic characters frequently attack from supernatural worlds, but much of the action is set on the dark and gloomy streets of Seattle. The series includes a number of mythological characters and a mystical labyrinth. The dark plots are complex, with many supernatural and mythical details.

Liu, Marjorie M. (cont.)

CRIMSON CITY

Liu is one of five authors for this series. See Maverick, Liz.

Lockwood, Cara

DEMON SERIES (CH—V3, S2, H5)

> Pocket Star: *Every Demon Has Its Day* (2010); *Can't Teach an Old Demon New Tricks* (2010)

Set in Dogwood County, Texas, Constance "Connie" Plyd, protagonist of this frenetically paced series, discovers that she is a prophet—selected by God to foretell future events that will keep humankind safe from Satan. Book 1 begins with the death of Connie's soon-to-be-ex husband, Jimmy (stabbed in the back by a demon), and Connie is the prime suspect. Complicating matters is the fact that the new sheriff is Nathan Garrett, who walked away without further contact after a one-night stand with Connie ten years ago. The plot includes a talking dog in training to be an angel, a renegade militant priest, the accident-prone ghost of Jimmy, and several bumbling members of Satan's demon army—all focused on Satan's desire to get together with the would-be mother of the Antichrist (Dante London—a Britney Spears clone). Lockwood uses more dialogue than narration, and the wisecracks come fast and furious—both from the demons and from the humans. Ratings are based on book 1. In book 2, Connie's friend Rachel must deal with a handsome supernatural bounty hunter who is after her demon-possessed husband, Kevin.

Love, Kathy

THE YOUNG BROTHERS (SMR—V4, S4, H4)

> Brava: *Fangs for the Memories* (2007); *Fangs but No Fangs* (2008); *I Only Have Fangs for You* (2009); *My Sister Is a Werewolf* (2007)

The series tells the erotic SMR stories of three handsome, wealthy, witty vampire brothers and their werewolf sister. Although there are a few relatively violent scenes in each book (with the heroine in danger), the emphasis is on the angst-ridden romances, with lots of graphic sex throughout.

MacAlister, Katie

DARK ONES (SMR—V2, S5, H5)

A Girl's Guide to Vampires (Love Spell, 2003; out of print, but available from libraries); *Sex and the Single Vampire* (Leisure, 2004); *Sex, Lies, and Vampires* (Love Spell, 2005); *Even Vampires Get the Blues* (Signet, 2006); "Bring Out Your Dead" in *Just One Sip* anthology (Love Spell, 2006); *Last of the Red, Hot Vampires* (Signet, 2007); *Ain't Mythbehaving*, two novellas (Pocket Star, 2007); *Zen and the Art of Vampires* (Signet, 2008); *Crouching Vampire, Hidden Fang* (Signet, 2009); *In the Company of Vampires* (Signet, 2010)

Each book follows one of the Dark Ones (soulless vampires) as he searches for and wins the love of his beloved (i.e., soul mate). With the winning of his beloved, the hero gets his soul back. Heroines are generally half-human, sassy, independent women with various preternatural abilities. Frequently, they have a physical defect (e.g., aftereffects of a stroke, scarred leg). Heroes are, of course, handsome, mysterious, and angst ridden. Minor characters provide comic relief.

AISLING GREY, GUARDIAN (SMR—V3, S4, H5)

You Slay Me (Onyx, 2004); *Fire Me Up* (Signet, 2005); *Light My Fire* (Signet, 2006); *Holy Smokes* (Signet, 2007)

More of the Otherworld of DARK ONES, this time focusing on the world of Aisling, a demon lord, and her beloved, Drake, leader of the green dragons. Jim, the demon dog, provides comic relief.

SILVER DRAGON (SMR—V3, S4, H5)

Signet: *Playing with Fire* (2008); *Up in Smoke* (2008); *Me and My Shadow* (2009)

MacAlister's tales of the DARK ONES Otherworld continue with May Northcott, a doppelgänger; her beloved, Gabriel Tauhou, leader of the silver dragons; and her sister Cyrene, a naiad who is May's twin. Many characters overlap from MacAlister's other series. Magoth, a sleazy, lesser-demon lord who controls May's life, provides comic relief. Jim, the demon dog, also joins in the merriment. Although the protagonists must battle a variety of supernatural villains, the stories are really all about the romantic relationships.

MacAlister, Katie (cont.)

LIGHT DRAGONS (SMR—V3, S4, H5)

> Signet: *Love in the Time of Dragons* (2010)

This series continues the stories of the dragons in MacAlister's AISLING GREY, GUARDIAN and SILVER DRAGON series. The light dragons are a newly developed dragon weyr led by Baltic and his mate, Ysolde, who spend much of their time at odds with the dragons of the other weyrs.

MacInerney, Karen

TALES OF AN URBAN WEREWOLF (UF—V2, S3, H4)

> Ballantine: *Howling at the Moon* (2008); *On the Prowl* (2008); *Leader of the Pack* (2009)

Sophie Garou has a great life in Austin, Texas, where she has a successful career with a prestigious accounting firm and a handsome attorney for a boyfriend. There's just one problem: Sophie is a werewolf, and up until now (book 1), the only person aware of that is her eccentric, psychic mother. But there are plenty of questions on Sophie's mind (resolved in books 2 and 3): What's going to happen when she's discovered by the local pack? Why is Heath (her human boyfriend) spending so many late nights at his office? Why is she so attracted to Tom, her best friend's werewolf lover? Who (or what?) is the mysterious Mark, Sophie's handsome client, who comes to her rescue one night with wings of fire?

Maclaine, Jenna

CIN CRAVEN (HIS—V3, S4, H3)

> St. Martin's: *Wages of Sin* (2008); *Grave Sins* (2009); *Bound by Sin* (2009); "Sin Slayer" in *Huntress* anthology (2009)

Dulcinea "Dulcie" (and "Cin") MacGregor Craven descends from a long line of witches. Book 1 introduces Dulcinea, who makes the difficult decision to give up her human life and become the vampire Cin, joining the Righteous, a band of warrior vampires who slay the rogue undead to defeat an ancient demon. Although she regrets leaving her human world, Cin (who was orphaned in the opening chapters) finds a new family with the Righteous and a lover and eventual husband in Michael, the vampire who turns her. The second book follows Cin and the Righteous to Edinburgh to determine if the resident vampire queen, Marrakesh, has turned rogue. Later books read much like mystery novels.

Maverick, Liz (books 1, 6–8); **Marjorie M. Liu** (book 2);
Patti O'Shea (books 3, 7); **Carolyn Jewel** (books 4, 7);
and Jade Lee (books 5, 7)

CRIMSON CITY (SMR—V4, S4, H1)

Love Spell: *Crimson City* (2005); *A Taste of Crimson* (2005); *Through a Crimson Veil* (2005); *A Darker Crimson* (2005); *Seduced by Crimson* (2006); *Crimson Rogue* (2006); *Shards of Crimson*, collection of four novellas (2007); *Crimson and Steam* (2009)

Liz Maverick is the creator of this series, but she shares the writing with the other authors. Set in a slightly futuristic Los Angeles that includes airborne neon advertisements, helicopter taxis, and "mechs" (mechanized humans used as solitary attack soldiers), this is really an urban SMR series. The new nickname for the city comes from the blood spilled in a recent war among the rich and haughty vampires; the weaker, but treacherous, humans; and the poor, hardscrabble werewolves. The city is again on the brink of interspecies war, and each group is fighting for total control. Midway through the series, demons from Orcus enter the fray. In each book, a couple (generally cross-species) lives out the soul-mate experience as they help to fight the war.

Mayhue, Melissa

DAUGHTERS OF THE GLEN (SMR—V3, S4, H3)

Pocket: *Thirty Nights with a Highland Husband* (2007); *Highland Guardian* (2007); *Soul of a Highlander* (2008); *A Highlander of Her Own* (2009); *A Highlander's Destiny* (2009); *A Highlander's Homecoming* (2010)

The series tells the SMR stories of a group of fae women who trace their ancestry back to Pol, king of the fae. The modern-day descendants have a variety of magical talents, including time travel. Generally, the time travelers either go back to late-thirteenth-century Scotland to edit tragic events or they travel forward from ancient Scotland to the twenty-first century to escape death. The heroes are the fae and half-fae Guardians, protectors of mortals and of the Fountain of the Souls. Villains are the Nuadians, rogue fae who want to capture Pol's female descendents and use them to reenter and conquer the Land of the Fae. Not every book includes time travel.

McCarthy, Erin

VEGAS VAMPIRES (SMR—V3, S5, H5)

Berkley: *High Stakes* (2008); *Bit the Jackpot* (2008); *Bled Dry* (2009); *Sucker Bet* (2010)

The casino scene in Sin City serves as a backdrop for a series of humorous stories about a group of humans and vampires. In book 1, Ethan Carrick owns a casino on the Strip; Alexis Baldizzi is the county prosecutor who falls for him. Their friends, acquaintances, and family members make up the rest of the cast of characters for the series, and each has his or her own set of personal problems. In each book, love scenes and battles with various villains ensue as vamps and humans meet their soul mates.

SEVEN DEADLY SINS (SMR—V1, S5, H3)

My Immortal (Jove, 2007); *Fallen* (Jove, 2008); *The Taking* (Berkley, 2010)

Set in modern-day New Orleans, this series includes fallen angels, demons, and cursed immortals who fall in love with young human women.

CUTTERSVILLE GHOSTS (SMR—V1, S5, H4)

Berkley: *A Date with the Other Side* (2007); *Heiress for Hire* (2007); "Charlotte's Web" in *An Enchanted Season* anthology (2007)

This series is set in modern-day Cuttersville, a small town in rural Ohio with lots of ghosts—mostly friendly ones. Stories follow the love lives of various townspeople. No vampires, no werewolves, no demons—just ghosts.

McCleave, Annette

SOUL GATHERERS (SMR—V3, S4, H1)

Signet Eclipse: *Drawn into Darkness* (2009); *Bound by Darkness* (2010); *Surrender to Darkness* (2011)

The soul gatherers are immortal penitents, warriors for Death (an actual "person"—a woman—in the stories) who must atone for their sins by spending five hundred years collecting the souls of departed mortals and delivering them either to heaven or hell, always on the alert for demons who want to steal the souls for their own dark purposes. Each book tells the SMR story of one soul gatherer and his lady love. Plots revolve around the recovery of ancient, biblical artifacts (e.g., the coins used to pay Judas). McCleave has posted a glossary on her website that explains some of the vocabulary of her world (www.annettemccleave.com/soul-gatherers/).

McCray, Cheyenne
MAGIC (SMR—V5, S5, H2)
St. Martin's: *Forbidden Magic* (2005); *Seduced by Magic* (2006); *Wicked Magic* (2007); *Shadow Magic* (2008); *Dark Magic* (2008)

McCray describes this series as "urban paranormal," but it's really an SMR series. The series focuses on the San Francisco D'Anu witches, with such a huge cast of paranormal creatures (from elves to fairies to demons) that the reader almost needs a chart to keep track of who's who. Each book features a different witch as she meets and mates with one of the D'Danann Enforcers (fae warriors) and battles the Fomorii Demons. Despite their paranormal characteristics, the witches and the warriors spend a lot of time eating human foods like pumpkin bread, roast beef, and potatoes. A different twist: graphic sex is not limited to the hero and heroine; everybody has a good time, even the villainous demons. Humans serve primarily as demon fodder. The series includes coarse language and profanity.

NIGHT TRACKER (CH—V5, S4, H2)
St. Martin's: *Demons Not Included* (2009); *No Werewolves Allowed* (2010); *Do Not Disturb the Undead* (2011)

Nyx is a half-human, half-Drow (Dark Elf) princess who is also a private investigator of paranormal crimes. During the day, Nyx appears to be human, but at night she becomes Drow, with blue hair and amethyst skin (which really puts a crimp in her social life). Nyx is also a member of the Night Trackers, a group that hunts down evil demons on the streets of Manhattan. Nyx's supernatural powers derive from the four elements: earth, air, water, and fire. Her two love interests are New York City Police Department detective and Paranorm Liaison Adam Boyd (who serves as a buffer between the police department and the supernatural community), and Rodán, her Drow mentor. Although the author calls this series urban fantasy (and Nyx certainly does have some angst-ridden moments), the series contains so many fashion references and girlfriend moments that it is closer to chick lit.

McGuire, Seanan
OCTOBER DAYE (UF—V4, S1, H2)
DAW: *Rosemary and Rue* (2009); *A Local Habitation* (2010); *An Artificial Night* (2010); *Late Eclipses* (2011)

October "Toby" Daye is a changeling—daughter of a fae mother and a human father. As book 1 begins, Toby is a knight-errant of the Duchy of

Shadowed Hills, in San Francisco—the only changeling ever to be so honored. Her liege lord, Duke Sylvester Torquill, has commanded her to find his missing wife and daughter. By page 11, poor Toby has been put under a curse—turned into a fish for fourteen years—by the kidnapper. When Toby returns to human life, she finds that she has lost her fiancé and daughter and any semblance of her precursed life, so she exiles herself from the fairy community and tries to make it on her own. Book 1 takes Toby through her recovery period as she solves the murder of her longtime friend and adversary, Countess Evening Winterrose. In book 2, Sylvester sends Toby to a nearby fiefdom to determine why his niece is not returning his calls—seemingly a simple baby-sitting job, but initial appearances can be deceiving. Book 3 takes Toby to the realm of Blind Michael, where she must locate missing fae and mortal children while trying to avoid becoming the prey of the Wild Hunt. Toby's adventures constantly engage her in physical battles, and she is usually covered in blood, bandages, and scars. Besides Sylvester, the men of the series include Tybalt, fairy king of the cats, with whom Toby has an ongoing, antagonistic relationship; Devin, Toby's former lover, who is the Faginesque leader of a ragtag group of changeling runaways; Connor, Toby's former (and, maybe, still) childhood sweetheart, a selkie who is now married to Sylvester's nutty daughter, Raysel, who hates Toby with a passion; and Quentin, a teenage fae courtier from Sylvester's court who accompanies Toby in book 2.

Mead, Richelle

GEORGINA KINCAID (UF—V2, S4, H4)

> Kensington: *Succubus Blues* (2007); *Succubus on Top* (2008); *Succubus Dreams* (2008); *Succubus Heat* (2009); "City of Demons" in *Eternal Lover* anthology (2009); *Succubus Shadows* (2010)

Georgina is a demon—a succubus to be exact—who makes her daytime living as the assistant manager of a bookstore in Seattle. Her best friends include two vampires; a fallen angel; and her boyfriend, Seth, a famous mystery novelist. To maintain her own life force, Georgina must periodically drain some of the life force from a human male through some level of sexual activity. Frustratingly, she has to be very careful to avoid any sensual acts with Seth, lest she drain away his life—even kissing is dangerous. Understandably, their romance follows a heartbreakingly downhill road. Plot lines include the usual paranormal dangers, including fallen angels, powerful vampires, evil demons, and human religious fanatics.

DARK SWAN (UF—V4, S5, H3)

Storm Born (Zebra, 2008); *Thorn Queen* (Zebra, 2009); *Iron Crowned* (Bantam, 2011)

Eugenie Markham (aka "Odile Dark Swan") is a shaman living near Phoenix. She spends her time hunting down evil fae creatures from the Otherworld and the Underworld and either killing them or sending them back. During the course of book 1, she learns of a startling prophecy—one that uncovers dark secrets about both her past and her future. She also attracts two handsome boyfriends: Dorian, a fae king, and Kiyo, a shape-shifting fox (*kitsune*). When word of the prophecy gets out, every demon in the Otherworld is out to get her, and Eugenie must learn how to bring her powers to their fullest heights to save herself. In book 2, Eugenie has become the Thorn Queen and must decide whether to focus her talents on her human life or her fae life. Book 3 tells more of her story. Mead also writes the young-adult series VAMPIRE ACADEMY.

Meyer, Stephenie

THE TWILIGHT SAGA (SMR—V3, S2 [books 1–3], S4 [book 4], H3)

Little, Brown Books for Young Readers: *Twilight* (2005); *New Moon* (2006); *Eclipse* (2007); *Breaking Dawn* (2008)

Although this series is marketed to teens, many adults are also reading the books and watching the related movies. Isabella "Bella" Swan is an attractive high school student who moves from her mother's sunny Phoenix home to live with her father in damp and dreary Forks, Washington, where she meets and falls for a seventeen-year-old vampire, Edward Cullen, who lives with his extended vampire family just outside of town. The plot includes a pack of werewolves living on an adjacent Indian reservation, one of whom (Jacob) is also in love with Bella. Each book includes plenty of ups and downs in Bella's love life, as well as suspenseful, and sometimes violent, battles with the bad guys, who range from bloodthirsty rogue vampires to the Vultura, the ruling council of vampires worldwide.

Moning, Karen Marie

HIGHLANDER SERIES (HIS, SMR—V3, S4, H2)

Dell: *Beyond the Highland Mist* (1999); *To Tame a Highland Warrior* (1999); *The Highlander's Touch* (2000); *Kiss of the Highlander* (2001);

The Dark Highlander (2002); *The Immortal Highlander* (2005); *Spell of the Highlander* (2006)

Virginal women and alpha lairds become soul mates in medieval Scotland amid meddling fae, Knights Templar, and Odin's Berserker warriors. Some books include time travel. All of the stories end with weddings and babies. *The Highlander's Touch* won the RITA Award for best paranormal romance (2001).

Moning, Karen Marie (cont.)

FEVER SERIES (UF—V4, S3, H1)
Dell: *Darkfever* (2007); *Bloodfever* (2008); *Faefever* (2009); *Dreamfever* (2010); *Shadowfever* (2010)

When MacKayla "Mac" Lane travels to fae-infested Dublin to find her sister's murderer, she discovers that she is a sidhe seer (i.e., she can see the fae). Mac gets caught up in a search for ancient fae relics that will enable her to save the world from fae domination. She has several love interests, primarily Barrons, the mysterious owner of the bookstore she manages (and lives above), and V'lane, a handsome but sly fae prince.

Monk, Devon

ALLIE BECKSTROM (UF—V4, S4, H1)
Roc: *Magic to the Bone* (2008); *Magic in the Blood* (2009); *Magic in the Shadows* (2009); *Magic on the Storm* (2010); *Magic at the Gate* (2010); *Magic on the Hunt* (2011)

Allison "Allie" Beckstrom is a Hound—a wizardlike person who can analyze a magical spell and trace it back to its caster. In Allie's world, magic is available to the general public through a series of grids laid across the city, and Hounds help keep people from using dark magic to harm others. Every act of magic exacts a price from its user—generally in the form of physical pain—so most Hounds rely on narcotics or alcohol. Allie uses just aspirin, but her heavy use of magic causes migraines and bruising, as well as spotty memory loss, so she has to keep a daily journal to jog her memory of day-to-day events. Allie's love interest is Zayvion Jones, a handsome but mysterious man who comes to her rescue time and time again, and she thinks she loves him—if she could just remember! Allie's adventures include corporate espionage, black magic, ghostly apparitions, and involvement both with the police department's Magic Enforcement Response Corps and with the Authority, a secret organization of magic users.

Morgan, Alexis

PALADINS OF DARKNESS (SMR—V4, S5, H2)

Pocket Star: *Dark Protector* (2006); *Dark Defender* (2006); *In Darkness Reborn* (2007); *Redeemed in Darkness* (2007); *Darkness Unknown* (2009); *Defeat the Darkness* (2010)

The human world is in constant danger from the world of the Others, dangerous beings who live deep in the earth and who try to cross the barrier between the two worlds at times of geological upheaval (e.g., earthquakes, active volcanoes, electronic interference). Ironically, the Paladins—immortal warriors who hold back the Others—are, in fact, products of human-Other liaisons. Paladins live and die repeatedly, becoming more like the Others with each death, until they finally go mad and must be destroyed by their handlers. Set in cities located near fault lines (e.g., Seattle, St. Louis), each book tells the story of one Paladin's battles with the Others and his discovery of his soul mate.

TALIONS (SMR—V4, S4, H2)

Pocket Star: *Dark Warrior Unleashed* (2008); *Dark Warrior Unbroken* (2009); *Dark Warrior Untamed* (2010)

The Kyth are supernatural beings who derive their energy from humans. Normal Kyth can pull energy by simply mingling with a crowd of people, but Rogue Kyth, who have out-of-control energy addictions, drain and kill humans. The Talions are enforcers who deliver eye-for-an-eye justice by stripping away all of the Rogues' energy and life force. Set in Seattle, each book tells the story of one Talion's battles with the Rogues and his discovery and wooing of his recalcitrant soul mate.

Murphy, C. E. (Catie)

WALKER PAPERS (UF—V3, S1, H3)

Luna: *Urban Shaman* (2009); "Banshee Cries" in *Winter Moon* anthology (2009); *Thunderbird Falls* (2009); *Coyote Dreams* (2009); *Walking Dead* (2009); *Demon Hunts* (2010)

Siobhan Grania MacNamarra Walkingstick (aka "Joanne Walker") is a six-foot-tall, half-Cherokee, half-Irish police officer in Seattle. She is also a trained and experienced auto mechanic, which was her first job with the police department. Although Joanne has changed her Indian name and repressed her heritage for most of her life, a near-death experience triggers her abilities as a shaman, and she begins to use trances and dreams to move back and forth between astral realms, trying to solve both human and immortal problems. Her sidekick is cabbie Gary Muldoon, who drums Joanne into her trances; her partner is Billy Holiday, a medium whose wife (Melinda) is a witch. Joanne's nemesis (and possible love interest) is her boss, Captain Michael Morrison, who tries to ignore Joanne's magic but keeps being drawn into it. Story lines include an evil banshee who kills several humans in a quest for power, an ancient Celtic god who leads the Wild Hunt in search of a missing Rider, a coven of witches who try to reanimate an ancient spirit, and a zombie invasion of Seattle. Plots are mystically labyrinthine at times—particularly during Joanne's frequent dreams and trances.

Murphy, C. E. (cont.)

NEGOTIATOR TRILOGY (UF—V3, S3, H2)

Luna: *Heart of Stone* (2007); *House of Cards* (2008); *Hands of Flame* (2008)

Margrit "Grit" Knight is a no-nonsense Manhattan legal aid attorney when she comes face to face with the supernatural world in the person of Alban Korund, a thousand-year-old winged, shape-shifting gargoyle who is being framed for murder. There are five Old Races: djinns, vampires, gargoyles, selkies, and dragons—all in danger of extinction, both from human interference and from supernatural power plays. The series follows Grit's adventures as she single-handedly maneuvers her way into both business and personal relationships with the leaders of the Old Races and forces them to make sweeping changes in their laws, resulting in violent repercussions in both the human and the supernatural worlds. Grit's African American heritage and the fact that the Old Races are swept up in prejudicial species-based misunderstandings reinforce the underlying theme of racism. Plots are dialogue heavy and filled with action—from fistfights to full-blown, fiery battles—and lots of bumps, bruises, and broken bones for Grit. Grit's two love interests are Alban and Tony Pulcella, a tightly wound New York Police Department homicide detective. Grit's primary antagonists are Eliseo Daisani, crooked businessman and master vampire, and Janx, crime lord and dragon leader. Although book 3 provides plot resolution, the author adds a few potential conflicts to the epilogue, thus leaving the door open for future adventures.

Neill, Chloe

CHICAGOLAND VAMPIRES (UF—V4, S2, H3)

NAL Trade: *Some Girls Bite* (2009); *Friday Night Bites* (2009); *Twice Bitten* (2010)

. . . .

> "Surely some humans do consent to the drinking," I suggested . . . "I mean, they walk willingly into some kind of vampire feeding. It's not like they're heading out for a garden party. And we've all seen *Underworld*. I'm sure there are humans who find that kind of thing . . . appealing."
>
> Ethan nodded. "Some humans consent because they want to ingratiate themselves to vampires, because they believe they're positioning themselves to serve as Renfields—servants—or because they find an erotic appeal."
>
> Merit and Ethan discuss the motivations of humans who attend vampire raves as blood sources, in Chloe Neill's *Friday Night Bites*

. . . .

Merit is a University of Chicago graduate student when a rogue vampire mortally wounds her and then the master of the Cardogan House, Ethan Sullivan, rescues her from death (i.e., changes her over). Merit, daughter of a wealthy Chicago family, is initially devastated by her change. In this world, vampires live in "houses," each led by a master. A handful of rogue vampires live independently, with no allegiance to the houses. The houses submit to the rules of a governing council in England. Merit is a typical UF heroine: brash, stubborn, and outspoken. When Merit's powers develop to a much greater degree than is normal for an initiate, she is appointed to a position that includes guarding Cardogan House and its master. Merit's love-hate interests are Ethan, of course, as well as Morgan, a leader of the rival Navarre House. Other characters include Merit's roommate, Mallory, a newbie sorcerer; Mallory's boyfriend, Catcher Bell, a powerful sorcerer; and Merit's grandfather, who heads up the city's ombudsman program, which serves as a buffer in the investigation of crimes between humans and supernaturals. Villains include a variety of traitorous house vampires. Werewolves and fairies are also involved in the plots.

O'Shea, Patti

Light Warriors (SMR—V4, S4 [book 1 = 5+], H1)
Tor: *In the Midnight Hour* (2007); *In Twilight's Shadow* (2008); *Edge of Dawn* (2009); *In the Darkest Night* (2010)

The Gineal are supernatural beings sworn to protect humankind from evil. The books focus specifically on the adventures of several of the Gineal's Enforcers (Light Warriors), magical troubleshooters who protect the innocent from being harmed by dark magic while constantly fighting their own personal battles with the continuing temptations of the dark forces. Each book tells the story of one warrior as he or she fights off evildoers, tries to avoid going over to the dark side, and finds a soul mate. Book 1 is rated 5+ for sensuality because of several scenes of sadomasochism.

O'Shea, Patti (cont.)

CRIMSON CITY

O'Shea is one of five authors for this series. See Maverick, Liz.

Palmer, Pamela

FERAL WARRIORS (SMR—V5, S4, H1)

Avon: *Desire Untamed* (2009); *Obsession Untamed* (2009); *Passion Untamed* (2009); *Rapture Untamed* (2010); *Hunger Untamed* (2011)

The Feral Warriors are shape-shifting soldiers for the Therian race, each able to shift into his namesake animal (e.g., Lyon, Vhyper, Wulfe, Foxx). Now numbering only nine, they are in constant battle with their two enemies, the daemons and the mages. The daemons send their minions, the soul-sucking "dradens," to attack both warriors and humans, and the mages try to defeat the warriors through the use of dark magic and bewitching spells. In each book, one of the warriors gets involved with a woman, sometimes human and sometimes supernatural, who turns out to be his soul mate. The men are very alpha, and the women, though plucky, are relatively submissive. Plots center around the retrieval of the daemon blade in which the daemon leaders have been imprisoned for centuries. The blade has fallen into the hands of the mages, who are trying to complete the ceremony to free the daemons.

Parks, Lydia

EROTIC VAMPIRE SERIES (SMR—V5, S5+, H1)

Aphrodisia: *Addicted* (2008); *Devour Me* (2009)

Each book contains two vampire novellas written by one of the authors of *Sexy Beast*, a series of erotic paranormal anthologies. Each book has a warning on the back cover ("WARNING! This is a REALLY HOT book. Sexually Explicit"). Interwoven through the thin plots are many sexual scenes that include multiple partners and graphic bloodlust.

Peeler, Nicole

JANE TRUE (UF—V4, S4, H2)

Orbit: *Tempest Rising* (2009); *Tracking the Tempest* (2010); *Tempest's Legacy* (2011)

Jane True lives in small-town, coastal Maine with her father. Her mother disappeared years ago—never to be heard from again. Jane feels like a pariah because of her mother's strange behavior and because of her own connection with the drowning of her boyfriend several years ago. In book 1, Jane learns that her mother was not human and that her own strange attraction to the ocean is caused by her supernatural heritage. She meets Ryu, a vampire who is investigating the murders of several Halflings—half-human supernaturals—and love blossoms. Other supporting characters include Anyan, a sexy shifter; Nell, a gnome; and Trill, a "kelpie." Jane soon learns that a number of her hometown acquaintances are also supernaturals. Books 2 and 3 had not yet been released at the time of this writing.

Pettersson, Vicki

Signs of the Zodiac (UF—V4, S3, H1)

"The Harvest" in *Holidays Are Hell* anthology (prequel; Harper, 2007); *The Scent of Shadows* (Eos, 2007); *The Taste of Night* (Avon, 2007); *The Touch of Twilight* (Eos, 2008); *City of Souls* (Eos, 2009); "Dark Matter" in *Unbound* anthology (Eos, 2009); *Cheat the Grave* (Eos, 2010)

Welcome to one of the most complex plot lines in this bibliography. Joanna Archer (aka "Olivia," "Archer," and "Kairos") has spent an unhappy childhood as the daughter of the owner of the Valhalla Hotel and Casino in Las Vegas—only to discover that he isn't her real father. In reality, Joanna is the daughter of supernatural parents—one good and one evil. Her birth father is the leader of the Shadows, bad guys who love to kill, maim, and generally create chaos; her long-missing mother, Zoe, is an agent of the Light—the good guys who fight off the Shadows. Each side has twelve agents with enhanced senses, strength, and weapons—one warrior for each sign of the zodiac. Zoe was the archer (Sagittarius). Now, Joanna must take her place. In book 1, Joanna's sister is murdered, and Joanna receives plastic surgery to assume her sister's identity. Throughout the rest of the series, she wears a mask during battle scenes to keep her identity hidden—and no one ever rips it off! One other aspect of the story concerns a comic-book shop that publishes the adventures of the Light and the Shadows as superhero graphic novels. This shop is also the place where the changelings hang out: young children who protect the warriors on neutral ground and spread the superheroes' battle stories among their peers. The series follows Joanna and the Light heroes as they argue among themselves and battle the Shadows. Joanna's two love interests are Ben, her childhood true love, and Hunter, a sexy Light agent.

Readers must suspend logic as well as disbelief, as many incidents rely on truly tenuous coincidences and insights that don't necessarily track with previous events. A multitude of ever-changing metaphysical circumstances make plots even more complex.

Phoenix, Adrian

THE MAKER'S SONG (UF—V5, S5, H1)

Pocket: *A Rush of Wings* (2009); *In the Blood* (2009); *Beneath the Skin* (2009); *Etched in Bone* (2011)

Heavy on satanic mythology, the story follows Dante Baptiste (aka "Dante Prejean" and "S"), a New Orleans vampire who may have much more power and influence than he knows. In the mortal world, Dante is a rock musician whose early years were controlled by a mad doctor. As Dante attempts to retrieve the buried memories of his painful past, a serial killer is pursuing him and his loved ones. Dante's love interest is FBI Special Agent Heather Wallace, who is torn between her FBI duties and her feelings for Dante. Vampires are called "nightkind," and there are two types: true blood (born) vampires and made vampires. Supernatural characters include fallen angels and various underworld beings. Villains include shadowy government forces and the perpetrators of Project Bad Seed, a secret psychopathological experiment that corrupted young children (including Dante). Each book contains a glossary of Dante's Cajun phrases as well as many mythological terms.

Popp, Robin T.

NIGHT SLAYER (SMR—V3, S4, H1)

Warner Forever: *Out of the Night*, e-book only (2005); *Seduced by the Night*, e-book only (2006); *Tempted in the Night* (2007); *Lord of the Night* (2007)

In this series, El Chupacabra is a South American creature that feeds at night and turns to stone at sunrise. Humans bitten and killed by El Chupacabra change into vampires after death. Any vampire created by El Chupacabra also turns to stone in the daytime. The protagonists are vampire hunters (night slayers)—some human and some changelings (humans who have been bitten but not killed). Each book tells the SMR story of one night-slayer couple, with the usual plot interventions from evil vamps and other villains—both human and supernatural.

Pratt, T. A. (Tim)

Marla Mason (UF—V3, S3, H4)

Bone Shop (prequel; www.lulu.com, 2009); *Blood Engines* (Spectra, 2007); *Poison Sleep* (Spectra, 2008); *Dead Reign* (Spectra, 2008); *Spell Games* (Spectra, 2009)

Tough and pragmatic Marla Mason is the chief sorcerer of Felport, a large East Coast city. Marla is a martial magician, or battle sorcerer, who specializes in fighting her way out of bad situations, sometimes with the aid of her magical cloak. (The purple side of the cloak turns her into an unbeatable killing machine; the white side heals all of her injuries.) Marla runs a shadow government, working with Felport's human civic authorities to protect the ordinaries (i.e., humans) from magical dangers. Marla's consigliere is the wisecracking Rondeau, a "free-floating parasitic psychic entity of unknown origin" (*Poison Sleep*, p. 152) who has taken over the body of an attractive young man. Marla's adventures include battles with an ancient frog god, a monstrous nightmare creature, an evil mushroom god, and Death himself—along with a few recalcitrant sorcerers and her grifter brother, Jason. Although there is plenty of violence and some sex (including a brief sadomasochism scene), those scenes are described concisely and with so few details that the violence and sensuality ratings have been set at a moderate level.

Rardin, Jennifer

Jaz Parks (UF—V5, S2, H3)

Orbit: *Once Bitten* (2007); *Twice Shy* (2008); *Another One Bites the Dust* (2009); *Biting the Bullet* (2008); *Bitten to Death* (2008); *One More Bite* (2009); *Bite Marks* (2009); *Bitten in Two* (2010)

Jasmine "Jaz" Parks (aka "Lucille Robinson") is a CIA assassin with a few magical skills and plenty of sarcastic attitude. Her partner, and love interest, is Vayl, a three-hundred-year-old vampire. Together, they travel the globe, hunting down and killing supernatural enemies of the U.S. government—with many up-close and violent battles. Other members of their team are Cassandra, a seer; Miles Bergman, an inventive genius; Cole Bemont, former private investigator and skilled sniper; and special ops commander David Parks, Jaz's brother. Also part of the action is Raoul, Jaz's spirit guide who allowed her to come back to life after she was killed in a battle that took place just prior to book 1. Bergman's inventions are of the James Bond type (e.g., contact lenses that blink into either telescopic or night vision, impenetrable

. . . .

Jasmine, correct me if I am wrong. But in the past three months you have been murdered by a Kyron and brought back to life by Raoul. Spent weeks in hospital. Become an aunt. Endured killer nightmares. Come to terms with the loss of your fiancé. Saved the world at least twice. Freed your brother from a cursed existence only to see him die. Rescued your niece from otherworldly soul stealers. Sighed with relief when David did come back to this life, but then lost that relief because the next minute you found your father was the target of a murderer.

Ah, the life of a UF heroine! Vayl sums up the reasons Jaz
is feeling a bit tense, in Jennifer Rardin's *Bitten to Death*

. . . .

armor that bonds with the wearer's DNA). Sexual tension between Jaz and Vayl builds up to a fever pitch, book by book, with a release (finally!) in an extremely brief scene at the very end of book 5.

Raye, Kimberly

Dead End Dating (CH—V3–4, S2–4, H4)

Dead End Dating (Ivy, 2006); *Dead and Dateless* (Ballantine, 2007); *Your Coffin or Mine* (Ballantine, 2007); *Just One Bite* (Ballantine, 2008); *Sucker for Love* (Ballantine, 2009); *Here Comes the Vampire* (Ballantine, 2010)

Lilliana "Lil" Marchette is a born vampire and a fashionista who lives in Manhattan (think Carrie Bradshaw as a vamp). In book 1, she has just opened Dead End Dating, a matchmaking service. If Lil can't make this business work, she's destined for a career managing one of her family's copy stores. Lil's love interest is Ty Bonner, a bounty hunter who is a made vampire. Lil's snobbish family has taught her to shun made vamps, but this guy really turns her on. Villains include evil humans, vampires, warlocks, and spirits. With the exception of book 1, each book contains one or two sex scenes, with the level of graphic detail going up in the later books, but the emphasis in the series is definitely on the humor, especially Lil's attempts to keep her business afloat by recruiting nearly every unmarried person she meets, from cab drivers to handymen to computer geeks. Lowest levels of violence and sensuality are in book 1.

Reinke, Sara

THE BRETHREN (SMR—V5, S4, H1)

Dark Thirst (Zebra, 2007); *Dark Hunger* (Zebra, 2008);
Dark Passion (DDP Literary Press, 2009)

This trilogy tells the story of the Brethren—a vampire clan living in isolation in Kentucky horse country. The Elders strictly control clan members' lives. Members are not allowed to leave Brethren lands and must marry within the clan. These vampires are different from the usual in that they can procreate, tolerate sunlight, and eat regular food (in addition to blood, of course). Brandon Noble, the hero of book 1, is a deaf-mute because of a childhood injury. He sets the series plot in motion when he runs away to New York City to avoid having to kill his first human during a bloodlust ceremony. There, he gets together with his soul mate Angelina ("Lina"). Each book continues the story of the Brethren and follows the romance of a soul-mate couple.

Resnick, Laura

ESTHER DIAMOND (UF—V4, S3, H3)

DAW: *Disappearing Nightly* (2006; out of print, but available in some libraries; a reissue is in the works); *Doppelgangster* (2010); *Unsympathetic Magic* (2010); *Vamparazzi* (2011)

Resnick summarizes the plot of *Disappearing Nightly* in *Doppelgangster*, so readers could begin the series there. Esther Diamond has no magical skills of her own, but she hangs around with people who do. Esther is a struggling New York actress who earns money as a singing waitress in a mob-financed Italian restaurant, where she is on a first-name basis with many of the local wise guys. Her best friend, Max, is a 350-year-old sorcerer who appears to be in his seventies. Esther's love interest is straight-arrow detective Connor Lopez, who seems to be human—until a strange incident at the climax of book 2. Esther's adventures are all magic related, and they include a power-hungry sorcerer's apprentice, a serial killer who creates doppelgängers of his victims, and angry spirits who want to use Esther as a human sacrifice.

Richardson, Kat

GREYWALKER (UF—V3, S3, H1)

Roc: *Greywalker* (2009); *Poltergeist* (2009); *Underground* (2009); *Vanished* (2009); "The Third Death of the Little Clay Dog" in *Mean Streets* anthology (2009); *Labyrinth* (2010)

This series is urban fantasy insofar as it takes place in Seattle and has a protagonist who is an independent young woman. But Harper Blaine is missing the passionate, angst-ridden introspection that characterizes most UF heroines. For example, Harper mentions her estrangement from her mother in passing, but not until book 4 do we get a few specifics. Told in the first person, the dialogue-heavy plots deal primarily with Harper's day-to-day activities. She spends little time meditating about her life, except in book 1 when she has trouble adjusting to the Grey, and in book 4, when we finally meet Mom. In book 1, Harper, a private investigator, is declared dead for two minutes after a vicious attack and wakes to find that she can access the Grey—a foggy realm that is the home of ghostly preternatural creatures. The primary manifestation of this new ability is that Harper sees both the ghosts of the dead and the brightly colored auras of the living. The books detail her progress as she solves a variety of supernatural-related crimes (largely by interviewing lots of people), gradually learning to control the Grey and use it to her advantage. Although Harper has few friends, she does become close to a witch, who helps her deal with the Grey, and develops not-quite friendships with some vampires. The two men in her life (Will, a very nonmagical antiques auctioneer, and Quinton, a mysterious handyman with an awareness of the paranormal world) provide minimal diversion, but not much passion—out of sight, out of mind seems to be Harper's motto.

Roberts, Nora

Sign of Seven Trilogy (SMR—V4, S4, H4)

Jove: *Blood Brothers* (2007); *The Hollow* (2008); *The Pagan Stone* (2008)

This is a typical Nora Roberts trilogy, but with a supernatural twist. The books center on Hawkins Hollow, Maryland, where three best friends (Cal Hawkins, Fox O'Dell, and Gage Turner) accidentally awaken an ancient evil demon when they sneak into the woods and spill blood on the Pagan Stone during a blood brother ceremony on their shared tenth birthday. This demon returns to the town for a week every seven years and wreaks plague-style havoc on the townspeople. The friends are unsuccessful in their fight to stop this evil until three women, each with a connection to the demon, show up. The six join forces and, of course, a couple pairs up in each book.

Robertson, Linda

Circle/Persephone Alcmedi (UF—V3, S3, H2)

Juno: *Vicious Circle* (2009); *Hallowed Circle* (2009); *Fatal Circle* (2010)

Persephone ("Seph") Alcmedi is a solitary witch living in a rural area near Cleveland, Ohio. She doesn't like the politics of the coven and prefers a simple life, writing her newspaper column and getting used to having her cranky grandmother as a housemate. In this world, supernaturals have few civil rights, and shifters must "kennel" in safe houses at the full moon. Seph provides cage space in her basement for her shifter friends, one of whom is a possible love interest: Johnny, a mysterious goth musician who has been flirting with Seph for months. In book 1, Seph tangles with a master vampire (Menesso) and his right-hand assassin (Goliath) as she tries to solve the murder of a shifter friend. In book 2, Seph is nominated as high priestess of the coven and must pass a grueling examination along with several other powerful witches. In book 3, the fairies want Seph's help in destroying Menesso. The story line that connects the series is the possibility that Seph is the Lustrata—the magical one who will bring witches, shifters, and vampires together in a peaceful coexistence.

Rowe, Stephanie

IMMORTALLY SEXY (SMR—V2, S3, H5)

Warner: *Date Me Baby One More Time* (2006); *Must Love Dragons* (2006); *He Loves Me, He Loves Me Hot* (2007); *Sex and the Immortal Bad Boy* (2007)

This is a peek at the funny side of the Dark Realm, telling the stories of a strange group of characters, including Satan himself, his girlfriend, his half-human conniving son (Satan Jr.), his various levels of guardians, tricky angels, immortal warriors (both good and evil), and the innocent and not-so-innocent humans who get caught in the cross fire. Even the battles are presented in a humorous way. For example, in book 1, the heroine is the immortal guardian of the Goblet of Eternal Youth—a shape-shifting espresso machine named Mona—and her eventual soul mate (who is the inventor of the carb-free pretzel) initially tries to kill her so that he can grab Mona and break a family curse. Each book takes one Satan-connected couple from the first moments of attraction to soul-mate status, with lots of humorous adventures and sarcastic sniping along the way.

Rowen, Michelle

IMMORTALITY BITES (CH—V3, S4, H3)

Forever: *Bitten and Smitten* (2006); *Fanged and Fabulous* (2007); *Lady and the Vamp* (2008); *Stakes and Stilettos* (2009); *Tall, Dark, and Fangsome* (2009)

Most of the books focus on Sarah Dearly and her life as a newbie vampire as she tries to avoid being killed by vampire hunters and falls more and more in love with Thierry de Bennicoeur, a master vampire. Of course, her life has other complications: getting fired from her job, being tempted by other handsome vampiric men, shopping for designer shoes with her girlfriends, and coping with the fact that Thierry is already married to the beautiful Veronique—and has been for six hundred years. Book 3 has more of an SMR plot, as it tells the story of Janie Parker and Michael Quinn, who play supporting roles in the earlier books. Plots are paper thin and filled with relatively unbelievable coincidences and saved-by-the-bell incidents. These vampires are a bit wimpy—no real super strength or speed—and human vampire hunters frequently overpower and outmaneuver them. Book 4 resolves all of the series conflict.

Rowen, Michelle (cont.)

LIVING IN EDEN (UF—V3, S3, H3)
Berkley Sensation: *The Demon in Me* (2010); *Something Wicked* (2010)

Psychic Eden Riley is a police consultant who becomes possessed by the demon Darrak when his human host is killed in a police manhunt. By night, Darrak exists inside Eden, but by day (for reasons that are tied to Eden's psychic powers), he becomes a corporeal human—unsurprisingly, a tall, dark, and sexy human. Darrak needs Eden's help to break the curse that took away his body and forced his spirit to move from host to host over the centuries, draining his hosts' energy until they died. In book 1, Eden is caught between two love interests: Ben Hanson, a down-to-earth, nonmagical police detective, and Darrak, her personal demon. Villains include various evil supernaturals and the Malleus, a centuries-old magic-hating organization that was responsible for such tragedies as the Salem witch trials. Book 2 deals with Eden's father, who disappeared before she was born. Hmm, I wonder if Dad just might have some supernatural genes of his own! The plot for the series focuses on Eden's adventures as she helps Darrak try to break his curse and prevent her own death.

Rowland, Diana

KARA GILLIAN (UF—V3, S4, H3)
Mark of the Demon (Bantam, 2009); *Blood of the Demon* (Bantam, 2010); *Secrets of the Demon* (DAW, 2011)

Kara Gillian is a homicide detective in small-town Beaulac, Louisiana. She is also a newbie summoner—a person who can call forth demons. Kara's male friends (and love interests) include Rhyzkahl, a demon lord, and Ryan Kristoff, an FBI agent. This is a police procedural series with a side order of demons—all kinds of demons. In book 1, Kara gets more than she bargains for when she accidentally summons a demon lord, who eventually becomes a link to Kara's investigation of a serial killer. In book 2, Kara and Ryan catch another serial killer with assistance from Rhyzkahl.

Rush, Jaime

OFFSPRING (SMR—V4, S4, H1)
Avon: *Perfect Darkness* (2009); *Out of the Darkness* (2009); *Touching Darkness* (2010); *Burning Darkness* (2011)

Two decades ago, a secret government agency collected a small group of men and women with a variety of psychic abilities (e.g., telekinesis, out-of-body travel, ability to predict the future) and infected them with "booster" chemicals to enhance their talents. When the boosters caused the psychics to lose their minds, the project was abandoned. Now, one of the original project directors, a sociopath named Darkwell, has discovered that the offspring of the original group have psychic talents even more advanced than their parents'. Darkwell wants to pump the offspring full of boosters and use them as his personal assassin team until they go crazy. But some of the offspring have banded together to fight Darkwing and to discover the truth about their parents. The series follows the team as they discover more offspring and battle Darkwell and his minions.

Russe, Savannah

DARKWING CHRONICLES (CH—V5, S5, H2)
Beyond the Pale (Pocket, 2009); *Past Redemption* (Pocket, 2009); *Beneath the Skin* (Pocket, 2009); *In the Blood* (Pocket, 2009); *Under Darkness* (Signet, 2008)

Daphne Urban is a centuries-old vampire who is forcibly recruited (i.e., join or die!) by the U.S. government for its covert Project Darkwing, which uses a team of vampires to battle terrorists. Her love interests include Darius della Chiesa, a sexy vampire slayer who works for a different undercover government agency, and St. Julien Fitzmaurice, a charming Irish alcoholic human who works for yet another secret government agency. One continuing plot point is the inability of these various clandestine agencies to work together or to share information, which results in many dangerous situations for the characters. Two other important characters are J, Daphne's boss at Darkwing (who may be in love with her), and Marozia ("Mar-Mar"), Daphne's meddling vampire mother—who is the commander of Darkwing. Plots include a shady arms dealer with terrorist connections, a dangerous drug dealer, an attempted assassination of a presidential candidate, a raid on Opus Dei to retrieve secret documents, a terrorist bomb threat, and a kidnapping with terrorist connections. These vampires can transform at will into giant bats, and they have the usual characteristics of bloodlust and sun intolerance. Graphic bloodlust scenes and over-the-top sexual encounters take the series to its high ratings in violence and sensuality. Daphne's insatiable sexual appetite is similar to that of Keri Arthur's Riley Jensen character. Although the series has a few UF characteristics (e.g., urban setting, plenty of angst), the endless fashion references, shopping sprees, and girlfriend scenes push it into CH.

Russe, Savannah (cont.)

Sisterhood of the Sight (SMR—V3, S4, H2)
Signet: *Dark Night, Dark Dreams* (2008)

The CIA's Alternative Investigations Unit has created Project AngelWay and has forcibly recruited four young women with paranormal talents to form its first team: a psychic, a voodoo priestess, a witch, and an animal communicator. Their job is to solve crimes with paranormal elements. As each woman becomes involved in dangerous escapades, she, of course, meets her soul mate.

St. Giles, Jennifer

Shadowmen (SMR—V3, S4, H1)
Pocket: *Touch a Dark Wolf* (2006); *The Lure of the Wolf* (2007); *Kiss of Darkness* (2009); *Bride of the Wolf* (2009)

Each book tells the SMR story of a couple who is part of a small group of humans and shape-shifting Blood Hunters—elite warriors of the Shadowmen —who are sworn to protect mortals. The villains include the sinister Dr. Cinatas (spell his name backward), as well as the Vladarian Order—a group of evil vampires who kill mortals, particularly Elans (a special type of human with magical blood), for their blood. Dr. Cinatas is the director of an evil medical corporation called Sno-Med (spell it backward), which collects Elan blood for the Vladarians. Plots include various attempts by the Vladarians to capture, torture, and/or kill human Elans and Blood Hunters.

Saintcrow, Lilith

DANTE VALENTINE (UF—V4, S3, H1)

Orbit: *Working for the Devil* (2007); *Dead Man Rising* (2007); *The Devil's Right Hand* (2007); *Saint City Sinners* (2007); *To Hell and Back* (2008)

Dante "Danny" Valentine is a necromance who raises the dead in a mildly futuristic society that travels on hovercrafts and wears data bands (think Dick Tracy's wristwatch) to communicate. Danny's love interests include Jason "Jace" Morgan, a shaman who walked away from their love affair some years ago, and Japhrimel ("Japh"), a demon who was formerly Lucifer's right-hand man and assassin. Danny's adventures include many battles with Lucifer and his minions as well as skirmishes with rogue demons, dangerous mob enforcers, and crooked police officers. This dark and violent series takes place several years after the world's religions have collapsed, and the old Egyptian gods are back. Paranormal beings are part of society, and children with psychic abilities are trained for public service. Two governmental groups run the world: Hegemony (the Americas, Japan, and Western Europe) and Putchkin (Russia, China, and Central Asia). Saintcrow changes the spellings of cities and countries, but many are quite recognizable (e.g., *Merica* = *America*; *Kebec* = *Quebec*). She also renames many of the usual paranormal beings (e.g., Nichtvren = vampire; Werecain = shape-shifter). Each book contains a glossary of Saintcrow's "created" words.

. . . .

The single biggest blow to the Religions of Submission had been the Awakening and the rise of the science of Power. When anyone can contract a Shaman or Ceremonial to talk to the god of their choice, and spiritual experiences become commonplace—not to mention Necromances proving an afterlife exists and Magi definitively proving the existence of demons—most organized religions had died a quick hard death, replaced by personal worship of patron gods and spirits. It was, in all reality, the only logical response on humanity's part.

Danny explains the recent religious history
of her world, in Lilith Saintcrow's *Saint City Sinners*

. . . .

Saintcrow, Lilith (cont.)

JILL KISMET (UF—V5, S3, H2)

Orbit: *Night Shift* (2008); *Hunter's Prayer* (2008); *Redemption Alley* (2009); *Flesh Circus* (2009); *Heaven's Spite* (2010)

Jill "Kiss" Kismet is a psychic and a hunter (of demonic creatures) in Santa Luz in the American Southwest. Trained by her late teacher, Mikhail, Jill works as an occult consultant with the local police department. As the liaison between the paranormal community and the police, Jill's job description includes exorcism and spiritual extermination. Jill's police department contact is Montaigne ("Monty"), who provides human backup and tries not to know too much about the dark side of Jill's supernatural adventures. Jill's nemesis is Pericles ("Perry"), the powerful hellbreed (demon) who runs the supernatural part of town. On her right wrist, Jill wears Perry's hellbreed mark (in the shape of puckered lips—a kiss), which gives her demonic strength and near immortality. She accepted the mark with Mikhail's blessing to attain strength enough to make her town safe from even the most powerful dark forces. Jill's love interest is Saul Dustcircle, a Native American werecougar, who arrives in Santa Luz in book 1 in search of his sister's killer. Each book focuses on the rise and fall of an evil and violent creature, including a rogue were, several psychotic hellbreeds, and a wendigo. Battle scenes are graphic and brutal. Although Jill is nearly immortal, she does sustain an excessive number of horrible injuries and spends many conscious and unconscious hours healing from various traumas. The author includes a glossary of demonic terms in each book.

Saintcrow also writes stand-alone paranormal novels, such as *The Demon's Librarian* (ImaJinn Books, 2009).

Sands, Lynsay

ARGENEAU VAMPIRES (SMR—V4, S4, H3)

A Quick Bite (Avon, 2005); *Love Bites* (Leisure, 2009); *Single White Vampire* (Leisure, 2008); *Tall, Dark and Hungry* (Leisure, 2009); *A Bite to Remember* (Avon, 2006); *Bite Me If You Can* (Avon, 2007); *The Accidental Vampire* (Avon, 2007); *Vampires Are Forever* (Avon, 2008); *Vampire, Interrupted* (Avon, 2008); *The Rogue Hunter* (Avon, 2008); *The Immortal Hunter* (Avon, 2009); *The Renegade Hunter* (Avon, 2009); "Vampire Valentine" in *Bitten by Cupid* anthology (Avon, 2010); *Born to Bite* (Avon, 2010); *Hungry for You* (Avon, 2010)

Books are listed in the reading order that Sands suggests on her website (www.lynsaysands.net), not in the order of their publication. These vampires prefer to call themselves immortals. Their vampiric condition is caused by bioengineered nanos in their blood, which work furiously to cure diseases and mend injuries, with the side effect of requiring excessive amounts of blood to keep them going. Each book tells the SMR story of a member of the Argeneau family, a wealthy, many-branched family that traces its lineage back to ancient Atlantis, where the nanos were first created. Sands provides a family tree on her website. The tone of the books varies greatly, from dark (e.g., *The Immortal Hunter*) to humorous (e.g., *The Accidental Vampire*). Female soul mates (called life mates) are generally petite, independent mortals. Villains range from misguided locals to evil immortals, with some books more plot driven than others.

Shayne, Maggie

WINGS IN THE NIGHT (SMR—V4, S4, H3)

Twilight Phantasies (Harlequin e-book, 2007); *Twilight Memories* (Harlequin e-book, 2007); *Twilight Illusions* (Harlequin e-book, 2007); *Born in Twilight* (Harlequin e-book, 2007); *Twilight Hunger* (Mira, 2010); *Embrace the Twilight* (Harlequin e-book, 2007); "Run from Twilight" and "Twilight Vows" in *Two by Twilight* anthology (Harlequin e-book, 2009); *Edge of Twilight* (Mira, 2010); *Blue Twilight* (Mira, 2010); *Prince of Twilight* (Harlequin, 2010); *Demon's Kiss* (Harlequin, 2007); *Lover's Bite* (Harlequin, 2008); *Angel's Pain* (Harlequin, 2008); *Prince of Twilight* (Harlequin, 2010). Early books in this series are available only in e-book format but are gradually being republished by Mira; titles are listed in the original reading order for the series.

Only the Chosen (humans who carry the Belladonna antigen in their blood) can be changed over to vampirism. This series tells the SMR stories of various vampires, humans, and shape-shifters as they battle a variety of villains and find their soul mates. The primary villains are rogue CIA agents who want to brainwash the most powerful vamps and use them as assassins and mad scientists who capture, torture, and experiment on the vampires. One of the scientists, Frank Stiles, seemingly has nine lives, as he continually gets caught, escapes, and strikes again in the next book.

Mira: *Bloodline* (2009) (SMR—V3, S4, H1)

In the related novel *Bloodline*, Lilith and Ethan have spent their childhoods in an experimental program run by the Division of Paranormal Investigations (DPI), a secret U.S. government agency. The DPI steals Chosen children and trains them to be vampire soldiers, brainwashing them into complete obedience. When Ethan and Lilith (both vampires by now) get together after escaping from the DPI farm, they must decide whether to escape for good or go back and rescue the other captives. Complicating their efforts is Ethan's brother, James, who may be working against them.

Shayne, Maggie (cont.)

IMMORTAL WITCHES (HIS, SMR—V3, S4, H2)

Eternity (Jove, 1998); *Infinity* (Jove, 1999); *Destiny* (Jove, 2001); *Witch Moon Rising, Witch Moon Waning* (Spilled Candy Publications, 2001); "Immortality" in *Out of This World* anthology (Jove, 2001); "Anytown U.S.A." in *Words of the Witches* anthology (Berkley, 2002); *Eternal Love*, contains *Eternity* and *Infinity* (Berkley, 2007); *Immortal Desire*, contains *Destiny* and *Immortality* (Berkley, 2007)

Immortal witches can be killed by fire or by having their hearts cut out. There are two kinds of witches: light and dark. Light witches become immortal by saving the life of another witch. Dark witches become immortal only by feeding off power from the cut-out heart of a light witch. Thus, the conflict for the series: dark witches constantly trying to cut out the hearts of light witches. Each book moves back and forth in time as a witchy couple fall in love, get separated, and then find each other after centuries apart. *Infinity* won the 2000 P.E.A.R.L. Award in the fantasy/magical category.

Showalter, Gena

LORDS OF THE UNDERWORLD (SMR—V4, S4, H3)

Harlequin: *The Darkest Fire*, e-book only (prequel; 2008); *The Darkest Night* (2010); *The Darkest Kiss* (2010); *The Darkest Pleasure* (2010); *The Darkest Prison*, e-book only (2009); *The Darkest Whisper* (2009); "The Darkest Angel" in *Heart of Darkness* anthology (2010); *Into the Dark*, all of the e-books combined in print (2010); *The Darkest Passion* (2010); *The Darkest Lie* (2010)

The Lords of the Underworld were immortal warriors battling the enemies of the gods. When Zeus chose Pandora to guard a special box full of demons (e.g., death, violence, pain), the warriors became jealous. They killed Pandora and opened the box, allowing all of the demons to escape. Zeus then decreed that each escaped demon would be bound to one of the warriors, who would spend eternity under its effects (e.g., Torin is bound to Disease, so everyone he touches gets a deadly plague). The box disappeared after the theft, and for centuries, bands of hunters have searched for the box and for the Lords. The hunters believe that the Lords are to blame for all of the troubles in the world. They want to capture the Lords, find the box, tear the demons out of the Lords, and lock them back in the box. The Lords have spent the past thousand years learning to control their demons, living quiet lives in a castle in Budapest. Now there are rumors that the box will soon be found. The Lords know that if the hunters rip out their demons their bodies will die, so they want to find the box first. The series focuses on the search for the box. Each book also tells one Lord's story as he meets and falls in love with his soul mate—generally a virginal human woman who is able to mitigate the effects of his curse through her own particular supernatural skill. *The Darkest Pleasure* won an honorable mention for the P.E.A.R.L. Award for best fantasy or magical romance (2008).

ALIEN HUNTRESS (SMR—V4, S4, H2)

Awaken Me Darkly (Downtown Press, 2006); *Enslave Me Sweetly* (Downtown Press, 2006); *Savor Me Slowly* (Pocket Star, 2007); *Seduce the Darkness* (Pocket Star, 2009); *Ecstasy in Darkness* (Pocket Star, 2010); "Tempt Me Eternally" in *Deep Kiss of Winter* anthology (Pocket, 2009)

The series is set in a mildly futuristic world populated by both mortals and "otherlanders"—aliens from other realms who travel through portals between their lands and ours. Many of the otherlanders are out to harm mortals in various ways. The protagonists are mostly human and half-human hunters and huntresses who police the alien population. Each book tells the SMR story of a female huntress and her man (frequently an alien).

ATLANTIS (SMR—V4, S4, H3)

Harlequin: *Heart of the Dragon* (2009); *Jewel of Atlantis* (2009); *The Nymph King* (2007); *The Vampire's Bride* (2009); *The Amazon's Curse*, e-book (2009) and included in *Into the Dark* anthology (2010)

The series tells the SMR stories of a group of supernaturals who live under the sea in Atlantis but make occasional trips to the surface (i.e., the contemporary mortal world). Each book focuses on one soul-mate couple but generally tells at least one other SMR story as well. The cast of characters includes nymphs, vampires, and shape-shifting dragons. Various Greek gods and goddesses are mixed in to stir up the plots. Several of the soul mates are mortal—generally virginal—young women. The conflict for most of the books is an interspecies war that has been going on for centuries, with the dragons versus the nymphs and vamps.

Showalter, Gena (cont.)

TALES OF AN EXTRAORDINARY GIRL (UF—V4, S4, H3)
Harlequin: *Playing with Fire* (2009); *Twice as Hot* (2010)

Belle Jamison is working at the Utopia Café when a mad scientist drops an experimental drug in her mocha latte and changes her life forever. Now, Belle has the power—but not the control—to harness the four elements: fire, water, air, and earth. She spends much of book 1 lighting objects—and buildings—on fire as she swings back and forth through an emotional maelstrom. Belle is the target for two rival groups: Paranormal Studies and Investigations, the good guys, and a group called Observation and Application of Supernatural Sciences, the bad guys. Each group wants to experiment on her and exploit her powers. One of the good guys, Rome Masters, rescues Belle from the baddies and helps her learn some control. By the end of book 1, they are in love, and Belle has decided to join Rome's team. Book 2 continues their adventures.

Silver, Eve

COMPACT OF SORCERERS (SMR—V5, S5, H2)
Demon's Kiss, e-book only (Grand Central, 2007); *Demon's Hunger* (Forever, 2008)

The Continuum, or Dragon Current, is the connecting "river" that keeps the forces of light and dark in perfect balance. The protagonists are sorcerers whose sole job is to guard the Continuum, protecting humankind against the evil demons that keep trying to cross over to the human world. Set in Toronto, each book tells one sorcerer's story as he battles the enemy and finds his soul mate.

Simmons, Wm. (William) Mark

CHRIS CSÉJTHE: HALF/LIFE CHRONICLES (UF—V5, S3, H4)

Baen: *One Foot in the Grave* (1996); *Dead on My Feet* (2005); *Habeas Corpses* (2007); *Dead Easy* (2008)

In this series, a supervirus made up of two lesser viruses—one carried in vampire saliva and one carried in vampire blood—causes vampirism. Since Christopher Cséjthe (pronounced "Chay-tay") received only one of the viruses during his transformation, he is only half a vampire. Neither fully human nor technically undead, he is not totally sun sensitive and can eat regular food, but he has super strength and does enjoy blood. Chris pulls strength and magic from the various supernatural creatures from whom he drinks. In Chris's world, groups of vampires live in demesnes, each headed by a Doman. The Domans are in a constant power struggle with one another, and Chris gets caught up in that struggle in a variety of ways. Chris's love interests include the ghost of Jennifer, his dead wife; Volpea, his shape-shifter lover; and Deirdre, a sexy young vampire. An overriding theme for the series is Chris's continuing hatred for his undead state. Another theme is Chris's family history, which extends back to Count Dracula himself. Chris has frequent nightmares in which he travels to the past and interacts with ancient relatives. Many literary and pop cultural references are scattered throughout the books. Plots include a wide variety of mythological monsters as well as an ancient Babylonian demon, cloned Nazis, vampire assassins, paramilitary black ops, lycanthropic lynch mobs, undead assassins, and lots of zombies. Chris is the usual UF hero—cocky, smart mouthed, and angst ridden. Plot structures are complex, with relatively straightforward action scenes alternating with Chris's freaky, time-travel nightmares.

Singh, Nalini

PSY-CHANGELINGS (SMR—V3, S4, H3)

Berkley: *Slave to Sensation* (2006); *Visions of Heat* (2007); *Caressed by Ice* (2007); "Beat of Temptation" in *An Enchanted Season* anthology (2007); *Mine to Possess* (2008); *Hostage to Pleasure* (2008); "Stroke of Enticement" in *The Magical Christmas Cat* anthology (2008); *Branded by Fire* (2009); *Blaze of Memory* (2009); *Bonds of Justice* (2010); *Play of Passion* (2010). The author has a link on her website (www.nalinisingh.com/books .html) to two free, online PSY-CHANGELINGS short stories: "The Cannibal Princess" and "A Gift for Kit."

Set in San Francisco in 2080, the series tells the SMR stories of couples from three different "races" (table 5 lists them in order of their power). One hundred years ago, the Psy Council found itself faced with a growing number of killers, driven insane by their inability to live a normal life with their powerful psychic abilities. They decided to strip Psy citizens of all emotions (the Silence), allowing them to use their talents without harming their minds. As the series begins, an ever-growing group of Psy is revolting against both the Silence and the Council itself. The changelings have always hated the supremacy of the Psy, but a successful business relationship has evolved between the two groups so that they have, on the surface, a relatively civil relationship. The humans also hate the Psy, and their leaders have begun trying to take down the Psy Council. The series story line involves growing revolutionary movements within the three groups. Each soul-mate couple crosses species lines (e.g., Psy-changeling, leopard-wolf, human-changeling), and one series theme is the contrast between the ever-growing Psy-Web of the changelings and the dying PsyNet of the Psy. Because each couple must overcome great personal difficulties before mating, the scenes with the highest sensuality come in the final third of most of the books, with the exception of book 6, which has scenes of graphic sex scattered throughout. The underlying message of the series is that emotions are a necessary and valuable part of life and love.

TABLE 5   Psy-Changelings "Races," in Order of Power

"RACE"	CHARACTERISTICS	LED BY
Psy	Not human but appear human; have a variety of psychic talents (e.g., healing, empathy, telekinesis); must be connected to the PsyNet, an interconnection of the minds of all Psy, or they die	Psy Council, a cynical and corrupt group that connects through the PsyNet
Changelings	Shape-shifters, particularly leopards and wolves; connected by the Web, an interconnection of the minds of the top members (alphas and sentinels) in each changeling group	Alpha of each group: Hawke (SnowDancer wolves) and Lucas (DarkRiver leopards)
Humans	Weakest group, generally at the mercy of the Psy	Human Alliance leaders, a mysterious and violent group headquartered in Venice, Italy

Singh, Nalini (cont.)

Guild Hunter (UF—V4, S3, H3)

Berkley: *Angels' Blood* (2009); "Angels' Pawn: A Companion Novella to Angels' Blood," available electronically on Amazon.com's Kindle only (2009); "Angels' Judgment" in *Must Love Hellhounds* anthology (2009); *Archangel's Kiss* (2010); *Archangel's Consort* (2011)

Elena Deveraux hunts down vampires who have run away from their angel masters. In this world, society looks relatively realistic, except that angels are the ultimate rulers. Elena works for the Guild, which, in turn, works for the angels. In book 1, Elena is assigned to hunt down a rogue archangel who is killing humans. Elena's nemesis–love interest is (gulp!) the archangel Raphael—the very alpha head of the New York angels. Elena, of course, hates Raphael at first sight but also, of course, becomes more and more attracted to him each time they meet. Book 1 ends with the couple facing off with the rogue in a battle that changes both their lives. Book 2 continues their story as Elena learns some new skills before she and Raphael take off for a danger-filled trip to Beijing.

Sizemore, Susan

Laws of the Blood (SMR—V4, S3, H2)

The Hunt (Roc, 1999); *Partners* (Ace, 2000); *Companions* (Ace, 2001); *Deceptions* (Ace, 2002); *Heroes* (Ace, 2003); "Cave Canem" in *First Blood* anthology (Berkley, 2008)

Although each book includes a couple's developing relationship, the plots do not focus entirely on those relationships, and the relationships do not have traditionally happy endings. These vampires call themselves strigoi, and they live in nests in urban areas. Each nest is headed by a strigoi, with a "companion," several young vamps, and a handful of "slaves." The companion is the strigoi's blood partner, lover, and assistant; the slaves are the strigoi's minions. As soon as the baby vamps mature, they must leave their maker's nest and start their own nest. Companions eventually become vampires and must also leave the nest—a source of heartbreak—because in this world, two vampires cannot be lovers. The Strigoi Council assigns enforcers in each city to reinforce the council's many Laws of the Blood, the rules by which all of the strigoi must live. A general story arc for the series involves various attempts by the younger vamps and companions to get rid of the council's restrictive laws. The enforcers make sure that vampires don't kill humans, and enforcers are the only ones allowed to kill other vampires. Each book tells the SMR story of an enforcer and his companion. Plots are complex and include a revolt by several strigoi against their enforcer, the serial murders of vampires, a demon-sorcerer plot to take over all of the strigoi, and a disgruntled companion's attempt to take down an enforcer. Book 5 (*Heroes*) brings together many characters from the previous four books for a shared adventure in Las Vegas.

* * *

A Prime is a fully sexually mature male in control of his powers, a male who accepts responsibility for his actions, and responsibility for the safety, comfort, and happiness of those he takes under his protection.

> Alec, a Prime, explains to Josephine what it means
> to be a Prime, in Susan Sizemore's *I Thirst for You*

Primes are . . . proud, imperious, possessive, strong, territorial, intensely sexual, stubborn, haughty, protective, arrogant, handsome. Depending on the situation, they can be the most wonderful men in the world or complete pricks.

> A second opinion on being Prime, from a female
> strigoi, in Susan Sizemore's *I Burn for You*

* * *

Sizemore, Susan (cont.)

PRIMES (SMR—V4, S4, H2)

Pocket Star: *I Burn for You* (2003); *I Thirst for You* (2004); "A Touch of Harry" in *The Shadows of Christmas Past* anthology (2004); *I Hunger for You* (2005); *Crave the Night* (2005), a collection of the first three books; *Master of Darkness* (2006); *Primal Heat* (2006); *Primal Desires* (2007); *Primal Needs* (2008); *Primal Instincts* (2010)

These vampires are not undead; they have simply evolved separately from mortals. Their matriarchal world is divided into three social strata: Clans, Families, and Tribes, with the Clans at the top as the primary protectors of mortals. Clan members take special medications that allow them sun and garlic immunity and the ability to eat regular food so that they can blend into the mortal world. The Families are the "middle class," and the lawless Tribes are at the bottom of the heap. In each group, adult males are called Primes, meaning that they are the "alphas," with designated cultural responsibilities, special strengths, and seemingly insatiable sexual appetites.

The vampires—particularly the women—live within a net of strict rules that regulate all aspects of their lives. Each book follows the soul-mate relationship of one couple—usually a vampire Prime and a human woman with some type of psychic ability. Most of the supernaturals are vampires, but by book 4, shape-shifters (called werefolk) join the cast of characters. The same set of vamps and weres makes up the core group of characters for the series, playing starring roles as they find their soul mates and taking supporting roles in other books. Several story lines wind together throughout the series, including Tribe vampires selling drugs, neo-Nazi werewolves trying to start a revolution against both vampires and mortals, mortals doing scientific experiments on kidnapped vampires, and fanatical vampire hunters (Purists) trying to destroy immortals. Each book ends with one or two battles won, but the really bad guys always escape, so the final resolution is still ahead.

Smith, Kathryn

BROTHERHOOD OF BLOOD (HIS, SMR—V3, S5, H2)

> *Be Mine Tonight* (Avon, 2006); *Night of the Huntress* (Avon, 2007); *Taken by the Night* (Avon, 2007); *Let the Night Begin* (Avon, 2008); *Night after Night* (Avon, 2009); "The Wedding Knight" in *Weddings from Hell* anthology (Harper, 2008)

The crux of the overall series plot is explained in the prologue to book 1. In 1307, five soldiers of King Philip are sent to steal the secrets and treasures of the Knights Templar. The soldiers believe that they have found the Holy Grail, and they drink from it, only to find that it is actually the Unholy, or "Blood," Grail, which turns them all into vampires. The suicide of one of their own and the events that follow drive them apart, but six centuries later, an ancient evil conspires to reunite them once more. Each book in the series takes place in 1899 and tells the story of one of the five as he battles against an enemy who wishes to capture him and steal his Templar blood for the enemy's own dark purposes. Each soldier finds his soul mate in the midst of his adventures.

NIGHTMARE CHRONICLES (UF—V3, S4, H2)

> Avon: *Before I Wake* (2008); *Dark Side of Dawn* (2009)

Dawn Riley is a Ph.D. sleep therapist and a Nightmare—the half-human daughter of Morpheus, king of the Dreamworld. Her Dreamworld job is to protect humans from the nightmares that plague them, but she has always rejected her father and his people, so she has no training for these duties.

Noah Clarke is her human boyfriend. Together they battle evildoers, including rebellious Dreamworld creatures who want Morpheus's power and who hate the idea that the half-breed Dawn is Morpheus's heir.

. . . .

> Shane once explained the vampires' obsessive-compulsive behaviors to me. The world moves so far beyond them, they need to feel like they control something. It's the only way to feel sane, he says.
>
> Ciara explains why vampires feel the compulsive need to sort,
> arrange, and count, in Jeri Smith-Ready's *Bad to the Bone*

. . . .

Smith-Ready, Jeri

WVMP RADIO (UF—V5, S4, H3)

Pocket: *Wicked Game* (2009); *Bad to the Bone* (2009); *Bring on the Night* (2010)

When Ciara gets a marketing job at a failing radio station in small-town Sherwood, Maryland, she soon learns that the station's DJs are all vampires, so she turns the station into "WVMP—the Lifeblood of Rock 'n' Roll," and the vampires are an instant success with the listeners. Each vampire plays only the music that was popular during the decade preceding his or her death, and each book includes a playlist of the songs that are intricately woven into the plot. Ciara's love interest is the DJ Shane, a 1990s grunge rocker. Ciara and her friends battle evil in several forms, including a powerful and violent vampire who wants to keep vampires out of the public eye and a group of fanatics who want all vampires dead. Humor is both situational and conversational and includes the consequences of an odd vampiric trait of obsessive-compulsive behavior (e.g., alphabetizing a CD collection, compulsively counting things). The sudden reappearances of Ciara's double-dealing father and a paramilitary group called the Control, which governs many aspects of the vampires' lives, complicate the lives of Ciara and the vampires.

Sniegoski, Thomas E.

REMY CHANDLER (UF—V4, S2, H2)

Roc: *A Kiss before the Apocalypse* (2009); *Dancing on the Head of a Pin* (2009); "Noah's Orphans," in *Mean Streets* anthology (2009); *Where Angels Fear to Tread* (2010); *A Hundred Words to Hate* (2011)

SERIES DESCRIPTIONS **195**

Imagine Philip Marlowe with angelic powers (Remy actually names his dog Marlowe). Remy is not a fallen angel; he chose to reject his heavenly life after being disillusioned by God's actions toward Lucifer Morningstar. Now a human, Remy has to fight constantly to keep his angelic side hidden. A complex hierarchy of angels populates the series, from fallen angels to good and bad Seraphim, the Grigori (or Watchers, disgraced angels forced to live forever as humans), and the Black Choir (who tried to take both sides in the showdown between God and Morningstar and lived to regret it). Remy has a human friend in Steven Mulvehill, a police detective who knows what Remy really is but doesn't want to know much more. The series is set in Boston in the noir detective tradition. The angels have many human emotions—mostly negative. Adventures generally focus on angel-related supernatural crimes, with plenty of battles involving flying combatants wielding magical swords. A bittersweet aspect of Remy's life is his mourning over the death of Madeline, his human wife. In book 1, heaven hires Remy to find the angel of death and to recover some missing scrolls. In book 2, Remy must retrieve some stolen weapons that have the power to destroy heaven and earth. In book 3, Remy takes a case involving a missing child and winds up playing an important part in the Samson and Delilah story: the sequel (and conclusion).

Sparks, Kerrelyn

Love at Stake (CH, SMR—V4, S5, H4)

Avon: "A Very Vampy Christmas" in *Sugarplums and Scandal* anthology (2006); *How to Marry a Millionaire Vampire* (2005); *Vamps and the City* (2006); *Be Still My Vampire Heart* (2007); *The Undead Next Door* (2008); *All I Want for Christmas Is a Vampire* (2008); *Secret Life of a Vampire* (2009); *Forbidden Nights with a Vampire* (2009); *The Vampire and the Virgin* (2010); *Eat Prey Love* (2010)

Plots revolve around Roman Draganesti and his friends. Roman, a vampire, is a former medieval monk who became a twenty-first-century millionaire when he invented synthetic blood. The good guys are the Vampires and the two bad-guy groups are the Malcontents (vamps who reject synthetic blood and keep draining humans) and the Stake-It Squad (a CIA-sponsored group dedicated to killing all vamps—both good and bad). Each book follows one couple (male vamp and female human) from the time they meet until they overcome all obstacles and become soul mates. Most stories take place in Manhattan. Humorous touches include the beverages that Roman invents to increase vampiric food choices (e.g., Blissky [synthetic blood + whiskey],

Bubbly Blood [synthetic blood + champagne]). Another bizarre touch of humor comes in book 2, when a harem of vamp females rocks the vampire world by asserting their feminine independence.

Spear, Terry

WOLF SERIES (SMR—V4, S4, H2)

Sourcebooks Casablanca: *Heart of the Wolf* (2008); *Destiny of the Wolf* (2009); *To Tempt the Wolf* (2009); *Legend of the White Wolf* (2010); *Seduced by the Wolf* (2010); *Wolf Fever* (2010)

In each book, a werewolf soul-mate couple graphically explores their sexual relationship while constantly fending off male werewolves who want the heroine for themselves—at any cost.

Spencer, Jorrie

STRENGTH (SMR—V4, S4, H2)

Samhain: *Strength of the Pack* (2007); *Strength of the Wolf* (2008)

The series revolves around sibling werewolves who try to hide their shape-shifting identities. Book 1 tells the story of Seth and his human mate, Jamie. Book 2 focuses on Seth's amnesiac sister, Veronica, and her true love, David. Villains include humans who want all werewolves dead. Although the books' covers contain warnings of "explicit sex," the sex scenes actually contain fewer details than expected. Spencer has written other erotic paranormal novels, including *Puma* (Samhain, 2009).

Squires, Susan

THE COMPANION (HIS, SMR—V5, S5, H1)

St. Martin's Paperbacks: *The Companion* (2004); *The Hunger* (2005); *The Burning* (2006); *One with the Night* (2007); *One with the Shadows* (2007); *One with the Darkness* (2008); "Beyond the Night" in *Dead after Dark* anthology (2008); *Time for Eternity* (2009); *A Twist in Time* (2010)

Not your grandmother's Regency romance! Most of the books are set in England in the early 1800s, with some flashbacks to ancient times. The general plot for each novel revolves around a vampire who meets and falls for a human and eventually changes that human over to vampirism. In this world, vampirism is caused by a virus, termed the "Companion," a highly infectious parasite that lives in the blood. In this series, a small group of born vamps, who live by rules and regulations set by the Elders, lead the vampire world. One of these rules is that no new vamps can be made, and if a made vamp is discovered, he or she must be destroyed. Several of the plots revolve around one evil female vamp (Asharti), who creates her own vampire army and tries to rule the world. Other plots involve the friction between born and made vampires. Later books involve a time machine created by Leonardo da Vinci. Bloodthirsty pirates, murderous Arabs, and sea monsters also make appearances. The high violence and sensuality ratings are due to the many sexual torture scenes, with dominatrix-submissive and sadomasochistic acts described in graphic detail, particularly in the Asharti plots.

Stein, Jeanne C.

ANNA STRONG CHRONICLES (UF—V4, S3, H2)

Ace: *The Becoming* (2006); *Blood Drive* (2007); *The Watcher* (2007); *Legacy* (2008); *Retribution* (2009); *Chosen* (2010)

In book 1, Anna is a bounty hunter in San Diego when she is turned into a vampire. Anna hates her vampiric state and spends the entire series trying to maintain her humanity while all of her otherworldly friends and acquaintances urge her to make peace with her new "monstrous" self and turn her back on her human family and friends. There are also hints that Anna may be "the one"—but no one will tell her what that means. In Anna's world, humans are unaware of the existence of vampires, even though vampires hold a number of respected positions (e.g., deputy mayor, police chief). Supporting characters include Anna's partner, David, a former NFL player; her human boyfriend, Max, an undercover agent for the Drug Enforcement Agency; Williams, an ancient vampire who is the San Diego police chief; Frey, a shape-shifting panther who befriends Anna; and Culebra, a shape-shifting rattlesnake who runs a Mexican hideaway for humans and vampires living on the dark side of the law. Other boyfriends/sexual partners for Anna also turn up in the stories. Sexual scenes occur, but few graphic details are included. Anna is a typical UF heroine, with her sarcastic sniping, angst-ridden interior monologues, and rough-and-ready approach to her problems. She doesn't carry as many weapons as Anita Blake, but she was definitely created in Anita's image. Bad guys include the villainous revengers, vampire hunters who also work as highway patrol officers; a rogue vampire who poses as Anna's friend; a Latino mobster who threatens Max; and a powerful black-arts witch who terrorizes Anna and her friends. Some characters come and go randomly throughout the series, appearing as major characters for a while and then either going to the background or disappearing completely.

Stone, Juliana

JAGUAR WARRIOR (SMR—V4, S4, H1)

Avon: *His Darkest Hunger* (2010); *His Darkest Embrace* (2010)

This series tells the SMR stories of a team of good-guy warriors and assassins —Jaxon, a jaguar shifter; Jaxon's brothers, Julian and Jagger; Libby, a human with mysterious ancestry; Ana, a vampire; and Declan, a mage—who travel the globe battling various villains.

· ·

> Zombies. After work hours, they were almost motionless as they clacked softly away at the keyboards before them, no longer working at the pace I had seen them filing and typing on my first visit here. It made perfect sense that they were still here. At the end of the workday, where did these corporate zombies have to go, really? They didn't have homes, and without a single working brain among them, they would sit there silently until their masters returned in the morning. Their faces reminded me of so many I saw among the commuters here in New York—lifeless and slack-jawed.
>
> Simon muses on the lives of zombies, in Anton Strout's *Deader Still*

· ·

Strout, Anton

SIMON CANDEROUS (UF—V4, S3, H4)

Ace: *Dead to Me* (2008); *Deader Still* (2009); *Dead Matter* (2010); *Dead Waters* (2011)

Simon is a psychometrist; he has the power to touch an object and divine information about its history. In his younger years, he used his power for illegal gain, but now he's gone straight. Simon has been hired by New York City's Department of Extraordinary Affairs (DEA), which handles all of the city's supernatural problems. With its enchanted furniture, supernaturally empowered workers, endless paperwork, and office behind a horror movie theater, the DEA is a cross between Simon R. Green's NIGHTSIDE and Terry Gilliam's mind-numbing bureaucracy in the movie *Brazil*. The DEA has many divisions (e.g., Haunts-General, Greater and Lesser Arcana), each with its own director and its own rules and regulations, and all of them require reams of paperwork for even the simplest action. The DEA controls the public's knowledge of the supernatural through the Mayor's Office of Plausible Deniability. (A zombie attack at a fashion show is spun as just a new style of runway walking.) Simon, along with his ghost-catching partner, Connor, and his technomancer girl-friend, Jane, gets involved with a variety of bad guys, from ghost-sucking cult-ists to *chupacabra*-stealing gypsies and a (literal) corporate headhunter. And there are always plenty of zombies to mix up the action.

Sunny

MONÉRE: CHILDREN OF THE MOON (UF, but not very urban— V5, S5, H2)

> Berkley: *Mona Lisa Awakening* (2008); "Mona Lisa Three" in *Over the Moon* anthology (2007); *Mona Lisa Blossoming* (2008); "Mona Lisa Betwining" in *On the Prowl* anthology (2007); *Mona Lisa Craving* (2008); *Mona Lisa Darkening* (2009); *Mona Lisa Eclipsing* (2011)

This is an erotic fantasy series. In book 1, Lisa is a nurse in New York City when she meets Gryphon, who claims that he is a warrior of the supernatural Monére race (children of the moon) and that Lisa is a Monére queen. Lisa turns her back on her human life and joins the Monére. Eventually Lisa—now called Mona Lisa—is recognized as a queen among the Monére. Plot lines involve attacks on Lisa by rogue Monére warriors, other queens, and a variety of demonic creatures. Lisa's love (i.e., sex) interests are too numerous to list here. The Monére race is matriarchal, and each queen's warriors serve her in the bedroom as well as on the battlefield. Sex scenes in the early books are rated 4–5, but the later books go up to 5+, with explicit, over-the-top scenes that include threesomes, sadomasochism, and voyeurism.

DEMON PRINCESS CHRONICLES (UF, but not very urban— V5, S5, H2)

> Berkley: "Mona Lisa Betwining" in *On the Prowl* anthology (2007); *Lucinda, Darkly* (2009); *Lucinda, Dangerously* (2009)

In a related erotic fantasy series, Lucinda is the daughter of Blaec, the High Lord of Hell. Her character is introduced in "Mona Lisa Betwining." In *Lucinda, Darkly*, she begins to gather her own group of warriors as she comes to terms with the mysteries of her parentage. Violence and sensuality match the MONÉRE series.

Swendson, Shanna

ENCHANTED, INC. SERIES (CH—V2, S2, H3)

Ballantine: *Enchanted, Inc.* (2005); *Once upon Stilettos* (2006); *Damsel under Stress* (2007); *Don't Hex with Texas* (2008)

Katie Chandler is a small-town Texas girl who comes to Manhattan with her college roommates to begin a career in advertising. She is amazed at all of the weird people she sees as she walks to work (e.g., women with wings, gargoyles who wink at her). Then she meets the recruiters from Magic, Spells, and Illusions (MSI), who prove to her that magic is real and that she is immune to it. They offer her a job as a verifier—someone who checks over contracts to ensure that they are not bespelled. Soon, Katie finds herself in the middle of a magical war between MSI and Phelan Idris, a former MSI wizard who was fired for dabbling in black magic. Now, Idris is selling harmful spells on the open market, and MSI has to stop him. Katie is also pulled into a friendship, and more, with Owen Palmer, a powerful and sexy MSI wizard, so shy that he doesn't even kiss Katie until the end of book 2. Plots revolve around MSI's attempts to stop Idris, as he lashes out at Owen and Katie in a number of magical, but not very violent, ways.

Thompson, Ronda

WILD WULFS OF LONDON (HIS, SMR—V4, S4, H2)

St. Martin's: *The Dark One* (2005); *The Untamed One* (2006); *The Cursed One* (2006)

The Wulf brothers, lords of Wulfglen, are under a witch's curse. As soon as they fall in love, their lycanthropic beasts will be released—they will become werewolves. As a result, the brothers vow never to fall in love or marry. Of course, every romance reader knows what happens next. Each brother meets his soul mate and tries to break the curse. Set in 1820s London, the series follows three of the brothers on their SMR journeys, with a variety of villains standing in their way.

The author has also written stand-alone werewolf fiction and has contributed stories to a number of anthologies listed at the end of this bibliography.

. . . .

"Come on." He shoved his feet into his work boots. "Let me show you my Big Knob."

Maggie grinned as she reached for her shoes. "I don't think I know you well enough for that."

"Bad choice of words." He tied the laces on his boots. "I meant the rock outside."

Sean and Maggie get acquainted in Big Knob,
Indiana, in Vicki Lewis Thompson's *Over Hexed*

. . . .

Thompson, Vicki Lewis

HEX SERIES (SMR—V1, S4, H5)

Onyx: *Over Hexed* (2007); *Wild and Hexy* (2008); *Casual Hex* (2009)

Banished to Big Knob, Indiana, because they cast a bad spell, the husband-wife team of Ambrose (wizard) and Dorcas (witch) Lowell spend their time matching up the locals with their soul mates. Each story includes a supernatural element: a delinquent dragon in the Whispering Forest just outside of town, a lonely lake monster who needs a mate, an arrogant fairy prince who tries to take the local florist for his queen. Stories are fast paced and quite humorous. The quirky local townspeople seem to have stepped out of a cozy mystery. And there's plenty of sex—they don't call it Big Knob for nothing!

Thurman, Rob (Robyn)

CAL LEANDROS (UF—V5, S3, H4)

Nightlife (Roc, 2006); *Moonshine* (Roc, 2007); *Madhouse* (Roc, 2008); "Milk and Cookies" in *Wolfsbane and Mistletoe* anthology (Ace, 2008); *Deathwish* (Roc, 2009); *Roadkill* (Roc, 2010); *Blackout* (Roc, 2011)

Caliban ("Cal") and Niko Leandros are tough, streetwise half brothers. Although Niko is fully human, Cal is half Auphe—a violent and cannibalistic elf-related supernatural race. Cal has spent his life constantly trying to prove to others—and to himself—that he isn't the monster that his name and his heritage imply. The series follows the brothers as they escape from the Auphe (or do they?) and strike out on their own as detectives and bodyguards serving the supernatural community in New York City, a community brimming over with every kind of paranormal being that you have ever heard of—and some that you haven't. (Do you know what a *boggle* is?) Love interests for the brothers are Niko's Promise, a beautiful vampire, and Cal's Georgina, a young psychic. Robin "Puck" Goodfellow is the boys' sidekick. The stories are very dark and violent, as the boys are constantly under attack by someone—or something. Sarcastic sniping adds humor to the dialogue—primarily from smart-mouthed Cal, who serves as narrator for the first three books (he shares that duty with his brother in the fourth).

Thurman, Rob (Robyn) (cont.)

TRICKSTER (UF—V4, S2, H4)
Roc: *Trick of the Light* (2009); *The Grimrose Path* (2010)

Trixa Iktomi owns a bar off the Vegas strip and spends her spare time hunting down and killing demons with her friends Zeke Hawkins (a telepath) and Griffin Reese (an empath), who work for Eden House, a demon-hunting organization sponsored by angels—yes, real heavenly angels. Trixa is a streetwise, tough, wisecracking modern woman. She is the only female character in book 1, and her fighting skills and weapons easily match or exceed Anita Blake's. Other characters include two demons, Eligos and Solomon, who fight for Trixa's favor as well as for the treasure for which she is searching. Leo, Trixa's American Indian bartender buddy, and Lenore, her pet raven, make up the rest of the cast of off-beat characters. In the first novel, Trixa searches for her brother's killer and for the magical Light of Life, with angels, demons, and Eden House bigwigs trying to beat her to the punch. Although parts of the surprise ending are telegraphed early on, there is still plenty of mystery left to be unveiled during the final "apocalyptic throwdown," as the back cover describes it. Ratings are based on book 1 because book 2 had not yet been released at the time of this writing.

Troop, Alan F.

DRAGON DELASANGRE (UF—V5, S3, H1)
Roc: *The Dragon DelaSangre* (2003); *Dragon Moon* (2003); *The Seadragon's Daughter* (2004); *A Host of Dragons* (2006; out of print, but available from libraries)

The series follows the adventures of Peter DelaSangre, a shape-shifting dragon, or as he calls his race, People of the Blood. The series begins as Peter's father is dying in their isolated home on an island south of Miami, and Peter is on the verge of finding his first mate. Peter narrates his adventures as he mates, meets his in-laws, raises his children, and gets involved in a variety of dangerous situations. The dragons are matter-of-fact and absolutely non-sentimental about killing their human prey. Humans are either servants or they are lunch—nothing in between. Peter heads up a huge, slightly sinister corporation that stops at nothing to get its way—from bribing politicians to killing interlopers.

· ·

> "Wolves hunt by moving. I want to be out there looking for this thing. Tracking it down."
>
> "And vampires are like spiders," Rick said. "We draw our quarry in and trap it."
>
> I suddenly pictured Rick as a creature at the center of his web, patiently waiting, watching, ready to strike. A chill ran down my spine, and I shook the image away.
>
> Kitty the werewolf and Rick the vampire discuss
traits of their respective species, in Carrie Vaughn's
Kitty and the Dead Man's Hand

· ·

Vaughn, Carrie

KITTY NORVILLE (UF—V3, S3, H3)

Kitty and the Midnight Hour (Grand Central, 2005); *Kitty Goes to Washington* (Grand Central, 2006); *Kitty Takes a Holiday* (Grand Central, 2007); *Kitty and the Silver Bullet* (Grand Central, 2008); *Kitty and the Dead Man's Hand* (Grand Central, 2009); *Kitty Raises Hell* (Grand Central, 2009); *Kitty's House of Horrors* (Grand Central, 2010); *Kitty Goes to War* (Tor, 2010); *Kitty's Big Trouble* (Tor, 2011)

Kitty is an independent young werewolf who escapes from her abusive pack leader and establishes a career as the increasingly well-known host of a late-night radio talk show with an audience of angst-ridden vampires and lycanthropes. Think Ann Landers as a werewolf, with a bit of Howard Stern mixed in. Characters include her lawyer and (*spoiler alert!*) eventual husband, Ben O'Farrell, and her friend (and Ben's cousin), Cormac Bennett, a werewolf hunter. Adventures include battles with Kitty's original pack leader, serial killers, religious fanatics, an evil skin walker, and nasty vampires.

Viehl, Lynn

THE DARKYN SERIES (SMR—V5, S5, H3)

If Angels Burn (Signet, 2005); *Private Demon* (Signet, 2005); *Dark Need* (Signet, 2006); *Night Lost* (Signet, 2007); *Evermore* (Signet, 2008); *Twilight Fall* (Onyx, 2008); *Stay the Night* (Onyx, 2009)

The novels tell stories of the Darkyn, or Kyn (the heroic Knights Templar who came back from the Holy Land with the curse of vampirism), and the Brethren (the villainous secret, unsanctioned sect of the Catholic Church dedicated to hunting down and eradicating the Darkyn). Each book takes place in modern times as a Darkyn-human couple become soul mates while battling the Brethren and other villains. One twist is that the Darkyn's vampirism appears to be caused by a blood disorder, which one of the soul mates, a former human doctor, tries to pin down and cure over the course of the series. Another twist: some famous characters from literature and history turn up as members of the Darkyn (e.g., Robin Hood, Will Scarlet).

Vincent, Rachel

WERECATS (UF—V5, S4, H3)

Mira: *Stray* (2007); *Rogue* (2008); *Pride* (2009); *Prey* (2009); *Shift* (2010); *Alpha* (2010)

Faythe Sanders is a werecat, only daughter of the alpha of the Southwestern Pride. She begins the series with a human boyfriend (Andrew) and a werecat ex-lover (Marc), whom she deserted at the altar five years earlier. The series follows Faythe's adventures as her need for independence and her inability to control her big mouth lead her into deeper and deeper troubles, both inside and outside the Pride. Faythe's rocky road through the series includes some extremely deep potholes as she must deal with a surprising and unpleasant development in her relationship with Andrew and enormous emotional swings in her relationship with Marc. Villains include rogue strays, dangerous jungle cats, and a power-hungry Pride leader who is out to get both Marc and Faythe's father.

Walker, Shiloh

THE HUNTERS (SMR—V3, S4, H1)

Legends: Hunters and Heroes (prequel; Samhain, 2006); *The Hunters: The Beginning* (Ellora's Cave, 2004); *The Hunters: Interlude* (Ellora's

Cave, 2005); *The Hunters: Ben and Shadoe,* e-book only (Ellora's Cave, 2005); *The Hunters: Rafe and Sheila* (Ellora's Cave, 2005); *I'll Be Hunting You* (Ellora's Cave, 2009); *Hunting the Hunter* (Ellora's Cave, 2009); *Hunters: Heart and Soul* (Berkley Heat, 2007); *Hunter's Salvation* (Berkley Sensation, 2007); *Hunter's Need* (Berkley, 2009)

This erotic series focuses on various members of the Hunters, a supernatural organization (vampires, witches, and shape-shifters) that administers vigilante justice to human and supernatural evildoers in cities in the Midwest and South-Central states (e.g., Nashville, Memphis, Indianapolis, Cincinnati). Each book follows a couple from first lust to final soul-mate status, with plenty of angst-ridden scenes of self-doubt and second thoughts, closely followed by countless detailed scenes of over-the-top sex—with a few very light plot interruptions by a variety of evildoers, including rogue vampires, dangerous witches, and mad scientists.

Ward, J. R. (pseudonym for Jessica Bird)

BLACK DAGGER BROTHERHOOD (SMR—V5, S5, H3)

Dark Lover (Signet, 2005); *Lover Eternal* (Signet, 2006); *Lover Awakened* (Signet, 2006); *Lover Revealed* (Signet, 2009); *Lover Unbound* (Signet, 2007); *Lover Enshrined* (Signet, 2008); *Lover Avenged* (Signet, 2009); *Lover Mine* (NAL, 2010); *The Black Dagger Brotherhood: An Insider's Guide* (NAL, 2008)

The Black Dagger Brotherhood is a team of highly trained vampire warriors who protect their species against the Lessening Society—soulless, immortal slayers who are attempting to eradicate the vampire species. Each book tells one warrior's story as he battles the Lessers and finds his soul mate. *Lover Revealed* won the RITA Award for best paranormal romance (2008).

FALLEN ANGELS (SMR—V4, S4, H2)

Signet. *Covet* (2009); *Crave* (2010)

Covet begins a series about a fallen angel who must save the souls of seven humans, each of whom is guilty of one of the seven deadly sins. The fallen angel is Jim, who has led a life of violence. Now, his weapon is love, and he must battle the evil and powerful demonic powers that oppose him. In the first book, the sinner to be saved meets up with his soul mate, so I'm calling this an SMR series. Ratings are based on book 1 because book 2 had not yet been released at the time of this writing.

Warren, Christine

THE OTHERS (SMR—V4, S4, H4)

St. Martin's: *Wolf at the Door* (2008); *She's No Faerie Princess* (2006); *The Demon You Know* (2007); *Howl at the Moon* (2007); *Walk on the Wild Side* (2008); *One Bite with a Stranger* (2008); *You're So Vein* (2009); *Big Bad Wolf* (2009); *Born to Be Wild* (2010); "Any Witch Way She Can" in *No Rest for the Witches* anthology (2007); *Prince Charming Doesn't Live Here* (2010). Early titles were published as e-books and are no longer available. According to the author's website, the current publisher (St. Martin's Press) will be publishing expanded versions of those titles in the near future, probably with different titles. The list here includes the stories in the order of original publication, along with new titles (according to the author's website).

Each book takes a paranormal couple (handsome alpha male; sassy, independent female) through the SMR process. The premise is that the Others of the paranormal world have revealed themselves to the human world. Book 1 takes place just before the Unveiling, and the remaining books move through the following months and years. The Others include all manner of supernatural beings, from vampires, shifters, and fairies to the more unfamiliar doppelgängers, *oni* (Japanese demons), fox women (women who shift into foxes through magical powers), and fiends. Some characters appear in several books. In each book, a group of Others and their human friends/lovers work together to battle evildoers, including rogue humans and Others, human mad scientists, and powerful demons.

Warren, J. D.

WORLD OF THE STORM RAVENS (UF—V2, S2, H4)

Love Spell: *Bedlam, Bath and Beyond* (2008); *Crate and Peril* (2008)

Corydonais is a Peri ("Kin"), a shape-shifting raven who is the commander of the Order of the Storm Ravens. The Ravens battle the Order of Crow (rogue Kin who make deals with the devil to gain power). Samantha is a half-Peri and half-human young woman who gets caught up in the devilish doings. Set in Venice, California, the center of Peri activity in the United States, the stories have quirky characters who engage in endless humorous sniping at one other.

Weldon, Phaedra

Zoë Martinique (UF—V4, S2, H2)

Ace: *Wraith* (2009); *Spectre* (2008); *Phantasm* (2009); *Revenant* (2010); "Out of the Dark," a bridge novella between *Wraith* and *Spectre*, available free on the author's website, at www.phaedraweldon.com— I recommend reading the novella in the proper sequence to get a better understanding of the ensuing books.

Zoë is a twentysomething city girl who uses her ability to travel outside her body to conduct investigations (e.g., domestic surveillance, corporate espionage) for people who don't mind operating beyond the legal system. At the beginning of *Wraith*, Zoë calls herself a traveler and thinks that she is the only such creature in existence. Soon, however, she has a run-in with a supernatural assassin who has similar abilities. When that monster leaves his mark on Zoë, her abilities begin to change—and not for the better. Now, she is a wraith, with the ability to devour souls or set them free to go somewhere else—where, she does not know. In addition to marking Zoë, the villain steals her voice and her good health, turning her into a mute diabetic. Zoë's two love interests are both Atlanta police detectives: Lieutenant Daniel Frasier, who says he loves Zoë but vehemently denies the existence of the supernatural world (so she can't tell him about her true self), and Sergeant Joe Halloran, who has his own supernatural side and knows exactly who, and what, Zoë is. A third love interest shows up in *Phantasm*. Supporting characters include two witches—Zoë's mother (Nona) and their friend (Rhonda)—and a pair of gay ghosts. Villains include various supernaturals (e.g., symbionts, phantasms, horrors) from several spiritual planes (e.g., the Ethereal, the Abysmal). A related series is Grimoire, which tells the story of Dags McConnel, the friendly but mysterious bartender from the Zoë Martinique series. The first novella of that series, "Ministering Angels," is available free on the author's website. Also part of Zoë's world is "Ghoul," another free novella—vampires, this time—on the website.

Wellington, David

Laura Caxton (UF—V5, S3, H0)

Three Rivers Press: *13 Bullets* (2007); *99 Coffins: A Historical Vampire Tale* (2007); *Vampire Zero: A Gruesome Vampire Tale* (2008); *23 Hours: A Vengeful Vampire Tale* (2009)

• •

The vampire jumped up onto the jagged lower edge of the broken window. . . . His skin was the color of cold milk, his eyes red and dully glowing. He had no hair anywhere on his body, and his ears stood up in points. His mouth was full of row after row of sharp teeth.

. . . His body was emaciated, . . . thinner than any human being she'd ever seen. His skin stretched tight over prominent bones, and the muscles on his arms and legs were wasted away to thin cords. His ribs stuck out dramatically, and his cheeks were hollow with starvation. His skin was dotted with dark patches of decay and in some places had cracked open in weeping sores.

Laura Caxton describes a typical vampire,

in David Wellington's *99 Coffins*

• •

Laura begins the series as a Pennsylvania State Trooper, but she is soon assigned to assist Special Deputy Jameson Arkeley (U.S. Marshals Service), a legendary vampire killer. This dark and violent series graphically describes many bloody battles with vicious vampires. All of the vampires are blood-thirsty, Nosferatu-like monsters. The premise of the series is that Arkeley supposedly killed all but one vampire back in the 1980s. The U.S. government is holding prisoner the surviving centuries-old vampire, Justinia Malvern. Theoretically, there should be no more vampires running wild, but several have turned up in the Pennsylvania countryside, and they are killing innocent citizens by the dozens. The series follows Laura's adventures as she is promoted, demoted, and imprisoned—fighting vampires all the way. The 3 rating for sensuality is based on a few romantic kisses between Laura, a lesbian, and her girlfriend.

Wells, Jaye

SABINA KANE (UF—V4, S3, H3)

"Vampsploitation" in *The Mammoth Book of Vampire Romance*, vol. 2 (prequel; Running Press, 2009); *Red-Headed Stepchild* (Orbit, 2009); *The Mage in Black* (Orbit, 2010); *Green-Eyed Demon* (Orbit, 2011)

In this world, all vampires have red hair, and all mages (magic users) have black hair. Because Sabina has red-streaked black hair, the world knows that she is of mixed blood and, therefore, an outcast. Contributing to her isola-

• •

> All vampires have red hair—ranging from the young strawberry blondes
> to the ancient mahogany reds. The darker the shade, the older the vamp.
> My own hair, since I was half vampire and half mage, was a streaky
> combination of bright red and black. We owed this telltale sign to Cain,
> whom God had marked with a shock of red hair after the infamous
> murder of Abel. After he was cast out, he met up with Lilith, who'd left
> Eden after she grew bored with Adam. Cain's affair with Lilith resulted in
> the creation of the vampire race. We got our blood thirst and immortality
> from Lilith, and our inability to go into the sun and our red hair from Cain.
> . . . Like a scar, it's the ultimate proof of our lineage.
>
> Sabina explains the vampire mythology for this
> series, in Jaye Wells's *Red-Headed Stepchild*

• •

tion is the fact that her aristocratic vampire grandmother has raised Sabina to
be a mage-hating slayer who hunts down and kills at the behest of the Council. Sabina's primary love interest is Adam, a mage from New York City, but
an old flame—a fellow hunter—turns up in book 2 to complicate matters.
Near the end of book 1, Adam unveils to Sabina the secrets of her mysterious
birth and the mage family she never knew she had. In each book, Sabina and
her friends fight against political and personal enemies in both the vampire
and the mage worlds. Although humans are included in the series, they serve
mostly as a backdrop to the supernatural happenings. An interesting note:
applewood stakes and apple-juice-filled bullets can kill these vampires—a
connection with the forbidden fruit of Adam and Eve's downfall.

Whiteside, Diane

TEXAS VAMPIRES (SMR—V4, S5, H2)

Berkley: *The Hunter's Prey* (prequel; 2006); *Bond of Blood* (2006),
Bond of Fire (2008); *Bond of Darkness* (2008)

Don Rafael Perez, a medieval knight, was captured, turned as a vampire, and
tortured for seven hundred years before he escaped to the New World and
established his own *esfera* (territory) in Texas. Now, in the twenty-first century, enemies from his past have caught up with him and with the men of
his ranching empire. To save themselves and the women who become their
cónyuges (soul mates), they must win many battles against dangerous vampiric

forces. Each book tells one couple's story, beginning with Don Rafael and his soul mate, Grania O'Malley. The reader will need to refer frequently to the glossary of medieval and modern Spanish terms listed at the end of each book.

Wilks, Eileen

WORLD OF THE LUPI (SMR—V4, S4, H3)

Berkley: *Tempting Danger* (2004); *Mortal Danger* (2005); *Blood Lines* (2007); *Night Season* (2008); *Mortal Sins* (2009); *Blood Magic* (2010); "Human Nature" in *Inked* anthology (2010); *Blood Challenge* (2011)

The protagonists are FBI agent Lily Yu and her Lupi (werewolf) soul mate, Rule Turner—prince of the Nokolai clan. Their SMR story begins in book 1 and progresses throughout the series. Books 3 and 4 add a second SMR story to the mix—that of Lupi sorcerer Cullen Seabourne and FBI agent and finder Cynna Weaver. Set in San Diego and in various paranormal realms, the plot lines are more complex than in most SMR series. The good guys battle demons, evil goddesses, and rogue Lupins. This series might be considered urban fantasy if there were more focus on the plots and less on the ups and downs of the romantic relationships.

Wilson, F. Paul

REPAIRMAN JACK (UF—V5, S3, H4)

The Tomb (Tor, 1998); *Legacies* (Tor, 2008); *Conspiracies* (Tor, 2008); *All the Rage* (Tor, 2001); *Hosts* (Tor, 2003); *The Haunted Air* (Tor, 2004); *Crisscross* (Tor, 2006); *Infernal* (Tor, 2006); *Harbingers* (Tor, 2007); *Bloodline* (Tor, 2008); *By the Sword* (Tor, 2009); *Ground Zero* (Tor, 2009); "A Day in the Life" in *The Barrens and Others* anthology (Forge, 2000); "Interlude at Duane's" in *Aftershock and Others* anthology (Forge, 2009); "The Wringer" in *Night Screams* anthology (Roc, 1996)

Jack is an extremely paranoid underground mercenary who lives in New York City, totally off the grid: no Social Security number, no bank accounts, no registered vehicle, no property ownership, no taxes. As his nickname "Repairman" implies, Jack fixes situations for ordinary people who want to avoid legal means. The situations are frequently related to real problems in today's world (e.g., drugs, terrorism, scientific experiments, conspiracy groups, biological experiments). *Conspiracies* is among the funniest of the series, as it pulls together all manner of conspiracy buffs (e.g., UFOs, crop circles, men in black, new world order) into one big convention. Although

Jack uses only his own wits, strength, and real-world weapons, he does occasionally seek supernatural assistance from others. Jack has a "family": Gia DiLauro (his girlfriend, a commercial artist), Vicky (Gia's daughter), and Abe Grossman (his best friend, the owner of a sporting goods and illegal weapons store). In *The Tomb*, Jack has an adventure involving Rakoshi, huge humanoid creatures with cobalt blue skin and razor-sharp claws. Indestructible by most means, iron weakens them but only fire destroys them. The Rakoshi haunt Jack's life in subsequent novels. Except for the Rakoshi, the majority of Jack's life is spent with normal human beings. Each book covers about a week in Jack's life. On his website (www.repairmanjack.com/faq_III.htm), Wilson provides the following read-alikes for the REPAIRMAN JACK series: Dennis Lehane's KENZIE/GENNARO novels; Lee Child's JACK REACHER series; Andrew Vachss's BURKE novels; Dan Simmons's JOE KURTZ novels; Robert Crais's COLE/PIKE novels; Barry Eisler's JOHN RAIN novels; Douglas Preston and Lincoln Child's AGENT PENDERGAST series; Joe R. Lansdale's HAP AND LEONARD novels; and Stephen Hunter's BOB LEE SWAGGER novels.

Windsor, Anna

DARK CRESCENT SISTERHOOD (SMR—V4, S5, H3)

Ballantine: *Bound by Shadow* (2008); *Bound by Flame* (2008); *Bound by Light* (2008); *Captive Spirit* (2010); *Captive Heart* (2010); *Captive Soul* (2010)

In the three *Bound* books, Riana, Cynda, and Merilee are Sybils, supernatural female warriors. Each has connections with an element (earth, fire, air) and talents that come from her element. A fourth woman, Andrea, is a cop who goes through a series of changes during the series to achieve her own destiny as a Sybil (water). The four women meet their soul mates in a group of handsome good guys who are half-human and half-demon New York Police Department detectives. Together they battle the evil demons of New York City and beyond. The *Captive* books continue the demon battles and tell the SMR stories of friends of the Sybils and the cops.

Wisdom, Linda

HEX SERIES (UF—V5, S4, H5)

Sourcebooks Casablanca: *50 Ways to Hex Your Lover* (2008); *Hex Appeal* (2008); *Wicked by Any Other Name* (2009); *Hex in High Heels* (2009); *Best Hex Ever* (2010); *Give Me Your Best Hex* (2010)

In the first two books, Jasmine "Jazz" Tremaine is a powerful witch who, along with her friends, was banished from the Academy of Witches back in 1313 for misusing magic. For centuries, she has been trying to redeem herself but keeps getting herself in more trouble, largely because of her smart mouth and impulsive behavior. These days, she splits her time between driving a limousine for All Creatures Limo Service and working for private clients as a curse breaker. Her on-and-off boyfriend is vampire detective Nikolai Gregorivich (aka "Nick Gregory"). Quirky secondary characters add to the humor (e.g., Norma, the chain-smoking ghost who haunts Jazz's 1956 T-Bird; Dweezil, the ghoul who owns All Creatures; Fluff and Puff, a pair of hungry bunny slippers with sharp teeth and a taste for sweets and human ankles). Later books focus on romances among Jazz's friends and acquaintances.

Yarbro, Chelsea Quinn

SAINT-GERMAIN (HIS—V4, S4, H3)

Roman Dusk (Tor, 2008); *Burning Shadows* (Tor, 2009); *Dark of the Sun* (Tor, 2005); *Come Twilight* (Tor, 2001); *Better in the Dark* (Orb, 1995); *Blood Roses* (Tor, 1999); *A Feast in Exile* (Tor, 2002); *States of Grace* (Tor, 2006); *Darker Jewels* (Orb, 1995); *Mansions of Darkness* (Tor, 1997); *Communion Blood* (Tor, 2000); *A Dangerous Climate* (Tor, 2008); *Borne in Blood* (Tor, 2007); *Out of the House of Life* (Orb, 1994); *In the Face of Death* (Benbella, 2004). Novels are listed here in historical order, as suggested on Yarbro's website (www.chelseaquinnyarbro.net); out-of-print novels are not included here.

Saint-Germain is an alchemist, an apothecary, and a vampire. This saga follows our hero through the centuries of his life, beginning with his birth in Egypt in 1495 B.C. Saint-German needs blood as nourishment, and he generally takes it from sleeping neighbors, leaving them with pleasant dreams. The vampiric rules also include a need to place his native earth in his shoes and the requirement that he take blood from a person no more than five times. After the sixth time, that person is doomed to vampirism following his or her natural death. Yarbro presents the stories as historical slices of life, with Saint-Germain participating in historic events (e.g., Attila the Hun's attacks, the black plague). The plots are thick with dialogue and are carried along by a series of letters to and from various primary and secondary characters.

York, Rebecca (pseudonym for Ruth Glick)

MOON SERIES (SMR—V4, S4–5+, H1)

Killing Moon (Berkley, 2007); *Edge of the Moon* (Berkley, 2003); *Witching Moon* (Berkley, 2003); "Burning Moon" in *Cravings* anthology (Jove, 2004); *Crimson Moon* (Berkley, 2005); *Shadow of the Moon* (Berkley, 2006); *New Moon* (Berkley, 2007); *Ghost Moon* (Berkley, 2008); *Eternal Moon* (Berkley, 2009); *Dragon Moon* (Berkley, 2009)

Set for the most part in Maryland, this series focuses on the Marshall clan—werewolf brothers and cousins who meet and mate with women who each have some type of paranormal ability, from witchcraft to tarot reading to psychic trances. The series story arc involves solving the problem of the deaths of female werewolves in this family at birth and the deaths of many of the Marshalls' male siblings at the time of the first "Change," as well as the inability of the family's males to get along with one another (an alpha problem). In each book, the soul-mate couple, with the help of clan members, battles serial killers, evil sorcerers, paramilitary terrorists, demons, and more. Later books include characters who come from an alternate universe, crossing through a portal on Marshall property. The sensuality rating goes up as the series goes on, with *Shadow of the Moon* rating 5+ for scenes of sadomasochism.

CHAPTER 3

anthologies

Note: Ratings of violence, sensuality, or humor are not provided for anthologies. Readers should be guided by ratings of authors' individual novels and/or series.

Aftershock and Others: 19 Oddities (Forge, 2009): F. Paul Wilson's third collection of short fiction, including one from REPAIRMAN JACK.

Awakening the Beast: A Collection of Six Sexy Bites (Silhouette Nocturne, 2009): Six novellas: Olivia Gates, Barbara J. Hancock, Linda O. Johnston, Lisa Renee Jones, Lydia Parks, and Caridad Pineiro.

The Barrens and Others (Forge, 2000): F. Paul Wilson's second collection of short fiction, including one from REPAIRMAN JACK.

Beyond the Dark (Jove, 2009): Four novellas: Emma Holly (TALES OF THE DEMON WORLD), Angela Knight, Lora Leigh (WOLF BREEDS), and Diane Whiteside.

Bite (Jove, 2004): Five erotic novellas: MaryJanice Davidson (QUEEN BETSY), Laurell K. Hamilton (ANITA BLAKE), Charlaine Harris (SOUTHERN VAMPIRE [SOOKIE STACKHOUSE] MYSTERIES), Angela Knight (MAGEVERSE), and Vickie Taylor.

Bitten by Cupid (Avon, 2010): Three novellas: Pamela Palmer, Jamie Rush, and Lynsay Sands (ARGENEAU VAMPIRES).

Blood Lite: An Anthology of Humorous Horror Stories Presented by the Horror Writers Association (Pocket, 2008): Twenty-one stories, including Kelley Armstrong, Jim Butcher, Charlaine Harris, Nancy Holder, Sherrilyn Kenyon, Steven Savile, and Matt Venne. The book won the P.E.A.R.L. Award for best anthology (2008).

Burning Up (Berkley, 2010): Four novellas: Meljean Brook, Angela Knight (MAGEVERSE), Virginia Kantra (CHILDREN OF THE SEA), and Nalini Singh (PSY-CHANGELING).

By Blood We Live (Night Shade, 2009): Thirty-six vampire stories. Authors include Kelley Armstrong, L. A. Banks, Stephen King, Anne Rice, Lilith Saintcrow, and David Wellington. Most stories were written in the twenty-first century, but a few date back to the 1980s and 1990s.

Cravings (Jove, 2004): Four novellas: MaryJanice Davidson (QUEEN BETSY), Laurell K. Hamilton (ANITA BLAKE), Eileen Wilks, and Rebecca York (MOON SERIES).

Cupid Cats (Signet Eclipse, 2010): Three kitty novellas: Connie Brockway, Vicki Lewis Thompson, and Katie MacAlister.

Dark and Stormy Knights (St. Martin's Griffin, 2010): UF stories from Ilona Andrews (KATE DANIELS), Jim Butcher (DRESDEN FILES), Shannon K. Butcher, Rachel Caine, P. N. Elrod, Deidre Knight, Vicki Pettersson (SIGNS OF THE ZODIAC), Lilith Saintcrow, and Carrie Vaughn (KITTY NORVILLE).

Dark Dreamers (Leisure, 2006): two novellas from Christine Feehan (THE CARPATHIANS) and Marjorie Liu (DIRK & STEELE).

Dates from Hell (Avon, 2006): Stories from Kim Harrison (prelude to THE HOLLOWS), Lynsay Sands, Lori Handeland, and Kelley Armstrong (WOMEN OF THE OTHERWORLD).

Dead after Dark (St. Martin's, 2008): Authors include Sherrilyn Kenyon (DARK-HUNTERS), Dianna Love, Susan Squires (THE COMPANION), and J. R. Ward. This book won the P.E.A.R.L. Award for best anthology (2008). Ward's story won the P.E.A.R.L. Award for best novella (2008).

Death's Excellent Vacation (Berkley, 2010): Thirteen stories with a vacation theme, including Charlaine Harris (SOUTHERN VAMPIRE [SOOKIE STACKHOUSE] MYSTERIES), Jeaniene Frost (NIGHT HUNTRESS), L. A. Banks, Katie MacAlister, and Lilith Saintcrow.

Deep Kiss of Winter (Pocket, 2009): Two novellas, from Kresley Cole (IMMORTALS AFTER DARK) and Gena Showalter (ALIEN HUNTRESS).

Demon's Delight (Berkley, 2007): Four novellas: MaryJanice Davidson, Emma Holly (TALES OF THE DEMON WORLD), Catherine Spangler, and Vicki Taylor.

An Enchanted Season (Berkley, 2007): Four novellas: Jean Johnson, Erin McCarthy (CUTTERSVILLE GHOSTS), Maggie Shayne, and Nalini Singh (PSY-CHANGELINGS).

Eternal Lover (Kensington, 2009): Authors include Hannah Howell, Jackie Kessler (HELL ON EARTH), Richelle Mead (GEORGINA KINCAID), and Lynsay Sands.

Faeries Gone Wild (St. Martin's, 2009): Four sensuous novellas: MaryJanice Davidson, Lois Greiman, Michele Hauf, and Leandra Logan.

Fantasy (Jove, 2002): Four erotic novellas: Christine Feehan, Emma Holly (FITZ CLARE CHRONICLES/UPYR); Sabrina Jeffries, and Elda Minger.

A Fantasy Medley (Subterranean, 2009): Five novellas: Kelley Armstrong (WOMEN OF THE OTHERWORLD), Kate Elliott, Robin Hobb, Yanni Kuznia, and C. E. Murphy (NEGOTIATOR TRILOGY).

First Blood (Berkley, 2008): Four vampire novellas: Meljean Brook (THE GUARDIANS), Chris Marie Green (VAMPIRE BABYLON), Erin McCarthy (VEGAS VAMPIRES), and Susan Sizemore (LAWS OF THE BLOOD).

Four Dukes and a Devil (Avon, 2009): Five novellas: Elaine Fox, Jeaniene Frost, Cathy Maxwell, Sophia Nash, and Tracy Anne Warren.

Full Moon City (Pocket, 2010): Werewolf short stories by twelve authors, including Carrie Vaughn (KITTY NORVILLE), Holly Black, and Chelsea Quinn Yarbro.

Heart of Darkness (Harlequin, 2010): Three novellas: Susan Krinard, Maggie Shayne, and Gena Showalter (LORDS OF THE UNDERWORLD).

Hellbound Hearts (Pocket, 2009): Twenty-one tales inspired by Clive Barker's *Hellraiser* universe. Authors include Kelley Armstrong, Neil Gaiman, Christopher Golden, Tim Lebbon, Dave McKean, Mike Mignola, and Steve Niles.

His Immortal Embrace (Kensington, 2003): Four novellas: Sara Blayne, Hannah Howell, Kate Huntington, and Lynsay Sands.

Holidays Are Hell (Harper, 2007): Four novellas: Kim Harrison (prequel to THE HOLLOWS), Marjorie M. Liu, Vicki Pettersson (prequel to SIGNS OF THE ZODIAC), and Lynsay Sands (sequel to novella in *Dates from Hell* anthology).

Hot Blooded (Jove, 2004): Four novellas: Christine Feehan (THE CARPATH-IANS), Emma Holly (FITZ CLARE CHRONICLES/UPYR), Angela Knight (MAGEVERSE), and Maggie Shayne (WINGS IN THE NIGHT).

Hot for the Holidays (Jove, 2009): Four novellas: Anya Bast, Allyson James, Angela Knight (MAGEVERSE), and Lora Leigh (FELINE BREEDS).

Hot Spell (Berkley Sensation, 2006). Four novellas. Meljean Brook (THE GUARDIANS), Emma Holly (TALES OF THE DEMON WORLD), Lora Leigh (FELINE BREEDS), and Shiloh Walker (THE HUNTERS).

Hotter Than Hell (Harper, 2008): Thirteen stories: Keri Arthur, L. A. Banks, Heidi Betts, Kim Harrison, Tanya Huff, Denise Little, Susan Krinard, Marjorie Liu, Cheyenne McCray, Lilith Saintcrow, Susan Sizemore, Carrie Vaughn, and Linda Winstead Jones.

Huntress (St. Martin's, 2009): Four novellas: Caitlin Kittredge (BLACK LONDON), Marjorie M. Liu, Jenna Maclaine (CIN CRAVEN), and Christine Warren (THE OTHERS).

Immortals: The Reckoning (Love Spell, 2009): Three novellas from THE IMMORTALS series, by Jennifer Ashley, Joy Nash, and Robin T. Popp.

Inked (Berkley, 2010): Four novellas featuring magical tattoos: Karen Chance, Yasmine Galenorn (SISTERS OF THE MOON), Marjorie M. Liu (HUNTER KISS), and Eileen Wilks (WORLD OF THE LUPI).

Just One Sip (Love Spell, 2006): Three novellas: Jennifer Ashley, Katie MacAlister (DARK ONES), and Minda Webber.

Lilith Unbound (Popcorn Press, 2008): Short stories about Lilith, mother of demons, from twenty-five authors, including Jackie Kessler (HELL ON EARTH).

· ·

> Zombies weren't complicated. It wasn't like werewolves or ghosts or vampires. Vampires, for example, were the middle/upper-middle management of the supernatural world. Some people thought of vampires as rock stars, but really they were more like Martha Stewart. Vampires were prissy. They had to follow rules. They had to look good. Zombies weren't like that. You couldn't exorcise zombies. You didn't need luxury items like silver bullets or crucifixes or holy water. You just shot zombies in the head, or set fire to them, or hit them over the head really hard.
>
> Link muses on the differences between zombies and vampires, in Kelly Link's "Some Zombie Contingency Plans," in *The Living Dead* (originally published in *Magic for Beginners*)

· ·

The Living Dead (Night Shade, 2008): Thirty-four zombie tales. Authors include Clive Barker, Poppy Z. Brite, Neil Gaiman, Laurell K. Hamilton (the first ANITA BLAKE story), Joe Hill, Stephen King, Kelly Link, and George R. R. Martin. The anthology won the 2008 Publishers Weekly Best Book Award.

Love at First Bite (St. Martin's, 2006): Four novellas: L. A. Banks (VAMPIRE HUNTRESS LEGEND), Sherrilyn Kenyon (DARK-HUNTERS), Susan Squires (THE COMPANION), and Ronda Thompson (WILD WULFS OF LONDON).

The Magical Christmas Cat (Berkley, 2008): Four feline Christmas novellas: Lora Leigh (FELINE BREEDS), Erin McCarthy, Nalini Singh (PSY-CHANGELINGS), and Linda Winstead Jones. This anthology won an honorable mention for the P.E.A.R.L. Award for best anthology (2008).

Magical Seduction (Pocket, 2008): Three hardcore erotic novellas (three-somes, sadomasochism): Anya Bast, Cathryn Fox, and Mandy M. Roth.

The Mammoth Book of Paranormal Romance (Running Press, 2009): Twenty-five short stories. Authors include Keri Arthur, Karen Chance, Sherrilyn Kenyon, Caitlin R. Kiernan, Lilith Saintcrow, and J. R. Ward.

The Mammoth Book of Vampire Romance (Running Press, 2008): Thirty short stories. Authors include C. T. Adams, Keri Arthur, Amanda Ashley, Jenna Black, Karen Chance, Cathy Clamp, Delilah Devlin, Barbara Emrys, Sherri Erwin, Colleen Gleason, Raven Hart, Nancy Holder, Dina James, Caitlin R. Kiernan, Jenna Maclaine, Alexis Morgan, Vicki Pettersson, Kimberly Raye, Savannah Russe, Lilith Saintcrow, Susan Sizemore, Rachel Vincent, Shiloh Walker, and Rebecca York.

The Mammoth Book of Vampire Romance 2 (Running Press, 2009): Thirty short stories. Authors include Ann Aguirre, Jennifer Ashley, Dawn Cook, Caitlin Kittredge, Jaye Wells, Diane Whiteside, and Eileen Wilks.

Many Bloody Returns (Ace, 2009): Thirteen vampire stories: Kelley Armstrong (WOMEN OF THE OTHERWORLD), Jim Butcher (DRESDEN FILES), Rachel Caine, Bill Crider, P. N. Elrod (VAMPIRE FILES), Christopher Golden, Carolyn Haines, Tate Hallaway (GARNET LACEY), Charlaine Harris (SOUTHERN VAMPIRE [SOOKIE STACKHOUSE] MYSTERIES), Tanya Huff, Toni L. P. Kelner, Jeanne C. Stein, and Elaine Viets.

Mean Streets (Roc, 2009): Four novellas about paranormal investigators: Jim Butcher (DRESDEN FILES), Simon R. Green (NIGHTSIDE), Kat Richardson (GREYWALKER), and Thomas E. Sniegoski (REMY CHANDLER).

Midnight Cravings (Silhouette, 2009): Six novellas: Vivi Anna, Lori Devoti, Michele Hauf, Anna Leonard, Bonnie Vanak, and Karen Whiddon.

Midnight Pleasures (St. Martin's, 2003): Four novellas: Amanda Ashley, Sherrilyn Kenyon, Maggie Shayne, and Ronda Thompson (WILD WULFS OF LONDON).

Moon Fever (Pocket, 2007): Four novellas: Lori Handeland, Caridad Pineiro, Maggie Shayne, and Susan Sizemore.

The Morgue the Merrier (Zebra, 2007): Four Christmas-themed novellas: Dianne Castell, Karen Kelley, and Rosemary Laurey.

A Mother's Way (Love Spell, 2002): Stories from Lisa Cach, Lynsay Sands, Susan Grant, and Julie Kenner (SUPERHERO CENTRAL).

Must Love Hellhounds (Berkley, 2009): Four novellas: Ilona Andrews (KATE DANIELS), Meljean Brook (THE GUARDIANS), Charlaine Harris, and Nalini Singh (GUILD HUNTER).

My Big Fat Supernatural Honeymoon (St. Martin's Griffin, 2007): Nine stories: Kelley Armstrong (WOMEN OF THE OTHERWORLD), Jim Butcher (DRESDEN FILES), Rachel Caine, P. N. Elrod (VAMPIRE FILES), Caitlin Kittredge, Marjorie M. Liu (DIRK AND STEELE), Katie MacAlister, Lilith Saintcrow, and Ronda Thompson.

My Big Fat Supernatural Wedding (St. Martin's Griffin, 2006): Nine stories: L. A. Banks, Jim Butcher (DRESDEN FILES), Rachel Caine, P. N. Elrod, Esther M. Friesner, Lori Handeland (NIGHTCREATURE), Charlaine Harris (SOUTHERN VAMPIRE [SOOKIE STACKHOUSE] MYSTERIES), Sherrilyn Kenyon (DARK-HUNTERS), and Susan Krinard.

Mysteria (Berkley, 2006): *Desperate Housewives* meets *X-Files*! Four novellas: P. C. Cast, MaryJanice Davidson, Susan Grant, and Gena Showalter.

Mysteria Lane (Berkley Sensation, 2008): Four novellas: P. C. Cast, Mary-Janice Davidson, Susan Grant, and Gena Showalter.

Nature of the Beast (Zebra, 2009): Three erotic vampire novellas: Adrienne Basso, Hannah Howell, and Eve Silver.

Night Screams (Roc, 1996): Twenty-three short horror stories from well-known authors, including Ray Bradbury, Charles de Lint, Clive Baker, Katherine Ramsland, and F. Paul Wilson (REPAIRMAN JACK).

Night's Edge (Harlequin, 2009): Three novellas: Barbara Hambly, Charlaine Harris (SOUTHERN VAMPIRE [SOOKIE STACKHOUSE] MYSTERIES), and Maggie Shayne.

No Rest for the Witches (St. Martin's, 2007): Four novellas: MaryJanice Davidson, Lori Handeland, Cheyenne McCray (MAGIC), and Christine Warren (THE OTHERS).

On the Prowl (Berkley, 2007): Four novellas: Patricia Briggs (prequel to ALPHA AND OMEGA), Karen Chance (CASSANDRA PALMER), Sunny (MONÉRE; DEMON PRINCESS CHRONICLES), and Eileen Wilks (LUPI).

The Only One (Leisure, 2003): Three novellas by Christine Feehan (THE CARPATHIANS), Susan Grant, and Susan Squires.

Out of the Light, into the Shadows (Berkley, 2009): Three novellas: L. L. Foster, Lori Foster, and Erin McCarthy (VEGAS VAMPIRES).

Out of This World (Jove, 2001): Novellas from J. D. Robb, Laurell K. Hamilton, Susan Krinard, and Maggie Shayne (IMMORTAL WITCHES).

Over the Moon (Berkley, 2007): Four novellas: MaryJanice Davidson (QUEEN BETSY), Virginia Kantra, Angela Knight (MAGEVERSE), and Sunny (sequel to *Mona Lisa Awakening* in MONÉRE).

Primal Heat (Ellora's Cave, 2004): Four erotic novellas: Jaci Burton, Sherri L. King, Lora Leigh (prequel to WOLF BREEDS), and Lorie O'Clare.

A Red Hot Valentine's Day (Avon Red, 2009): Novellas from Jess Michaels, Lacy Danes, Megan Hart, and Jackie Kessler (HELL ON EARTH).

Running with the Pack (Prime Books, 2010): Werewolf stories from Laura Anne Gilman, C. E. Murphy, Carrie Vaughn, and others.

Sexy Beast (Aphrodisia, 2001–2010) (*Sexy Beast I* through *Sexy Beast IX*): Kate Douglas coauthors this X-rated anthology series with other writers (e.g., Lucy Danes, Morgan Hawke, Crystal Jordan). This hard-core urban paranormal fantasy anthology series is populated primarily by shape-shifters, and the plots revolve around their graphic sexual acts.

The Shadows of Christmas Past (Pocket Star, 2004): Two novellas, by Christine Feehan and Susan Sizemore (PRIMES).

Shards of Crimson (Love Spell, 2007): Four CRIMSON CITY novellas: Carolyn Jewel, Jade Lee, Liz Maverick, and Patti O'Shea.

Shifter (Berkley, 2008): Four erotic novellas: Alyssa Day (WARRIORS OF PO-SEIDON), Virginia Kantra (CHILDREN OF THE SEA), Angela Knight, and Lora Leigh (FELINE BREEDS).

Strange Brew (St. Martin's Griffin, 2009): Nine novellas: Patricia Briggs (ALPHA AND OMEGA), Jim Butcher (DRESDEN FILES), Rachel Caine, Karen Chance (CASSANDRA PALMER), P. N. Elrod (VAMPIRE FILES), Charlaine Harris (SOUTHERN VAMPIRE [SOOKIE STACKHOUSE] MYSTERIES), Faith Hunter (JANE YELLOWROCK), Caitlin Kittredge (NOCTURNE CITY), and Jenna Maclaine (CIN CRAVEN).

Strange Candy (Berkley, 2007): Laurell K. Hamilton's first short story collection, including two from ANITA BLAKE, one of which is the first story that Hamilton wrote about Anita.

Sugarplums and Scandal (Avon, 2006): Short stories from Dana Cameron, Mary Daheim, Lori Avocato, Cait London, Suzanne Macpherson, and Kerrelyn Sparks (LOVE AT STAKE).

These Boots Were Made for Stomping (Love Spell, 2008): Three novellas: Julie Kenner, Jade Lee, and Marianne Mancusi. Lee's story won an honorable mention for the P.E.A.R.L. Award for best novella (2008).

Two by Twilight (Mira, 2005): Two novellas from Maggie Shayne's WINGS IN THE NIGHT.

Unbound (Eos, 2009): Five novellas: Jocelynn Drake (DARK DAYS), Jeaniene Frost (NIGHT HUNTRESS), Kim Harrison (THE HOLLOWS), Melissa Marr, and Vicki Pettersson (SIGNS OF THE ZODIAC).

Unusual Suspects: Stories of Mystery and Fantasy (Ace, 2008): Authors include Donna Andrews, Michael Armstrong, Mike Doogan, Carole Nelson Douglas, Laura Anne Gilman, Simon R. Green (NIGHTSIDE), Charlaine Harris (SOUTHERN VAMPIRE [SOOKIE STACKHOUSE] MYSTERIES), Laurie R. King, Sharon Shinn, Dana Stabenow, Michael A. Stackpole, and John Straley.

Vampire Archives: The Most Complete Volume of Vampire Tales Ever Published (Vintage, 2009): Eighty-six vampire stories from Anne Rice to Stephen King, including Ray Bradbury, D. H. Lawrence, and H. P. Lovecraft. The excellent bibliography (110 pages) includes just about every piece of vampire fiction in print, past and present, including a chronological listing of the vampire novels written by modern paranormal authors. Vampire books for children and teens are also included.

Weddings from Hell (Harper, 2008): Four novellas: Jeaniene Frost (NIGHT HUNTRESS), Terri Garey (NICKI STYX), Maggie Shane, and Kathryn Smith (BROTHERHOOD OF BLOOD).

What Happens in Vegas . . . After Dark (Spice, 2009): Four erotic novellas: Anya Bast, Jodi Lynn Copeland, Lauren Dane, and Kit Tunstall.

Wild Thing (Berkley, 2007): Four novellas: Meljean Brook (THE GUARDIANS), Alyssa Day (WARRIORS OF POSEIDON), Marjorie M. Liu (HUNTER KISS), and Maggie Shayne.

Winter Moon (Luna, 2009): Three novellas, from Mercedes Lackey, Tanith Lee, and C. E. Murphy (WALKER PAPERS).

Wolf (Changeling Press, 2008): Four novellas: Dakota Cassidy, Sierra Dafoe, Marteeka Karland, and Kira Stone.

Wolf Mates (Changeling Press, 2006): Previously published e-books from Dakota Cassidy: *An American Werewolf in Hoboken, What's New, Pussycat?, Moon over Manhasset,* and *Ruff and Ready.*

Wolf Tales (anthology series) (*Wolf Tales I* and *Wolf Tales II,* Kensington, 2006; *Wolf Tales III* through *Wolf Tales X,* Aphrodisia, 2007–2010): Hard-core urban fantasy, with plots revolving around shape-shifters' graphic sexual acts. Extremely coarse language.

Wolfsbane and Mistletoe (Ace, 2008): Fifteen stories: Donna Andrews, Keri Arthur (RILEY JENSEN, GUARDIAN), Patricia Briggs (MERCY THOMPSON), Dana Cameron, Karen Chance (CASSANDRA PALMER), Simon R. Green (NIGHTSIDE), Alan Gordon, Charlaine Harris (SOUTHERN VAMPIRE [SOOKIE STACKHOUSE] MYSTERIES), Toni L. P. Kelner, J. A. Konrath, Nancy Pickard, Kat Richardson, Dana Stabenow, Rob Thurman (CAL LEANDROS), and Carrie Vaughn (KITTY NORVILLE).

Words of the Witches (Berkley, 2002): Stories from Yvonne Jocks, Maggie Shayne (IMMORTAL WITCHES), Rosemary Edghill, Lorna Tedder, and Evelyn Vaughn.

WEB RESOURCES

Fantastic Fiction: www.fantasticfiction.co.uk. This site offers a searchable database of information for 20,000 authors and 270,000 books.

How Stuff Works: http://science.howstuffworks.com/strange-creatures-channel .htm. This site, which you may know better as a science and technology site, offers the Strange Creatures library, which includes vampires, werewolves, *chupacabras*, zombies, the Grim Reaper, and Bigfoot. Information includes origins, history, characteristics, images of each monster, and links to other Internet sources.

Paranormal Readers Advisory for Librarians: http://readersadvisory.org/ paranormal.html. This site is a place to test and share ideas, projects, notes, and so on. Designed for librarians who provide readers' advisory services. Included are a cheat sheet and a guide that lists titles and series by type, a bibliography of sources, and lists of paranormal music, films, and television shows. There is also a long list of web links.

ParaNormalRomance Site: www.paranormalromance.org/PNRpearl.htm. This is the official homepage for the ParaNormal Romance Groups, designed for lovers of the paranormal romance subgenre. Members meet online via Yahoo! Groups and share an interest in science fiction, fantasy, and romantic fiction with paranormal elements, including time travel, futuristic, magical, ghost, vampire, and shape-shifter themes. The site presents P.E.A.R.L.—the Paranormal Excellence Award for Romantic Literature. P.E.A.R.L. is a reader's choice evaluation conducted annually by members of the ParaNormal Romance Groups, naming the "best of the best" for the year in ten categories related to paranormal romance and romantic science fiction and fantasy.

SciFan: Books and Links for the Science Fiction Fan: http://scifan.com. The database is frequently updated, with the ambition to make it a comprehensive and accurate resource for bibliographies and biographies in this genre. To date, the site includes 70,934 books, 19,647 writers, 8,832 series, and 4,490 web links. The focus is on classifying books into series and themes, with a close watch on upcoming releases.

SciFi Guy: www.scifiguy.ca. The site focuses on urban fantasy, paranormal romance, and science fiction and fantasy and includes book reviews, author interviews and articles, and blog links.

SF Bookcase: www.sfbookcase.com. The site includes the latest novels and reviews of science fiction and fantasy authors. Select the novel's title to display the details about the book. Select the author to list the novels written by that person.

The Ultimate Vamp List: www.vampire-books.com. The site lists vampire books by category and provides title links to Amazon.com. Categories include hot blood; horror; romance and erotica; mystery; sci-fi/fantasy; anthologies and short stories; children and young adult; role-playing; vampire nonfiction; movie and television; manga, comics, and graphic novels; Buffy/Angel; and not quite vamps (includes other paranormal creatures).

The Ultimate Zombie Book List: www.zombiebooklist.com/USA.php. This site is powered by Amazon.com and provides information on an extensive number of zombie titles. A plot summary is provided for each book listed.

Urban Fantasy Land: http://urbanfantasyland.wordpress.com/welcome/. The site includes links to books, movies, and television programs.

Vampire Library: www.vampirelibrary.com. A searchable database of vampire books, detailed book information, and links to purchasing information where available. In association with Amazon.com.

VampireGenre.com: www.vampiregenre.com. Book reviews, upcoming releases, free downloads (e.g., wallpaper, screensavers, e-novellas, podcasts), and chances to win copies of new paranormal novels.

Werewolf News: www.werewolf-news.com. Everything werewolf—books, television, movies, blogs, action figures, and toys.

Who Writes Like . . . ? www.erl.vic.gov.au/readers/who.htm?c=a. Have you read every novel by your favorite author? Are you looking for more suggestions? Browse the alphabetical list or do a search.

REFERENCES

Clute, John, and John Grant, eds. 1997. *Encyclopedia of Fantasy.* New York: St. Martin's Press, 1997.

Collins, Lauren. 2009. "How Nora Roberts Became America's Most Popular Novelist." *New Yorker*, June 22, 60–69.

Donohue, Nanette Wargo. 2008. "'Urban Fantasy': The City Fantastic." *Library Journal*, June 1, 64–67.

Holman, Tim. 2009. "The Publisher Files: Urban Fantasy Confirmed Undead." www.timholman.net/posts/urban-fantasy-confirmed-undead.

Huston, Charlie. 2005. *Already Dead.* New York: Ballantine.

Stuart, Anne. 1996. "Legends of Seductive Elegance." In *Dangerous Men and Adventurous Women: Romance Writers on the Appeal of Romance*, edited by Jayne Ann Krentz, 85–88. New York: HarperPaperbacks.

Vnuk, Rebecca. 2005. "'Chick Lit': Hip Lit for Hip Chicks." *Library Journal*, July 15, 42–45.

INDEX

Note: Authors, titles, subjects, and series are interfiled in one alphabet. Authors and series are printed in roman, titles in italic, and subjects in boldface.

Page numbers in bold indicate annotations. Page numbers in italic indicate excerpts from the author or work.

You may also be interested in

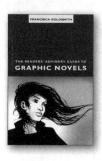